Advance P

Aware, Awake, Alive reflects Dr. Elliot............................n scientific medicine and his life-changing journey to the East. It is the result of the legendary hero's journey, in which a courageous individual travels to distant lands and returns with profound wisdom to share with the rest of us. Health is more than the absence of disease, and it is more than normal physical function. It is also about joy, fulfillment, inspiration, and contribution. If you are tired of merely going through the motions of life and aspire to the upper echelons of health, *Aware, Awake, Alive* is for you.

—Larry Dossey, MD, Author of *Healing Words* and *The Power of Premonitions*

Aware, Awake, Alive details the essential needs of our inner spirit. The author's personal wisdom, professional knowledge, and mastery of sacred teachings ensure that this book fulfills its promise to lead the reader into a deep and profound inner journey of self-awakening. *Aware, Awake, Alive* is absolutely stunning. I hope millions of people will read this book.

—Caroline Myss, Author of *Anatomy of the Spirit* and *Defy Gravity*

Elliott Dacher has the heart of a sage, the voice of a muse, and the skill of a trained physician. His writing offers an approach to healthcare that blends contemplative practice and optimal health practices. As we embody the wisdom of *Aware, Awake, Alive*, we find a roadmap that can lead each of us to healthier and happier lives. I strongly recommend this book.

—Marilyn Schlitz, President/CEO, Institute of Noetic Sciences

We can all use guides and coaches on our journey through life. *Aware, Awake, Alive* contains practical wisdom and resources which can assist you in developing your mind, opening your heart, and living your greatest potential.

—Bernie Siegel, MD, Author of *365 Prescriptions for The Soul* and *Faith, Hope & Healing*

Elliott is a wise, gentle, and deeply reassuring teacher and companion on the journey toward a more joyful, peaceful life. Read this book and weave timeless wisdom into the fabric of your daily life.

—James Gordon, M.D., Founder and Director The Center for Mind-Body Medicine

What Students Say

This has opened my hands, my eyes and my heart. It has shown me a path I can walk, through any tangle of thorns, to a place of stillness and merciful acceptance. It has sweetened my perception of beauty and delicacy, and has deepened my love. This is a teaching on how to be and let be.

Elliott's straightforward, no-nonsense approach demystifies the subject and brings you to a place where you can clearly understand and experience the benefits of this inner work.

Throughout the years I've tried meditation, but not with any consistency. I feel now that I am more prepared to make the necessary changes. The changes within me are subtle but with patience and persistence my life will be made different. I no longer ignore the urgency of now.

I can't imagine not having these insights as an integral part of my life. I am no longer sweating the small stuff and it is so much easier for me to keep things in perspective.

Now I realize that our thoughts are as fleeting as the spring flowers. Through meditation I have gained control over my busy mind and I'm more mindful and compassionate. Life is less stressful.

There is a profound and rare generosity of spirit that shines through Elliott Dacher's teachings. These teachings are intellectually and spiritually rich and practically helpful.

I see everything differently now and in a much more positive light. My interactions with others are more relaxed, more connected, more fulfilling.

When I began Dr. Dacher's program I was recovering from a serious brain injury. With his unique guidance and support, my ability to focus, concentrate, and remember has increased dramatically. Stable daily practice has brought me deep peace and enjoyment of everyday life and I have never been happier.

Aware

Awake

Alive

A Contemporary Guide to the Ancient Science
of Integral Health and Human Flourishing

Previous Books by the Author

Integral Health

Intentional Healing

Whole Healing

Aware
Awake
Alive

A Contemporary Guide to the Ancient Science
of Integral Health and Human Flourishing

Elliott S. Dacher, M.D.

PARAGON HOUSE
St. Paul, Minnesota

First Edition 2011

Published in the United States by
Paragon House
1925 Oakcrest Ave, Suite 7
St. Paul, MN 55113
www.paragonhouse.com

Cover design by Jessica Dacher

Library of Congress Cataloging-in-Publication Data

    Dacher, Elliott S., 1944-
      Aware, awake, alive : a contemporary guide to the ancient science of integral health and human flourishing / by Elliott S. Dacher. -- 1st ed.
        p. cm.
      Summary: "Presents a physician's program of self-study and practices to guide the reader towards a life of happiness and well-being. Topics include: meditation, mindfulness, overcoming afflictive emotions, integral health, and human flourishing. Applies this knowledge and these practices to common disorders such as stress, heart disease, addictions, and attention deficit disorder (ADD)"-- Provided by publisher.
     ISBN 978-1-55778-895-5 (pbk. : alk. paper)
    1. Health--Philosophy. 2. Mind and body. 3. Self-care, Health. I. Title.
    RA776.5.D333 2011
    613--dc23
                        2011020678

The paper used in this publication meets the minimum requirements of American National Standard for Information Sciences—Permanence of Paper for Printed Library Materials, ANSI standard Z39.48-1992.

Manufactured in the United States of America
10 9 8 7 6 5 4 3 2

For current information about all releases from Paragon House, visit the website at http://www.paragonhouse.com

For the many current and past participants in this course who have shown the courage and persistence to fully engage the path to a larger life and health. They have inspired me with their efforts and taught me how to teach this program. They have truly partnered with me in the writing of this book.

Permissions

"The Woodcarver" by Thomas Merton, from *The Way of Chuang Tzu*, copyright 1965 by The Abbey of Gethsemani. Reprinted by permission of New Directions Publications Corp.;

From *Letters to a Young Poet* by Rainer Maria Rilke, translated by M.D. Herter Norton. Copyright 1934, 1954 by W.W. Norton &Company, Inc. renewed © 1962, 1982 by M.D. Herter Norton. Used by permission of W.W. Norton & company, Inc.

Integral Health by Elliott Dacher, published by Basic Health 2006. Reprinted by permission of Basic Heath Publications, Inc.

"The Art of Disappearing" from *Words Under the Words* by Naomi Shihab Nye, Far Corner Books, Oregon, 1965. Reprinted by permission of the author.

From *The Flight of the Garuda*, restricted series, translated by Erik Pema Kunsang, Rangjung Yeshe Publications, Kathmandu, Nepal, 1984. Reprinted by permission of Rangjung Yeshe Publications.

"Love after Love" from *Collected Poems* 1948-1984 by Derek Walcott. Copyright © 1986 by Derek Walcott. Reprinted by permission of Farrar, Straus and Giroux, LLC.

"On Work" from *The Prophet* by Kahlil Gibran, copyright 1923 by Kahlil Gibran and renewed 1951 by Administrators C.T.A. of Kahlil Gibran Estate and Mary G. Gibran. Used by permission of Alfred Al Knopf, a division of Random House, Inc.

Edelstein, Emma J., and Ludwig Edelstein. *Asclepius: Collection and Interpretation of the Testimonies.* pp. 212 © 1998. Reprinted with permission of Johns Hopkins University Press.

Tell me, what you plan to do
with your one wild and precious life?

—Mary Oliver, The Summer Day

Contents

Part I
The Vision

Part II
The Path

Part III
The Fruition

Part IV
The Integration

List of Practices

1. Mindfulness Breathing Practice

2. Mindfulness in Daily Life

3. Taking an Inventory

4. Mindful Listening

5. Turning Afflictive Emotions Into Practice

6. Observing The Moving Mind

7. Giving and Taking

8. The Daily Practice of Loving-Kindness

9. Becoming a Healer at Work

10. Turning Adversity into Practice

A Letter to the Reader

In the pages that follow, you and I will join together in a profound journey of learning and transformation that can take us toward an extraordinary state of well-being, one largely unknown in modern times. This extraordinary state of well-being goes far beyond anything that we would call "normal," yet the potential for it exists within each and every one of us. In modern times we call this optimal well-being by its traditional term, human flourishing. It is the crowning achievement of human development. It is a deeply satisfying way to live. It is a state of peace, wisdom, happiness, freedom, and love as we have never known them.

To our customary way of thinking such well-being is inconceivable. Yet there are wise men and women from across various cultures and times whose lives give evidence to this possibility. Using a consistent set of practices as their vehicle, they have journeyed to the center of their being and brought forth the full flowering of their own human potential. They prospered in the full sense of that word—body, mind, and spirit. They found this state of optimal well-being to be steadfast and enduring, even in the face of illness, aging, or death.

For most of us this experience is far from the norm. Fortunately, the wise women and men of times past who awakened this within themselves have carefully articulated the universal science of integral health and human flourishing so that we may follow in their footsteps. They have provided us with a time-honored and reliable path that leads to the alleviation of all forms of mental distress and suffering and the attainment of an unsurpassable quality of life.

Fortunately for us, their attainments and methods are no longer a mystery. They were caring enough to leave a roadmap that details the precise steps that will also take each one of us from an ordinary life to an extraordinary life, from ordinary health to extraordinary health, from a limited life to profound prosperity. This universal roadmap to human flourishing is the basis for our work together.

That is why we are meeting here, and it is a fortunate connection of potentially great magnitude.

This book represents my best attempt to share with you what I have learned from individuals that have fully awakened to life. It is my intention that this knowledge will help guide you in this journey. I have presented it in a format that is personal, practical, and accessible.

Before you accept me as a guide and spiritual friend on this very important journey, however, it is important that you know something about my life and work. You must be careful about choosing your guides. I have learned that from personal experience. You must be willing to examine their lives, motivations, and capacities. If you are certain that you have chosen the correct guide, you will find it easier to make the level of commitment that will assure more rapid progress.

As for myself, I don't claim to be a master or sage, but I have been fortunate. I have been able to travel down this road for a period of time. I have had wonderful teachers to guide me, two excellent educations that together fully embrace the inner and outer aspects of healing, the opportunity to learn from teaching others, and the experience gained from continuously integrating what I have learned into my day-to-day life. I have had a taste of human flourishing, a taste I would very much like to share with you.

Let us start with my education, both my educations. My first education culminated in medical school, internship, and residency training. After this formal education, I practiced full time internal medicine for 21 years and participated in over 50,000 patient visits. Over the years, I learned to cherish my medical education and the opportunity it gave me to assist individuals suffering from disease and seeking health.

However, it was not long before I discovered that my medical education did not fully prepare me to care for all of the needs of my patients. I was extensively and well-trained in matters of the body—physical diagnosis and therapy—and this was certainly of great value when considering issues of health and disease. But I learned little about the mind, and nothing at all about the spirit. I often felt helpless and powerless when faced with the day-to-day complexities of life that unquestionably had a powerful impact on my patient's well-being; factors such as stressful lifestyles, disheartening and painful relationships, unsatisfying work, deeply ingrained high-risk behaviors and subtle discontent, and not-so subtle unhappiness.

Even when I succeeded in helping a patient alleviate the immediate signs and symptoms of disease, I realized that only half the job was done. In a conventional sense, one could say that patient was once again healthy. But at a deeper level, that was far from the actual truth. Why? Because the underlying disturbances of lifestyle, mental distress, and spiritual darkness persisted. The fundamental causes of ill health were unchanged.

There were many times when I would look into the eyes of my patients and feel their longing for something more. It would trigger the same feeling and longing within me. At that time I knew nothing about the mind or subtle mind/body interactions. And I certainly knew little about human flourishing. I did not know how to respond to their inarticulate yearning for a more substantial and far-reaching health or that indefinable "something more," a yearning we each revisit in our quietest moments. I could not understand the deeper meaning and hidden potential of their disorder. I had arrived at the limits of my knowledge and capacities. I could not meet the longing of my patient's soul. I was not trained to be an authentic healer of body, mind, and spirit; a healer of the whole person.

Here it is important for you to understand my attitude toward biomedicine so that you will not misunderstand me. Medical science has been a remarkable achievement. I am grateful for its brilliance. We can count on it for an accurate understanding and diagnosis of disease, a host of targeted therapies, risk factor reduction, safe surgery, and efforts aimed at health promotion and wellness that include physical exercise and proper nutrition. Our health and lives are far better—more comfortable, more productive, and longer lasting—because of it.

Those strengths aside, it has its shortcomings. Its current understanding, tools, and practices are insufficient to address today's challenges to health, healing, and human flourishing.

Why? Because we now face very different and subtler challenges. New epidemics have replaced old ones. We suffer from high and persistent levels of stress, anxiety, and non-stop mind chatter. Mood disturbances, addictive behavior and attention disorders have become increasingly common. Our relationships are often troubled, and a source of ongoing mental distress. In addition, many of us suffer from feelings of discontent, and dissatisfaction. At times these are so subtle we hardly recognize their presence and at other times they are quite overt and troubling. At all times these modern day epidemics are real and significant threats to the health of body, mind and spirit. We know that something is amiss, but we don't know what it is or how to fix it.

The failure to understand and address the causes of these symptoms, and their practical interference in our lives, denies us the full richness of human life. It's ironic—while our superb medical science is capable of extending life, it *cannot* guarantee that life is happy, peaceful, meaningful, or prosperous.

Because my traditional medical education did not teach me how to address these modern threats to the quality of human life, I began to study psychology, wellness, holism, mind/body interactions and the dynamics of stress. I learned many things that enabled me to expand my knowledge and skills. Over time, my studies resulted in two books, many speaking engagements, and a more satisfying medical practice. I thought I had found the answers I was seeking, and I did, in part. I practiced medicine in this expanded way for many years. Those were satisfying years, and I thought I had touched as deeply as possible what was known about health and healing. But I soon discovered that I had barely scratched the surface. I had not yet touched below the surface to the core of health and healing. At that time, like most of you, I was unaware of the capacity for human flourishing. I was similarly unaware of the unexpected turn my life and work were about to take.

When my youngest daughter completed college, I finally had time to sit back and reflect. Busyness and constant doing does not leave much time for self-reflection, and my day-to-day life was as busy as anyone else's. I had spent years developing myself professionally, running my medical practice, writing, teaching, and raising my daughters. And now, finally, I had the luxury of some time to myself.

And that's how I came to hear the insistent longings of my soul. It did not "speak" to me directly, but through a nagging insistence that there was more to life, more to be experienced and enjoyed than what I had tasted in my personal and professional life. In its quiet and persistent way, it "spoke" to me about all that was not yet resolved in my life and heart. It insisted that there was more to life.

I would have preferred that this voice just disappear, but I knew it spoke truth. It told me that there was a deeper and more enduring happiness than I had yet experienced, a peace that surpasses brief moments of relaxation, a profound love that inspires authentic connection and intimacy, and a greater purpose in life that transcends ordinary doing and achieving.

It would have been a lot more convenient if these nagging doubts and questions had just disappeared, allowing me to continue with my life as I always had. Why push my good fortune? I had a satisfying practice, a good and stable income, and the respect customarily offered to physicians. I also had the opportunity to continue writing books, speaking, and teaching. Those were clearly not things to turn away from. I had spent many years cultivating them. But the insistent voice in my head just kept repeating: *there is more, there is more.* I did not know the precise way forward. But I did know that I did not want to look back later in life with regrets that I had failed to heed this inner call. If there was more, I needed to discover it, and if not now, when?

A month after my daughter's graduation, I left my medical practice, sold my house, gave my furniture to my children, packed my bags and headed north by car to a secluded island home that I had used infrequently over the years. I did not have a set agenda. However, what I did know, for the first time in my life, was that I needed to learn how to "be" rather than "do." And I knew that would be the hardest thing I had ever done!

I knew the great stories of transition and transformation. I had read them many times, old and new, traditional and non-traditional.

They spoke with a singular voice: "If you want to turn a corner in your life," they said, "you must first be willing to let go of your comfortable anchors and move into the unknown. Rearranging furniture in the same room just won't work."

Unwinding a carefully cultivated and "successful" life was difficult at first, but once I got in the car with my bare belongings, I knew something was right, very right. I had begun the long awaited journey of awakening.

My plan was to just sit still for an indefinite period of time and see what it was like to just "be" with nothing to do and no place to go. That is exactly what I did except for a brief winter sojourn each of the first two winters to serve as a fellow at the *Institute of Noetic Sciences*. Slowly I could feel the natural rhythms of life returning to body, mind, and spirit. I could feel the layers of years of accumulated stress and strain slowly dissipate. They were slowly and tentatively replaced by a newfound lightness of being. I could sense something was happening, and it was good.

And then it happened. An unexpected meeting occurred during my second winter at the institute. At the time, I was sharing a house with an Indian physicist from Eugene, Oregon, Amit Goswami. He was a visiting scholar at the same institute. You might recall him from the movie *What the Bleep*. For several months, we shared dinner each evening and talked for hours about physics, consciousness, and health. Towards the end of our time together, he asked me if I wanted to join him on a forthcoming trip to Asia. "I'll give you a soft landing," he said. So I thought, why not?

Three months later, I was on an airplane to Chennai. I could not have possibly known what lay ahead. I could not have known that I had just embarked on a journey that was to last for more than a decade and define the next phase of my life and work. After all my previous efforts to organize life and career, it was now about to naturally unfold in ways I could never have imagined. It was happening without any intervention from my "doing" mode.

There are times and places where you feel at home. One does not know the why and how of it. You just feel at home. For me, India was like that. It was an immediate hit. There was something special there, perhaps the better word is sacred, something which touched my soul and continues to defy explanation. Yes, there was the beauty, sensuality, authenticity, colors, rhythms, natural simplicity, and more. It was all of these and at the same time none of them. There was something even deeper, intangible, and very subtle. It was about soul and spirit—a soul and spirit that are deeply grounded in the soil of this land, in the people, and in a culture that has cultivated two of the world's great religions. India was like a mirror that reflected my own spirit and soul. Something inside told me that I had found the people and place that could teach me about a different level of health and wholeness.

At the end of my first visit, I knew I would return. I also knew that when I returned, it would not be to sightsee. I wanted to focus, instead, on studying the inner aspects of health and healing, and learning how to bring about the radical health and well-being I had seen in certain highly developed teachers. So, over the next 12 years, I made annual trips to India, and later, Nepal. Each of these trips lasted from two to six months. I studied in various locations with various teachers. I committed myself to my studies the same as I had done in medical school. I searched for the wisest, happiest, and most peaceful teachers I could find. And then I sat, listened, studied, reflected, and practiced.

This was my *second* medical education, and it felt right. It lasted 12 years in Asia and continues to unfold each day. My second formal medical education did not supplant my first education in medical science, rather, it complements and completes it.

My first medical education taught me about the outer biologic aspects of healing. It focused on disease, treatment, and longevity. My second medical education focuses on the inner aspects of health and healing. Here, the emphasis is on mind and spirit, on the quality of life rather than the biologic aspects of life. Together, they form the basis for a comprehensive and far-reaching understanding of health and healing. Together, they provide me with a scope of knowledge and skills that ranges from diagnosing and treating disease to guiding others along the path to human flourishing. *This* is what I had come to the East to learn.

In some ways, this period of study resembled my medical school training. My curriculum was divided into intellectual understanding and laboratory experience. The former was attained by listening to talks and reading texts. The latter required daily practice of mind training. Mind training enabled me to examine and understand the intricacies of my mind, much as the microscope is used to understand the intricacies of the body. I soon discovered that this inner science was as precise, practical, and relevant as medical science was in the West.

Slowly, I developed an understanding of the principles and practices of inner healing. Because I wanted to carefully assess the effects of this training on my life, my life became my laboratory. Could I begin to bring stress, distress, dissatisfaction and suffering to an end in my personal life? Could I intentionally cultivate a more profound health, happiness, and wholeness? Could I taste the qualities of human flourishing? Would these ideas and practices work? Surely this would be the ultimate way to prove to myself whether or not there was a larger health, one that could be self-created through inner development without the use of external remedies or the need for health practitioners.

Fourteen years of immersing myself in this deeper study of inner health and healing has convinced me that it is possible for every motivated individual to gain a complete understanding of the mind. It *is* possible to learn to tame its repetitive and habitual mental chatter, diminish and overcome disturbing thoughts and emotions, activate the mind/body relationship as a powerful healing force, transform dysfunctional relationships into gifts of intimacy, and gain a profoundly satisfying life. I know that this might seem inconceivable. However, I have verified these possibilities through my own experience and witnessed it in many others. The wise healers of the past have spoken the truth. Human flourishing is possible for each of us. In fact, it is a potential waiting for us to awaken to it. It is already and always there.

Let's be very clear, however, that you cannot take a pill or use some other external remedy to achieve this optimal state of well-being. Someone else cannot do it for you or give it to you. You need to do it for yourself, and you need to want it. You need to want it with your whole being. You need to feel within you the deep longing for a larger life that reaches beyond the bounds of what is now known to you. Desire it as intensely as you would a lover.

As I could slowly see the glimmer of the gem of human flourishing I knew it was possible for everyone. And I also knew it was time to come home to my own culture, as a physician, and do what I could to help others see the truth, goodness, and beauty of life, much as I had been helped to see it for myself. I knew it was time to practice medicine again, but this time, an inner and outer *whole* medicine.

There were obstacles to overcome in bringing this expanded vision to the West. I struggled with many questions: how do I tailor the ideas and practices learned in a different culture, to day-to-day life in the West? How do I integrate inner healing with the outer healing that dominates Western culture? How do I convey the age-old vision of optimal health and human flourishing to individuals who mistake "normal" for healthy? This became my prime focus.

I committed myself to making what I had learned about human flourishing accessible to Westerners. I decided to do an experiment in the form of a ten-week program of study, reflection, and practice, and offer it in a local hospital.

I chose the hospital setting because I wanted to make this opportunity available to individuals who would not usually consider such programs. I wanted to work with "ordinary" people who had no particular background in inner or spiritual approaches: individuals who knew there was something more to life and health and were willing to undertake the challenge.

My students and I met weekly for two hours. At the beginning of the class, they would share their progress and the challenges they confronted. This allowed me to tailor the process to individual needs, reinforce the instructions, and clarify certain issues I presented. Then I presented material related to that week's class, provided time for group support, and taught practices to be used daily for formal home sessions as well as for day-to-day life activities.

Although the participants had varied backgrounds, that class clicked, because everyone shared the same goal, worked together, and supported each other. Watching my students' progress taught me that any motivated individual could work this program, irrespective of his or her background or state of physical health. That was a *very* important discovery. It affirmed something wise healers have long known: the possibility of human flourishing is equally available to everyone,

Since that time, I have taught the course to hundreds of people, some of whom have taken it two or three times. My students have taught me what worked and what did not work. They showed me how to adapt the course material to their individual needs, and even more importantly, they showed me with their lives the value of this approach.

Every time I teach the course, I am astonished at the changes I see in individual's lives. I still cannot believe that so much can occur in such a short period of time. Results have been consistent. By the second or third week, my students find that their reactivity has diminished and inner calm has gained a foothold. By the fifth week, they report that their relationships have improved. Afflictive emotions (like anger or jealousy) have lessened, mindfulness progressively extends into daily life, the overactive mind calms down, and personal relationships improve. Even in that short time, it is possible to see tangible evidence of a new and richer life. Life changes. The possibility of truly having "more" becomes real. And *that* is a miracle.

As the course evolved, I developed a manual to help with the intellectual content. Over the years it was edited and re-edited many times to incorporate what I learned teaching this course. Finally, we had a course manual that was written as much by the participants as it was by me. It fit the Western mind and accomplished the task of supporting others in the inner development that is essential for a larger life and health.

Inspired by the consistent, positive changes I saw in my students in each of the 16 courses I taught, I decided to turn the course manual into a book. *Aware, Awake, Alive* incorporates all the material I give to my students. It is divided into four parts.

The first, *The Vision,* will awaken you to possibilities for your life that may be more thrilling than any you've ever contemplated.

The second, *The Path*, explains in a careful, precise, and step-by-step way, how to train your mind and progressively unfold the capacities that characterize human flourishing. The third section, *The Fruition*, explores the exquisite capacities of human flourishing that begin to emerge when the mind is quieted and the heart is free of emotional disturbance. These include the capacity for serenity, full-knowing wisdom, enduring happiness, natural self-arising compassion, boundless freedom, and the perfection of health. The fourth section, *The Integration*, discusses the part these practices can play in the healing of challenging, often treatment-resistant conditions such as addictive disorders, heart disease, chronic illness, depression, attention deficit disorders, and post-traumatic stress disorders.

Aware, Awake, Alive is unusual in that it incorporates the original 10-week course into the book, along with more advanced material for those who master the basics and want to continue on. The book includes "readings" for each of the 10 weeks; each was created to deepen your understanding of an underlying basic principle. This is the "study and reflection" part of the course. Chapters 4-13 will also teach you a formal daily practice as well as a progressive series of daily living "practices" that will put you solidly on the path to human flourishing.

Many participants retake this course two and three times. Repetition is important, so expect to find it in this book. Repetition is how you learn and become familiar with the material and practices. That is how to develop new and healthy mental habits. The material presented is rich and multi-faceted; with each reading the material takes on a subtler meaning. To assist you in learning it, I have also included a practice CD with this book. The use of this CD is discussed in chapter four. It will help you establish a stable and effective daily practice.

I suggest that you first read through the entire book *without* focusing on the practices. This will provide you with a complete overview of the journey to human flourishing—*vision, path, fruition,* and *integration*. You may then return to Chapters 4-13 (the practice chapters) and work through the practices at your own pace. With this second reading you can take your time re-reading the text, learning and integrating the practices into your life one step at a time. Alternatively, you can work with the practices during your first reading, pacing yourself as you slowly integrate each practice into your life. Choose what is best for you: get the full picture first or dive right into the process. Either will work. Whichever you choose, consider this a self-development course that requires your active participation. Merely reading the book will plant a seed but won't bring the same benefits.

Many others, throughout time and across diverse cultures, have followed this time-honored approach and successfully transformed their lives. This can serve as a source of reassurance and affirmation that *you* are on the right path. We do not get that many chances in a lifetime to shift gears. We do not get that many chances in a lifetime to unfold the precious gem of life. We cannot wait until it is too late. We cannot afford excuses and delays. There comes a time to get on with it. There comes a time to jump into the richness and vastness of life. And that time is now, today.

My commitment to you is twofold. First, this approach will definitely and decisively bring you to greater health, happiness, and peace. There is nothing new here, nothing which has not been demonstrated time and time again by those willing to undertake this journey. Second, I will stay with you throughout your effort, and beyond. I will offer you additional resources in this book and on my website. I will be available to you.

I began this letter by introducing myself to you. I wanted you to know about my two medical educations and what I learned about human flourishing from both of them. I wanted to inspire you to turn a corner in your life and to offer to partner with you in that precious and sacred process. I want you to taste human flourishing as I have, and to feel a thirst for the fullness and richness of life. When you have seen what is possible and travelled along this path for a while, it is only natural to want others to experience the same. That is what I wish for you and that is what I am certain you will wish for others as well.

I hope this note encourages you to accompany me on this extraordinary journey that is brought alive in the pages ahead. If you choose to grow your inner life, your inner calling will progressively unfold itself and be fully realized. You will actualize human flourishing in your life, and the dissatisfactions, uncertainty, and discontent of your earlier life will dissipate like morning dew.

I must acknowledge that the teachings given in these chapters are not mine. I cannot take credit for them. I did not invent them or discover them. I am merely transmitting as best I can what the great sages have taught us throughout the ages. I hope I am an acceptable conduit.

Blessings on the journey,
Elliott

PART I

The Vision

The ability to create, sustain, and actualize a vision is a unique human capacity. A vision orients and shapes our lives. We are accustomed to envisioning our career, relationships, and other day-to-day possibilities. But here we are referring to a broader vision, a holistic and far-reaching one that guides our entire life. Such an over-arching vision points us toward what is best and most satisfying in life.

Our vision is a long-held and cherished view of the full potential of human life. It is a vision that encompasses body, mind, and spirit. There have been many names given to designate the fulfillment of this human possibility. In accordance with the Western tradition, which dates back to Plato and Aristotle, we shall call this *Human Flourishing*.

To flourish is to move beyond the stress, dissatisfaction, and suffering that too often limits and diminishes our lives, and reclaim the profound well-being which resides at the center of our being. That is our vision, a vision of human flourishing.

chapter 1

Human Flourishing

I have never encountered an individual who did not desire happiness, peace, and well-being. That human desire is universal. It is our deepest impulse. It will never leave us. We all want to flourish and prosper.

Fortunately, it is definitely possible for each one of us to achieve this. Why? Because happiness, peace, and well-being are *innate* qualities of human life. They are in our genes. They are already present at the core of our being. We can lose sight of these qualities, and we do. But like the sun that is temporarily hidden by thick clouds, they are always there to be rediscovered.

With enough effort and a bit of luck, each of us will experience such moments during the course of our lifetime. We will enjoy a variety of pleasurable activities—loving connections with family, friends, and partners, worldly achievements, and material things of all sorts. That is the kind of well-being with which we are most familiar. That is fine and good, as far as it goes. But that is not what we are speaking about here.

Because we cannot control the outer world or other people, these moments are only temporary. Experiences change, others become preoccupied with their own needs, and over time material objects lose their luster. Happiness, peace, and well-being attained through outer efforts alone are by nature transient and unstable. They alternate with the distress and suffering resulting from change, loss, illness, and aging. That is why we continuously strive to sustain pleasure where it exists, and find new sources—new experiences, new relationships, or new things—to replace what is lost or naturally diminishes over time.

What we are concerned with here is quite different. It is the cultivation of a special sort of happiness, serenity, and well-being that is found inside rather than outside, endures over a lifetime, is reliable and trustworthy, and immune to the usual adversities of life. Our aim is to reclaim this inner treasure which lies dormant in each of us. It is who we are. It is at the core of our being. We do not have to look outside of ourselves or chase after it. We do not have to strive to replenish it. It is permanent and abundant.

So if this natural treasure resides in each of us, why can't we see or experience it right now and at all times without further effort? Why does it seem so scarce and inaccessible? Why do we exert so much energy and effort scavenging in the outer world for passing pleasures? Why don't we go directly to the source, to the center of our being where it is naturally present? The answer is quite simple. Out of habit we have learned to search in the wrong place for the great treasures of life. That is why we cannot find what we are searching for no matter how much effort we make.

We learned this a long time ago. We mistakenly learned to reach outside ourselves for happiness and serenity, health and healing, wholeness and love. This tendency is so deeply ingrained that it feels like a natural instinct. Even when this reaching out fails to truly satisfy our longing, we respond with greater striving and effort. We don't know what else to do. We rarely question our learned dependence on the outer world. We have an intractable faith that it will give us what we need, if we only try hard enough. It is this habit which distracts our attention and blocks our access to the real thing.

It is as if we are born on an island filled with gems. At all times they are right beneath our feet, but our vision is cloudy. We don't know they are there. We live in unnecessary poverty in the midst of enormous wealth.

There is, as we have suspected, *more to life*. There is a way to attain our most cherished and sought after human longing. That way is the inner way—the direct path to life's greatest treasures. If this were my view alone you would be right to question it. But it is not. It is the universal teaching of all wise philosophies and religions.

Out of the Cave

Let's first look for this teaching in the Western tradition. Twenty-five hundred years ago our ancestors in the West solved the riddle of distress and suffering and simultaneously pointed out the way to human flourishing. At the same time, their colleagues in the East were busy solving the identical riddle. Philosophers, scholars, and healers, West and East, asked the same question: "Why, if we are endowed with a unique and precious capacity for health, happiness, and peace do we live with so much struggle and suffering?" That was the riddle they set about to solve, and they did.

In the Western tradition Plato answered these questions with a simple parable about cave dwellers. In a few pages of text he identified the cause of suffering, the obstacles to alleviating suffering and the path that leads to the end of distress and suffering, and the subsequent attainment of the precious qualities of human flourishing. He describes the movement from darkness to light, from confusion to wisdom, from mundane existence to divine life on earth. He urges us to discover the profound *truth* of our being, the essential *goodness* that resides at the core of our soul, and the intense *beauty* of life as it is. He urges us to flourish and prosper.

But here is the problem. Plato suggests that the unexamined life, our day-to-day life, is like being shackled in a dark cave. I know this sounds harsh, but please stay with me for a moment. Plato means to be helpful. He does so by confronting us directly. He is not interested in softening his teaching. He values life, our life, too much to dilute the truth. He desires to teach us the actuality of our circumstance. He believes that we can overcome our confusion and illusions.

The dark cave he describes is our confused mind. The shackles he speaks about are not physical shackles like handcuffs. As restrictive and unwanted as these would be, at least we would be aware of them and do what we could to rid ourselves of them as soon as possible. The shackles he is

referring to are far more restrictive, insidious, and dangerous. Why? Because we are unaware of them?

What are the shackles he is referring to? They are psychological shackles. They are the learned beliefs and habits
conveyed to us early in life by family, educators, and culture. We are so accustomed to these tenacious beliefs and
behaviors that we consider them normal. We rarely question or examine them. They determine our thoughts and our
actions. We live in the confines of this world. Our lives are
determined and conditioned by the known, by the character
and content of previous life experience. We are chained to
the past. We are prisoners of the past, deeply asleep. That is
our cave. And we do not know it.

We might think that when Plato speaks about the dark
cave and its shackled inhabitants he is referring to others, to
more primitive people. But he is not. He is referring to you
and me, right now. Plato's student Glaucon, referring to the
parable of the cave and its inhabitants, remarked to Plato,
"You have shown me a strange image, and they are strange
prisoners." Plato responds, *"Like ourselves."*

Plato continually urges us on to the cave door and
finally beckons us to behold the sun itself. Each step out of
the cave towards the light of wisdom and authenticity is a
step towards truth, a step towards freedom, a step towards
human flourishing. Each step breaks the shackles of the past.
Finally, we discover what was already and always there, the
essence of our being. And that essence is the *truth* of being,
the *goodness* of compassion and love, and the intense *beauty*
of existence itself.

This is what Plato's contemporary Aristotle called *eudai-
monia*—the good life. Plato encourages us to start wherever
we are, grow incrementally, accommodate our self to our full
potential, and never turn back. That is the path to human
flourishing as described in the Western tradition.

Let us now shift to the East where we are given the same view of our existence. Here it is as shared through another story.

> Once upon a time many centuries ago a King buried a large treasure in a remote desert. The King died, his ancestors passed away and the treasure was forgotten. A thousand years later a poor farmer built his small hut in the same desert and for most of his lifetime struggled to make a meager living from the arid land that surrounded his hut. He lived in poverty with only a few pieces of clothing, little to eat and some old possessions.
>
> One day a clairvoyant, a wise man, came upon the farmer and his hut. He looked around with great interest and said to the farmer. "I can see you have lived your life in great poverty and struggle and that you will soon die. Yet this is unnecessary. Many years ago a wealthy king buried a great treasure under the ground where you built your hut. If you dig for it you will find it and have all the wealth you wish." The farmer takes his advice, digs for and finds the gold. He lives the remainder of his life in great wealth.

We are once again told that this is the story of our own life. We each have access to a great treasure. But we are unaware of its existence. We cannot see our great treasure because it is covered with the stress and distress of an overactive mental life, fixed perspective and automated habits. As a result we live our entire lives without the extraordinary well-being that is already and always within us. Like the farmer, we must dig through and remove this obscuring "dirt" in order to find the hidden gold.

In this short story the wise ones from the East reveal to us the same "secret" of life that is told by our elders in the West. In the ancient Greek tradition, human flourishing is called *the true, the good, and the beautiful.* In the Christian tradition it is called *divine love, agape, and heaven.* In the Buddhist tradition it is called *wisdom, compassion, and delight.* In the Hindu tradition it is called *satchitananda*—awareness, knowledge, and bliss. In the Eastern tradition it is referred to as the *tao.* Life lived in our deepest self has many names, but it is one. It is the flourishing of our deepest nature. Wise sages tell us that this is possible for each of us, right now, and that our capacity to progress toward this great goal can be measured by the intensity and reach of our longing. With a clear and constant voice our ancestors urge us to become *aware, awake, and alive.* Perhaps we should listen to them.

The Secret In the Symbols

In case we misunderstand their words and parables, our ancestors have wisely left us visual symbols that further elaborate the path to human flourishing. They describe, in a simple and profound way, the ancient and modern path to an authentic and full life.

The Caduceus

In the West the symbol of human flourishing comes to us from ancient Greece. It is the well-known medical symbol of the Caduceus, two snakes curled around the staff of the Greek god Hermes. What do these snakes represent? They represent the two aspects of human life, inner and outer. The inner aspect of life is our consciousness, our mental and spiritual life. The outer is our physical life, our biology.

Even though each of our lives has an inner and outer aspect, they are usually unequally developed. In modern times our focus has been on the outer aspects. We have mastered an understanding of biology. We know how to enhance our physical well-being, address physiological disturbances, reduce biological risk factors, and promote high levels of physical wellness. As the mythologist Joseph Campbell reminds us, "where there was once darkness there is now light." We once knew very little about our biology, and now we know a great deal.

But he also reminds us that, "where there was once light there is now darkness." There was a time we had a profound understanding of our inner life. We could describe and traverse, as Plato did, the full development of consciousness from darkness to light, from confusion to wisdom. But in modern times that is no longer the case. We have a mastery of the outer world but we have simultaneously lost touch with our inner life. It has become a buried and unseen treasure. Where once there was light there is now darkness and ignorance.

When we look carefully at the Caduceus we see that there are times when the two snakes join together in balance and union. At other times they remain separated. When they are unequally developed, one aspect of our existence, inner or outer, is more fully developed and dominates our life. At such times the other aspect of our being becomes a mere shadow of its full potential. Flourishing is not possible. That requires the harmonious and balanced interplay of both the inner and outer aspects of life. As a result of this uneven development we are left with partial knowledge, partial health and a partial life. That is our circumstance in modern times.

However, there are rare and special times in history when inner and outer aspects of life merge in a union that is genuine wholeness. When these two aspects of our being are equally and fully developed we experience a flourishing of human life and culture. Such was the case in the West at the time of ancient Greece and the European Renaissance. Inner knowing and outer knowing were in balance. The result was a flourishing of life, the arts, and humanities. That is what is conveyed to us through the healing symbol of the Caduceus— wholeness and human flourishing require a full and equal development of the two central aspects of life, inner and outer. Only then is life's great treasure revealed.

The Medicine Buddha

In the East the great symbol of healing is the Medicine Buddha. In Buddha's right hand he holds the sacred *Arura* plant which represents all outer forms of therapy, the outer way. In his left hand he holds a bowl that contains the nectar of wisdom, the inner way. Again we are informed that wholeness and human flourishing require the full development of both aspects of our being.

Each of these great symbols, West and East, are identical in their message. They inform us that to be fully human we must develop and completely integrate outer knowledge and inner wisdom. That is the way we behold our authentic self. That is the way in which we transform an ordinary life into a noble one.

An Ancient Center for Human Flourishing

There was once a time when individuals could visit healing centers that emphasized this balanced and whole approach to optimal well-being. That time was 2500 years ago in ancient Greece at the same time that Plato was urging us to move out of the darkness and into the light.

If you lived between the years 450 BC and 350 AD and were ill, dissatisfied with life as it was and wanted to turn a corner in your life, you would make plans to visit one of the hundreds of healing centers throughout ancient Greece and the larger Mediterranean region. These centers were called Aesclepian healing centers.

Asclepius was the ancient Greek god of healing and today, as in ancient times, all physicians are considered to be in the lineage of Aesclepius. The Oath of Hippocrates taken by physicians at the time of graduation from medical school begins with the words, "I swear to Apollo, Aesclepius, Panacea and Hygeia." Apollo was the mythical father of Aesclepius, and Panacea and Hygeia were his daughters.

You would make preparations for your visit and pack a bag as the journey by foot might last several days and the stay at the center an indefinite period. On your way to the temple you would likely meet those returning home. They might share a meal with you and relate their experience at the temple. Their healing stories would strengthen your faith and lift your spirits.

Finally you would end your journey at the temple gate. You would spend the next several days waiting outside the gate. But this was not like waiting in a modern medical office. This was an important time to prepare yourself for the healing process. Through fasting, ritual bathing or other practices you would slowly let go of worldly concerns and activities. You were about to enter a sacred and holistic healing experience of body, mind and spirit which required as much clarity as possible. After several days of such preparation, heart and mind were ready for the activities of temple life.

When you entered the environs of the center your first stop would be at the temple of Aesclepius. Standing before you would be the statue of the healing god. You would feel his strength, confidence, compassion, and wisdom. It was the custom to leave an offering, perhaps a honey cake or cheese, to honor these qualities of healing which were manifested in the symbol of the god Aesclepius.

You would then find your dormitory room, unpack your bag, and begin to participate in temple activities. There were many activities which touched body, mind, and spirit. There was the gymnasium with its baths, massage, fitness activities, and athletic competitions. You might become involved in one of many philosophical dialogues or enjoy minstrel singing as you walked about the streets of the center. You might wander and reflect in the beautiful gardens, enjoy the finest art of ancient Greece, the statues created by Phidias and Praxiteles. There would be plenty of time for contemplation and stillness.

Perhaps later in the day you would attend the theater. The finest theater in all of Greece was located at the healing temple at Epidaurus. Here you could hear one of the great Greek dramas of Aeschylus, Sophocles, or Euripides. These dramas depicted the human condition in all its aspects—tragedy, conflict, greed, nobility, violence and so on. Your small story, your piece of this drama, was elevated to the level of myth, as it became part of the larger movement of the human condition—the struggle between the forces of darkness and light, suffering and salvation, stagnation and flourishing.

Each night you would dress yourself in your sacred whites and walk along the promenade to the great temple of Aesclepius. You would solemnly enter with others, leave an offering at the statue of

Aesclepius, locate a spot to recline, quietly reflect on your circumstance, and then enter sleep asking the god for a healing dream.

This process had a special name. The name was *incubation*. Perhaps it might be more familiar to us if we call it prayer or meditation. It is the universal process of leaving ordinary awareness, taking refuge in sacred silence, and listening carefully within for the words of wisdom that come only in the incubation of stillness. The ancient Greeks were listening for the wisdom of Aesclepius. That was their way of projecting out their inner wisdom to the imagined god. But this is not our way. Our way is to claim that wisdom as our own birthright. But in either case the process and outcome are the same. "Go inside," we are told. Incubate your innerness in stillness and listen for the wise messages carried by the wind of pure awareness.

During the evening many participants had dreams. Others did not and would wait for another evening. Most often the dreams were shared with the temple priests. There was also a special name for these priests. That name was *iatromantis*, sacred or divine healers. These were the guides who helped to interpret the dreams. Now as then, wise and knowledgeable guides are essential if one is to heal ones inner life and flourish into a larger life. At times the dreams were healing in themselves. At other times they called for various activities such as certain diets, pharmaceuticals, physical exercise or psychological understandings. The instructions were followed and the process of inner looking through incubation continued day-to-day, along with the other activities of temple life.

Close your eyes for a moment and imagine this multi-dimensional inner and outer approach to healing mind, body and spirit. Imagine the retreat environment and an entire community committed to healing and "wholing." For that is what happened. And when this was accomplished you left the temple revitalized, renewed, and transformed. That was the nature of an inner and outer healing in ancient Greece. This was a center for human flourishing.

If you had the resources, when you left the healing center you might leave an inscription on paper or stone that conveyed the details of your healing as a source of reassurance and inspiration for others. Here is one such testimonial written in 450 BC.

Believe me men, I have been dead during all the years of life that I was alive. The beautiful, the good, the holy, the evil were all the same to me; such was the darkness that formerly enveloped my understanding and concealed and hid from me all these things. But now that I have come here, I have become alive again for all the rest of my life as if I had lain down in the temple of Aesclepius and had been saved. I walk, I talk, I think. This sun, so great, so beautiful, I have now discovered, men, for the first time; today I see under the clear sky, you, the air, the acropolis and the theater.

This was the experience of human flourishing in a culture which had access to and valued both the inner and outer aspects of life. For us the process would be somewhat different, tailoring itself to our culture and level of development. But the essential aspects would be the same.

Modern Science Meets Human Flourishing

The experience of human flourishing, first described in ancient times, is now receiving attention and validation from high-tech modern science. Richard Davidson, working at his laboratory at the University of Wisconsin, has been a leader in this field of research, research which has now spread to other universities. Davidson, studying electrical brain activity and variations in brain blood flow, discovered that a certain area of the right side of the brain, the right prefrontal cortex, is activated by mental distress and a corresponding area of the left part of the brain, the left prefrontal cortex, is activated by feelings of well-being.

In July 2003, Davidson reported in the journal *Psychosomatic Medicine* the results of a study done on a group of employees at a biotechnology firm who were offered an eight-week course in stress reduction and relaxation techniques. One group took the course while another group was waiting their turn. The first group was evaluated before the course, immediately after the course, and then four months following its completion. The participants who completed the course showed a reduction in mental distress and a corresponding enhancement of well-being. This shift in mental state was correlated with increased activation of the left prefrontal cortex, the area of the brain associated with well-being.

This study and others like it show that inner development contributes to greater well-being even for beginners. We are discovering that our mental life is not predetermined and fixed. Our capacity for well-being is flexible, dynamic, and expansive. We now know that optimal health can be cultivated through systematic inner development. But that is only the beginning of the story. What follows is even more exciting.

Davidson is currently conducting experiments with highly trained and skilled contemplative scholars who have made inner development and the fulfillment of the human possibility their life's work. He asked these individuals to participate in experiments which measured brain activity. Once hooked up to sophisticated technology they were asked to enter into what for them were well-developed mental states such as boundless compassion or pure awareness. The level of activation of the left versus right prefrontal cortex was carefully assessed with electrical measurements and functional MRIs.

What Davidson discovered is that these Olympians of mental fitness have levels of activation of the left prefrontal cortex, the site that correlates with well-being, which is way beyond those of the ordinary individual. They are "off the charts." Not only do these high levels of activation occur during inner practice, but they are also sustained throughout the day as well. These stable states of optimal well-being are cultivated through inner development.

Scientific research conducted on highly trained individuals with Olympic levels of mental fitness shows us that the far reaches of human flourishing can be developed through training and measured scientifically. Now we have the first scientific evidence that documents the ancient observation, West and East, that human flourishing—a profound and enduring state of health, happiness, and inner peace—can be attained though inner development, and it begins as soon as we begin to work with our mind.

A Glimpse of the Treasure, or at Least a Facsimile

Perhaps it would be helpful if we have a sense of what human flourishing feels like, a taste of radical aliveness, with its ease, peace, and delight. There are many such moments in our life—a moment of communion with nature, the experience of great beauty, the peak of sexual intimacy, the free flow of dance, music, or athletic activities. Imagine such a moment when your sense of "self" drops away. Your usual mind is suspended. You are in a state of full presence and being without any mental commentary. You are fully present in the "now." You are fully alive in the divine dance of moment-to-moment life.

At times this moment is completely still and other times you experience intense perceptions. There is a profound sense of ease. Everything is okay. Everything is complete. You are in the center of your being, in the center of life, not separate but one. And perhaps in this moment you may gain insight, experience an unexplainable feeling of love, or even feel transformed. And all around you is bathed in beauty and grace. There is no fear and no hope, no grasping and no attachment, neither a sense of past nor future, nothing to change and nothing to do. It is all there in the radical aliveness of the moment. For that brief glorious moment you know the truth, goodness, and the beauty.

That is the experience of human flourishing, or at least a glimpse or facsimile of it. Now imagine this was not an extraordinary occurrence but how human life is actually meant to be. Imagine this moment stretched out to an hour, a week, a year, or a lifetime. How would your life be?

But for most of us these moments are fleeting, because we have not yet created an inner foundation that can support them. We are quickly drawn back to the dark cave of our mental life, back to time, back to fixed perspectives and routine behaviors. We lose heaven and accept as a substitute a fragment of life. We call this normal.

But that does not have to be our final fate. We are very fortunate, well-endowed, and destined for something more. We have a unique intelligence that can envision a full and prosperous life. No other species can do that. We have everything that is necessary to dream large and to actualize our dreams.

chapter 2

Shaping the Future

We live our lives backwards rather than forwards. Our day-to-day lives are largely determined by beliefs, perceptions and familiar reactions acquired early in life from family and culture. These old, tenacious, and persistent mental habits shape today's behavior. They obscure our greatest possibilities. That is how our life usually progresses until we consciously intervene to create a different future. Only then can we live our life forwards, shaping it with today's choices rather than yesterday's imperatives. And it is only by living our lives forward that we can create the causes that lead to human flourishing.

We may feel that in each moment we bring free will into our day-to-day life. However, nothing could be more false than this comforting illusion. To take charge of our life and shape a prosperous future, we must be willing to recognize and acknowledge this mistaken and life-destroying view. If we cannot accept the truth—the reality that our lives are largely predetermined—we cannot move beyond this obedience to the past. We cannot move beyond a programmed life. We cannot move beyond Plato's cave. The unfortunate and unnecessary reality is that most individuals end life much as they began it, chained to their past rather than reaching for their full possibility.

But this is not the only way to live life. As an alternative to repetitively acting out old mental programs, we are about to try something entirely different. Together, we are going to undertake an experiment. We are going to try to shape our future, not with the past, but with intentional choices we make in the present. These new choices will be consistent with the life we *want* to live rather than a life which is fated by our past.

This is a radical shift. We actually take charge of our life, *today*. We envision and create the future we desire and act now in a way that will result in that future. We no longer subject ourselves to the forces of yesterday. We no longer condemn ourselves to repetitive patterns. We are free to be who we want to be tomorrow, beginning today. That is how we live life forwards rather than backwards. That is how human flourishing becomes an actuality.

Trial and Error or a Bit of Faith

We can spend a lot of time thinking about the kind of life we would like to live. But if we can muster a bit of informed faith we can save a lot of time and energy. As we have already discussed, wise teachers throughout time and across diverse cultures and religious and philosophical traditions have spoken with a single voice about the characteristics of the "good life." Their understanding was arrived at through a mature wisdom which was unaffected by cultural fads and trends of one time or another. Their vision of human flourishing was consistent, reliable, trustworthy, convincing, and soul deep.

I think we would all agree with their understanding of the basic qualities of a good life—a peaceful mind, enduring and profound happiness, optimal health, loving relationships, meaning, and a mature wisdom. Can we agree that this would be an ideal future for our lives? Is this a vision we are willing to invest in? If so, we can avoid years of personal searching that will invariably end with the same conclusion as that of our wise ancestors.

I am suggesting this approach because I would like you to join me on the quick path to human flourishing, rather than the slower path of trial and error. Trial and error takes a long time because it is not a direct path. Why? Because misunderstandings, beliefs, and behaviors that linger from the past obscure a clear vision of human flourishing. So we try one thing and then another and then another to improve our current situation. That is how it is in modern times. Trial and error is a tedious and time-intensive process which most often fails to take us toward the fully realized experience of human flourishing. We are reluctant to use the perennial wisdom of the ages, and even if we are willing to do so we rarely have access to those who can teach it. However, if you are willing to accept the wisdom of those who have arrived at this vision and follow their instructions, you will save considerable time and effort.

That is how it was for me. For years I studied and explored many paths. I tried this and that. Then I directly observed the joy, wisdom, peacefulness, and clarity of highly developed beings. I saw these qualities directly experiencing their presence and observing their behavior. I knew without question what human flourishing looked like. I had a strong and instant faith in their wisdom and accomplishments. I discarded all my previous explorations and said to myself, as if I was speaking directly to these wise ones, "Show me how you attained this quality of life and I will do the same." That was not a simple decision. I arrived at it only after close observation of the qualities, stability and character of these wise beings. I immediately abandoned trial and error for a path that was clear, direct, and time-tested.

Once I made a choice, I gave my word to myself to follow this path with faith and effort. I honored my word. This greatly accelerated my journey to a larger life. And slowly, what I had initially chosen on informed faith was progressively realized and validated in my life. So if you choose the direct path you must first be certain that you can accept the vision of human flourishing bequeathed to us by our wise ancestors. Once you give your word to this vision it is important that you maintain integrity with your word. It is important that you commit the time and effort required to test this vision in your own life. In time you will verity its authenticity through your own experience. That is how we shape our future. We choose a life goal today and then, through intention and effort, we live tomorrow's goal today. We condition the future with today rather than with yesterday.

Joseph Campbell explained it this way. We can spend many years of our life climbing a ladder we have set against a wall, reach the top, and look over, only to find that our ladder was against the wrong wall. What an incredible disappointment and loss of life. We would then have no choice but to climb down the ladder, find another wall and start over again. This sort of trial and error can take a lifetime, not to speak of the effort, energy and disappointments along the way. Our life is short and precious. We don't have to rediscover what is already well-known. We can save this effort and energy by listening to the advice and instructions of the wisest of the wise. They have shown us the right "wall," and precisely described the steps up the ladder to human flourishing. If we start in the right place we will end up in the right place. That is certain.

As we lay the foundation for a life of human flourishing these are the two well-informed acts of faith we will take—a faith in the *vision* of human flourishing and a faith in the *path* that takes us there. These two acts of faith will immediately place us on the fast track. The experiment in your life is to test out this vision and roadmap and to see for yourself if it will indeed unfold this future for you.

The Experiment

We are going to begin with an experiment that has been conducted throughout the ages by individuals just like you and me. Although we will use as guidance the wisdom gained by those who have come before us, it is necessary for each of us to travel the path to human flourishing in our own life, by ourselves. There is no other way. No one else can do it for us. A larger life can only be achieved through personal effort. The potential for human flourishing comes with our genes. Its realization requires intention and commitment. It is somewhat like this. Butter, like our own hidden potential, lies unseen within milk. To transform milk into butter we need to churn it. To transform the seed and possibility of a precious life into a life of exceptional health, happiness, and wholeness, we need to similarly "work" our life.

Here is what we are going to do. The sages have told us that human flourishing is the result of inner and outer development. We are going to test their assertions in our own life. We are going to discover for ourselves whether this claim is true or false. So if they are correct and we now focus on our inner life we should, over time, begin to experience the qualities of human flourishing.

This is not a complex endeavor. We simply begin the process of developing our inner life and watch to see the results of our efforts.

We will need some benchmarks to measure our progress. Here again we do not have to make it difficult. Although we can chart our progress in a variety of ways, it is best that we simply rely upon our own experience. You will observe your life carefully as an "inner" scientist. Are you more peaceful and less reactive? Do you have less of a tendency to get taken over by difficult circumstances? Is your mind quieter and more still? Are you happier? Are your relationships improving? Has the overall quality of your life improved?

We cannot take these measures each day. We must observe them over weeks, months, and years. If you follow this experiment in your own life you will see some of these changes within weeks. At first there will be movement back and forth, moments when you experience major progress and others that seem flat. But over time you will notice more consistency in the results. Eventually you will be certain that your life is changing and if we are correct these changes will be in the direction of a richer and larger life. So that is our experiment. We start with the vision of human flourishing left to us by our ancestors and then follow the path they recommended as a way to attain this result. If they were correct we will discover what they discovered. If they were wrong we will discover that as well.

Study, Reflection and Practice

The path they recommended has three elements: study, reflection, and practice. "Study" refers to reading pertinent information and listening at seminars and workshops. For the initial purpose of our experiment the reading will be the following chapters in this book. Later we will expand our study to include other resources. "Reflection" is carefully considering what you have learned from study. We want to get below the words to the deeper meaning of what we are studying. We want to consider what we have learned to see if it makes sense to us. We want to expand our understanding. Study and reflection are the *basis* of "practice." There are two aspects to "practice." The first is a formal daily session the aim of which is to tame, train, and develop our mind. The second extends our practice into our daily life, where we use routine activities as opportunities for further learning. In this way all of our entire life becomes the ground of our experiment. That is why we call this the quick path.

To repeat, the process is study, reflection, and practice. What we learn from studying is the basis for reflection, and study and reflection together are the basis for practice. Initially this requires effort and discipline. As you progress it will become increasingly effortless. It is like a physical workout. In the beginning you must get to the gym and do the exercises. In time it becomes a way of life, a new positive habit. It is how we live forwards rather than backwards.

Shaping the Future: Mind and Body

It is important to emphasize that our personal experiment with inner development not only relates to mind and spirit, but to the body as well. Our body also lives backwards rather than forward. Yesterday's mental habits and reaction patterns shape today's physiology. However, our physiology is not sculpted in stone. The body is quite plastic and can respond to choices we make today. So if we want an optimal biological future we begin by establishing the foundation for that today. Much attention has been given to the role of nutrition and fitness in promoting physical well-being, but we have largely disregarded the profound impact of mind on body. For over 50 years we have known about the powerful relationship of body, mind, and spirit, but because our understanding of the inner life has been quite limited we have been unable to fully use the mind-body connection to promote optimal physical well-being.

However, we now know that daily stress in the form of disturbing relationships and unsatisfying work are risks to our well-being. Research similarly shows that the loss of a loved one, separation, divorce, anxiety, and mood disturbances have a damaging effect on our health. How does this show up in our body? Hypertension, cardiac arrhythmias, immune dysfunction (which plays a critical role in cancer,) and degenerative diseases are examples of body systems exhausted by anxiety and stress.

In the East they say that a brief mental disturbance disappears rapidly from our mind and body like writing on water with a finger.

A more prolonged mental disturbance and its physical consequences remain a bit longer, like writing our name in sand. But chronic stress, which to most of us goes unseen because we have become so accustomed to it, results in a permanent reshaping of our mind and body that is as difficult to change as etching in stone. This relentless disturbance of our mind, which too often passes for normal, is the primary source of premature and chronic disease.

The mind and body are as inseparable as fire and heat. You cannot place fire on one side of the room and heat on the other. As we begin our journey toward human flourishing we should remember that our focus on inner development is simultaneously a focus on our body. It is perhaps the most important step we can take toward enhancing physical health and longevity. That is how it is—a healthy mind equals a healthy body, or as our ancient Greek ancestors said—sound mind, sound body. Flourishing of our mind means flourishing of our body. We get two for one!

Universal Responsibility

We do not live as isolated beings. We are part of a larger community. Although we cannot fully serve others and heal the problems of humanity until we have committed ourselves to personal development, we cannot fully develop our own life unless we are concerned with others similarly caught in the same web of a limited and partial life. They remain unaware, as we have been, of the possibilities of human flourishing. Personal development and concern for others go together. It is important to recognize that healing our self and healing the world is a seamlessly interwoven experience.

Gandhi said to us "Be the change you want to see happen in the world." That is what we will be doing. By taking on the journey to human flourishing we will be simultaneously committing ourselves to becoming the change we wish to see happen in the world. We begin by taking responsibility for our own development as the first step. As we become more skilled in our effort we extend our concern beyond ourselves to others and our planet. By shaping tomorrow's future today we do so not only for ourselves. The interdependence of all of life assures that our efforts have a far broader reach.

By progressing towards human flourishing in our personal life we are preparing ourselves to serve as instruments for participating in the creation of a better world for everyone. Dysfunctional, disturbed, and confused understandings cannot lead to optimal living. Human flourishing is the only sound foundation for an authentic and sustainable society, culture, and environment. That is why our quest for human flourishing is so essential.

A Moment for Reflection

It is perhaps best to stop here for a moment of reflection before we begin our shared journey. We have spoken about the nature of human flourishing, the capacity we each have to shape our future, and the central role of inner development as the basis of a vibrant well-being of body, mind, spirit, and culture. We have also spoken of the three elements of our journey toward human flourishing: study, reflection and practice. It is now time for a moment of reflection on what we have already discussed.

So perhaps you might take a moment at the conclusion of this chapter and reflect upon your life and your potential for human flourishing. Do you want this for your future life? Do you want this with all of your being? Are you ready to undertake the study, reflection, and practice that can create this future for you? Are you willing to set aside the time, firm your commitment and resolve, and place yourself directly on the path to human flourishing? Are you ready to keep your word to yourself through difficult moments? Are you ready now, today, to hold and realize this noble human vision? Consider this choice carefully, as we are about to begin the journey of a lifetime.

PART II

The Path

Now that we have set our vision in place, we can turn our attention to the path or process that will take us there. If we were able to immediately realize and live the vision of human flourishing there would be no need for the activities which enable us to progressively arrive at this destination. But we are not. Our final goal is obscured by an overactive mind, fixed perspectives, and habitual patterns which were set in place a long time ago. They hide us from our innermost truth. But, we cannot merely wish these obstacles away. We need to clear them away through a precise path, one which has been time-tested through the ages by wise women and men.

In the chapters which follow we will explore a series of steps which take us directly towards our goal—the end of distress and suffering and the attainment of human flourishing. We will slowly weave a tapestry of practices and knowledge which together form the basis for a fully lived life. We will learn how every aspect of life can be brought on the path and used to advance our efforts.

The qualities of human flourishing are waiting for us. We do not have to create them. We merely have to follow the proper instructions which will enable us to remove the concealing veils and reveal what is already and has always been our wondrous birthright. That is the certain promise of the path. Pursued correctly it will take us to its natural destination, human flourishing.

chapter 3
Clearing the Mind

The practice of taming and clearing the mind is an essential first step. This practice has been given many names. In the ancient Greek tradition it was called "incubation." The individual takes time away from daily life, usually at a healing center, to quiet the mind and listen to the inner wisdom which spontaneously arises in the spaciousness of mental clarity. In the Judeo-Christian tradition it is called prayer, a focus on the divine that lifts our mind from its ordinary activities, opening mind and heart to a higher knowledge. In the East it is called meditation, a process that similarly quiets the mind and cultivates inner clarity and stillness. Here we shall embrace each of these traditions by using the simple phrase "clearing the mind." That is the intent and result of incubation, prayer, and meditation.

Clutter or Clarity

Why is it essential to overcome unrelenting mental activity and clear the mind? Why have the great traditions consistently emphasized this in their practices? Just look for your self. The adult mind is very busy. It is filled with mental chatter—random thoughts, feelings, mental images, sensory impressions, and elaborate stories. We automatically latch on to this or that fragment of mental activity, then another and then another.

This old and repetitive internal conversation creates our day-to-day life by filtering and shaping all incoming information. We fit present moment experience into our preexisting ideas and beliefs. It is through the lens of past experience stored in memory that we create our world. It is our self image. It is our life. As a result, *we live in mind rather than life*. Unless we can overcome the overactive mind we will stagnate in the past rather than flourish in the present. That is why the great traditions have emphasized practices that clear the mind.

Stop for a moment and observe your mind. Notice how it produces one thought after another. Observe how you follow these thoughts like a flag moving aimlessly in the wind. Next, focus on your breath. Try to follow it from one breath to another. See how long you can remain attentive to your breath before you lose your focus and are again lost in mental activity. Similarly, try to focus on a conversation with another person. See how long you are attentive to listening before your mind talk takes over with judgments, interpretations, and reactivity. Take a beautiful walk and see how long it is before your mind strays from your present moment experience in nature and returns to its busyness. A simple look at daily life demonstrates how lost we are in our non-stop monkey mind. There is no space for anything new.

> In the East they tell the story of a wealthy merchant who visits an Eastern master to request the great teachings of life. The sage pours a cup of tea for his visitor, but does not stop when the cup is full. The tea continues to flow over the sides of the cup. The teacher continues to pour the tea. Confused and annoyed the merchant cries out "Stop! Stop!" The sage replies, "Your mind is like your cup, it is too full to receive anything else." And that was the teaching. Much the same can be said for ourselves.

If we do not take charge of our minds we cannot possess our life. It does not belong to us. It is left to the vagaries of uncontrolled mental activity and corresponding words and actions. If we do not gain control of our mental chatter we cannot protect the mind from the fears, anxieties, and host of disturbing emotions that occupy much of our mental life. If we cannot protect our mind we cannot hold to any choices we make. This may be as simple as a choice to maintain a certain diet or as important as a choice to practice inner development. Without control over our mind we are likely to abandon all good intentions as soon as a compelling thought or emotion arises and takes over our mind.

If we cannot clear the fog of mental chatter there is neither inner freedom nor space to learn, grow, or create a larger health and life. We are victimized by our out-of-control thoughts and emotions. We do not know how to stop them. If we wish to grow our lives and experience the qualities of human flourishing we must choose mental clarity over mental clutter.

The great Indian teacher, Shantideva, eloquently expressed this human dilemma in a few well-chosen words. Consider the following:

> Wandering where it will, the elephant of mind,
> Will bring us down to the greatest suffering.
> No worldly beast, however wild,
> Could bring upon us such calamities.
> For all suffering and fear,
> All sufferings in boundless measure,
> Their source and wellspring is the mind itself.

With these simple and precise words this wise sage identifies the greatest obstacle to human flourishing, *the uncontrolled mind*. A drunken elephant loose in a china shop could not cause as much damage to us as our lifelong inability to tame the mind and gain freedom from its powerful influence over our life.

And finally Shantideva tells us how to do it.

> To cover all the world with leather—
> Where could such amounts of skin be found?
> But simply wrap some leather round your feet,
> And it's as if the whole earth had been covered.

We cannot control all the people or adversities in the world. If we try we will exhaust ourselves spending a lifetime attempting to accomplish this to no avail. That is not necessary. When Shantideva speaks about wrapping leather around your feet, he is speaking about developing a clear mind. If we can take the simple action of learning to clear our mind, we will establish an inner stability that is immune to the uncontrollable circumstances of life.

Learning How to Clear the Mind

The great traditions recognized that taming the mind and creating a clear inner space is key to breaking the enslavement to mental chatter, accessing our deeper self, and promoting human flourishing. This need is expressed in the image of Christ in retreat for 40 days in the desert, monks in their caves or cabins, Buddha under the Bodhi tree, Hindu renunciants in the forest, or modern-day individuals seeking the inner silence of prayer or inner practice. In each case individuals have recognized the life-destroying nature of mental clutter and have sought similar methods for clearing the mind.

If we carefully examine their wisdom and practices, we can distill their wisdom into two types of practices which work together to clear the mind. The first is done in a daily formal session. Sitting quietly we use the methods we will shortly describe to practice creating a clearing in the mind. The second is a series of specific practices that we progressively integrate into our usual daily activities. Because we are not seminarians or monks who devote all their time to formal practice, it is important to learn how to use all the activities of our daily life as opportunities for practice.

By taking this coordinated approach we greatly enhance our progress, bringing what we learn in formal practice sessions directly into daily life. In the beginning these practices break our enslavement to the overactive mind. In the middle, they stabilize and expand a still and clear mind. In the end they become the ground for the spontaneous emergence of the qualities of human flourishing. That is why these two practices are the foundation of our efforts.

The formal daily practice is based on the concept of retreat. All great traditions assert that it is important for individuals seeking a larger life to take time away, called refuge or retreat, to cultivate a clear mind. This "time out" allows us a designated time each day that is used for inner development. We let go of our usual mental preoccupations to focus on clearing the mind. It is somewhat like taking time to go to the gym for a physical workout. Here we are going into inner silence for a "mental clearing," a mental workout.

Clearing the mind is a progressive process. In the beginning you will likely achieve momentary glimpses. Do not underestimate their significance. Once you have experienced a clear and still mind, even for a moment, you know it is possible. You know that in the midst of ceaseless and life-denying mental chatter you can find stillness. Once you know this, all that is left to do is to extend and stabilize this achievement. With patience and practice these small islands of stillness and clarity will coalesce into larger "land masses."

You will also notice that stillness, calm, and clarity, in very mysterious ways, slowly show up in daily life. I often hear this in class as individuals discuss their progress. "Life seems calmer and I notice I am less reactive. But I'm not sure it is the practice." That is how this shift is usually described. Of course, nothing has happened in their life to account for this change except for the introduction of practice. Change can be very subtle, and that is a good sign. At first these changes may seem fragile, but with further progress your mind will slowly revert to its natural state of ease, stillness, and presence.

We experience this clearing as a state of simple presence and being undistracted by mental activity. You can get a sense of this by becoming aware of the gap between two thoughts. There is a moment of mental stillness in the space between two separate thoughts. That is the clearing. If you become aware of this "gap" you will experience a brief taste of mind's natural clarity and openness. However, observe it carefully as the active mind will take over quite rapidly.

Another way to get a sense of the mind's natural resting state is to hold your breath at the peak of inspiration. While holding the breath the mind will become still, and the thought process will momentarily stop. Become aware of this experience. For a moment obscuring mental chatter has dissipated and the mind's basic resting state is revealed. These mini experiences are only glimpses, or perhaps we can say a brief touch of the real thing.

Participants in our course often relate how amazed they are that their mind can actually be clear and still, if even for a brief moment. "I've never experienced a still mind, what a relief." That comment occurs quite frequently. I then point out that this is actually the natural resting state of the mind, the essence of our mind. The busy mind is something we have nurtured and cultivated for many years. We consider it "normal," but it is not! It is acquired and therefore can be overcome with intention and effort. That is the good news.

The second series of practices relate to your daily life. These are quite important. They will be introduced one-at-time so that you may slowly integrate all of them into your usual activities. These practices tweak your daily activities just a bit so that these activities can be used as practices themselves. A good example is mindful listening, a practice we will introduce shortly. This takes a routine daily activity, listening, and turns it into a practice that enhances your ability to listen to others, calms your mind, and improves your relationships. Simultaneously, this supports your formal sitting practice. Progressively, your daily life becomes your practice.

Clearing the mind is the first step in renewing and revitalizing life. It is the gateway to human flourishing.

Consider once again the words of Shantideva that we referred to above. In their entirety they are a worthy source of daily reflection.

> Those who wish to take charge of life
> Must guard their minds in perfect self-possession.
> Without this guard upon the mind
> No discipline can ever be maintained.

> Wandering where it will, the elephant of mind,
> Will bring us down to the greatest suffering.
> No worldly beast, however wild,
> Could bring upon us such calamities.

> For all suffering and fear,
> All sufferings in boundless measure,
> Their source and wellspring is the mind itself.

> For if I carefully protect my wounds
> Because I fear the hurt of cuts and bruises,
> Why should I not guard my wounded mind,
> For fear of being crushed beneath the weight of suffering.

To cover all the world with leather—
Where could such amounts of skin be found?
But simply wrap some leather round your feet,
And it's as if the whole earth had been covered.

We are now ready to begin clearing a space in our mind. This is the first step in moving forward toward our vision of human flourishing. Let us first overview this process that begins in the next series of chapters.

The Practice Chapters

Chapter 4-13 focus on the progressive stages of understanding and practice which will place you directly on the path to human flourishing.

It is not enough to know that we are endowed with the treasured possibilities we have spoken of. It is not enough to know that there is more to life. Even our intention to pursue the qualities of such a life is not sufficient. Oil may lie at the core of a sesame seed, but unless we break the seed open we will not be able to access its oil. Gold lies hidden in ore. However, unless we chisel away the ore we will not find the gold. Although the qualities of human flourishing are innate to our being, we must take specific steps that will awaken and reveal these qualities so that they may be embodied in our lives.

The book in its entirety has four sections. The first, the *vision*, opens our awareness to the full possibilities of human existence. The second, *the path*, provides a step-by-step program of understandings and practices that takes us toward these possibilities. The third, *the fruition*, provides a detailed description and in-depth understanding of the qualities of human flourishing that develop in tandem with study and practice. And the fourth section, *the integration*, explores the application of what we have learned to the major epidemics of our time. That is the full scope of the book.

By now it should be quite apparent that it is not my desire to just provide you with information alone. That would be unfair to you. It would be like offering you a once-in-a-lifetime possibility but giving you a booby prize instead. It is my desire to help you improve your life and move toward human flourishing. That is my wish for you. And these chapters are key to realizing this vision.

So how should you approach these chapters? It is my suggestion that you first read the entire book *without* focusing on the practices described in the practice chapters. This will enable you to take a broad view of our intent. Then, with this broad view in mind, I suggest that you return to the practice chapters and go through them slowly, at least one week for each chapter, as it will take this amount of time for you to integrate what you are learning and practicing into daily life. Alternatively, you may choose to slow down when you reach the practice chapters that follow, working with each of them at the pace mentioned above until you are ready for the final two sections of the book. Either way will work. Choose what is best for you.

The following chart will provide you with an overview of these chapters. Each chapter covers an important topic that is meant for study and reflection, a daily formal practice that continues into the future, and daily life practices that are added to each other week-by-week. These daily life practices will become a regular part of your life.

Guide to the Practice Chapters

Chapter	Content	Daily Sitting Practice	Daily Life Practices*
4	Homework for Life: Introducing Practice	Mindful Breathing	*Mindfulness in Daily Life*
5	Cultivating & Abandoning	Continue Mindful Breathing	*Taking a Life Inventory*
6	End of Suffering	Continue Mindful Breathing	*Mindful Listening*
7	Transforming Emotional Afflictions	Continue Mindful Breathing	*Turning Afflictive Emotions Into Practice*
8	Overcoming the Overactive Mind	Continue Mindful Breathing	*Observing the Moving Mind*
9	The Noble Heart	Introduces Loving Kindness Practice **	*Loving Kindness in Daily Life*
10	Work as Practice	Continue Mindful Breathing	*Becoming a Healer at Work*
11	The Alchemy of Adversity	Continue Mindful Breathing	*Adversity as Practice*
12	The Lightness of Being	Naturally Settled Awareness***	—
13	The Essential Points	Return to Mindful Breathing	—

* Most chapters introduce a new *"Daily Life Practice."* Each practice should be continued as new practices are added. The goal is to integrate all of the practices as a regular part of your daily life.

** The *Loving Kindness Practice* can be substituted twice a week for your Mindful Breathing Practice. Alternatively, you can add 10 minutes of this practice onto your regular Mindful Breathing Practice, limiting the "giving and taking" to a loved one.

*** This is the third level of practice. It is presented here to provide you with a comprehensive view of the full scope of sitting practice. Add this practice only after you have stabilized inner stillness for six months to one year.

chapter 4

The Practice: Homework for Life

The chapters that follow will join us together in a sacred process. Why do I call this a sacred process? I use the word sacred because our concern is with the very essence of our life. There is nothing that could be of greater importance. These teachings and practices have been passed down as precious gifts across many centuries. Wise women and men have protected and nurtured them with great care for a singular purpose. They intended that you and I learn from their knowledge and experience and gain, as they did, access to the great treasures of life.

We will now introduce our first two practices: a daily sitting practice, mindful breathing, and a mindfulness practice that we will integrate into our daily activities. The purpose of both practices is to train in clearing the mind. They will enable us to transform our mind from a noise machine to a finely tuned instrument which can help us to progressively gain access to the great treasures of life. Fortunately we have two valuable pieces of "mental equipment" that will assist with both these practices, mindfulness and vigilance.

Mindfulness and Vigilance

We begin by learning how to use these mental capacities which are the basis of formal practice, as well as practice in daily life. Mindfulness is the mental capacity that brings our attention to the activity of the present moment and holds it there. It keeps our mind focused, reversing its habitual tendency to wander towards random mental activity. It opens the gateway to the present moment by counteracting our usual tendency to stray into abstract mental activity.

We practice mindfulness by training ourselves to maintain attention. In our formal practice we accomplish this with a mindful breathing practice. During routine daily activities achieve this by holding our attention on the activity of the moment. This may be as simple as washing dishes or driving the car, or as complex as truly listening to another. The point is that mindfulness training develops the capacity to focus and hold attention. We bring and sustain awareness to what is actually occurring in the present moment. We are developing a new habit. We are substituting mindfulness for mindless distractibility.

By practicing mindfulness we protect ourselves from constant distraction and the tendency to chase after random mental chatter. The result is a progressive clearing of the mind accompanied by a growing inner calm.

The second mental capacity is vigilance or alertness. This reminds us when our mind has wandered from our focal point. Vigilance protects us from drifting away from the present by keeping an eye out for the intrusion of automatic mental activity. When our mind wanders, vigilance notes this and reminds us to return to a mindful state. The systematic cultivation of mindfulness and vigilance allows us to take charge of our mind, life, and health—ending the tyranny of autonomous mental activity. These are the tools we use to clear the mind.

Before we begin the actual practice it is important to consider some issues and concerns that may arise during practice. By discussing these now you will be more able to address them when they arise. Training the mind is not as much about "doing" in our usual way but rather about "being." And this requires a very different mental attitude. So let us look at what we take into inner practice and what we leave out of it. It is important to start by examining our motivation.

The Motivation

Our motivation drives our efforts. That is why it is so important to be clear about why we want to practice. When we first start, frustration with the stress and distress of an overactive mind is usually our initial motivation. We come to a point in life where we want more out of life. We want to slow down. We want inner peace and greater happiness. Whatever else we have tried has not worked. We have heard about mind training. Perhaps we have heard about it from a friend or read about it in a book. Or, perhaps we know someone who is actively engaged in inner development. We can see the changes in their life and want this for ourselves as well. That is what brings us to this work.

There are others who come to this work suffering from recent loss or serious illness. Their motivation is usually quite strong. They want to feel better and use this work to assist with their healing practice. Too often we have to wait until we are shaken by our roots before we take action to grow a larger life. But if that is your current circumstance, it is a powerful motivation.

Whatever your motivation, I would ask you to expand it as you begin practice. Remember that you have a precious opportunity right here and right now to move beyond an ordinary life towards a unique and priceless human life of enduring happiness, serenity, and wholeness. This opportunity does not appear every day. The right set of circumstances must come together at the same time—your motivation, your time and attention, the teacher, and the actual teachings. This is a rare and fortunate occurrence. If you fail to take advantage of this opportunity now, then when will you? Reflect on this.

So maintain a strong motivation, reflect on it before each session. Let it drive your efforts.

Non-Judgment

You will soon discover that you bring into practice your usual mental habits. Because inner development is concerned with *being* rather than *doing*, many of these habits are counterproductive. It is helpful to address them now so that you will notice them as soon as they arise.

We are accustomed to judging just about everything. I like this and I don't like that. Or we regularly compare one thing to another. This is better or this is worse. That is good and this is bad. One of the fascinating things about practice is that it throws a spotlight on our usual approaches to life, as they unknowingly slip into practice sessions. Judgments and comparisons are usually a fixture in our day-to-day mental life, but there is no place for them in inner development.

When I ask individuals about the progress in their practice I often hear, "I had a good practice session on Tuesday and a bad one on Wednesday." This is neither accurate nor helpful. When we judge, compare, or otherwise categorize our experience we react to such judgments, according to our personality, with frustration, feelings of failure, doubt, impatience, and so on. These reactions do not help. To the contrary, they are simply mind chatter and distraction that diminishes our ability to move forward in practice.

There is no good or bad practice. Each practice session is different and we learn from everything. So remember—no judgments, comparisons, good or bad. Just practice as described in the instructions. The rest will unfold by itself. Of course there may be certain suggestions that point out mistakes in following the instructions. These will enhance your practice. That is different than negative, repetitive, and useless self-defeating judgments.

When judgments and comparisons arise just watch these attitudes and the disabling reactions to them. Notice how they are self-defeating and self-sabotaging. Then, let them go and continue your practice.

Non-Striving

Hand in hand with non-judgment is non-striving. As mentioned above, settling into a clear mind is not about "doing," but rather about "being." This is a very important distinction. We strive all day long to achieve this or that so it is not surprising that this attitude easily creeps into practice. In inner practice we do not strive, we just do the practice as taught and relax into it with no regard for a specific outcome. The results will arrive by themselves.

There is really nothing to do except to ease into the practice. Does a seed strive to grow through the soil, a flower to give off perfume, a bee to produce honey? When you settle into the natural clarity and stillness of your mind the proper results will follow. You do not have to seek this experience. You only have to let go and do practice as taught.

So just stay with your practice and let these mental tendencies come and go. Then, perhaps in time, the excessive striving will disappear from your day-to-day life as well.

Patience

Patience is essential to your practice. For many years your mind has been trained to relentlessly chatter. It takes time to retrain your mind. But it can be done. That is certain.

In this context patience means the ability to engage in daily practice while viewing it as a long-term endeavor with many "ups and downs." It is important to measure this process over months and years rather than from day-to-day, even though you will definitely see changes early on which will grow with ongoing practice.

Patience means neither becoming discouraged nor disabled by daily differences in practice, the days in which you miss practice or when your practice seems to be taken over by a busy mind. That happens to anyone who tries to clear the mind. Use the moments when things seem to be off track as motivation to return to practice and enhance your efforts. In this way patience becomes an asset rather than a liability. It motivates you rather than disabling you.

There are times when patience fails me and I am overtaken by reactivity to this or that. My first response is annoyance and irritation. "All of this effort over so many years and here I am again." And then I begin to laugh at the circumstance. How powerful these old patterns are. How insidious they are, and yet if I look beyond the moment and take the long view over months and years I see that there has actually been significant change. So from these experiences I learn both patience and humility.

Enthusiastic Effort

Taking charge of your life and unveiling its extraordinary qualities is not a chore. It is a joy. Why, because each time you sit down to practice you are beginning the adventure of a lifetime. You are touching the great meaning and nobility of human life. The only frontier unexplored by most of us is the inner frontier—the frontier of the mind with its promise of a natural and enduring peace, happiness, wisdom, and wholeness. What other adventure could be as simple and offer as much?

What a fortunate joy to have the opportunity to sit quietly, take time to relax, learn to take control of your monkey mind and invest in a healthier and happier future. There are few activities we pursue in our lifetime that offer as many rewards as inner development. So be joyful that you have this extraordinary opportunity, the leisure time to practice, a sound mind and body, and teachers and teachings. This is a special moment when all of the important and necessary factors have come together to provide the basis for this important and fortunate opportunity.

So when you sit down for formal practice or when you practice in daily life, remember with gratefulness the precious circumstances which allow for this opportunity. There are few things that you can do that will offer so much promise of a better and happier life. That calls for joy rather than struggle.

Commitment and Discipline

Learning requires commitment and discipline. We simply set aside the time, do the practice as taught, and return for the next session. We just do it. Individuals often relate how their initial efforts at practice are stymied by an internal conversation such as this: "I've got a list of things to do today. I don't have time to practice. I'm really not in the mood today. I woke up a bit too late, and so on." I suggest that you stay out of such a mental conversation, because you will not win it. In the beginning our mind will find many reasons to convince us to skip a session. So, do not allow such a conversation to continue. Drop it immediately and begin practice.

As we grow in understanding it will increasingly become an effortless habit. It is not as difficult as you may think. Just stay with it and one day you will have a breakthrough. Remember how you began your physical workout. You began with discipline and commitment. Then, in time, it became an automatic routine. It is the same with a mental workout.

Commitment and discipline are acts of integrity. If we wish to flourish we must take our decisions seriously and stick with them, even when difficult, as a way of affirming and supporting our desire for more out of life. Every time you sit down to practice that is what you are doing. Even if you choose to practice for one month it is important to stick with it.

When You Are Having Persistent Difficulties, Ask

If we tried to read, write, or do math without a teacher we would likely repeat the same errors and blame ourselves. Clearing the mind is a learned skill. It is easy to make mistakes in the actual practice. You may get frustrated, blame yourself and drop off of your practice. But that is not the way to go about it.

Clearing the mind has always been taught from teacher to student. Each student has a different temperament, disposition, and learning style. The specific character of the practice should be tailored to each individual. So when learning in a group or through a book you may easily fall into errors while applying a generic process to your own needs. So you must always ask a skilled teacher when you are having difficulties. I will try to simulate that in the following chapters by providing you with "practice tips" that were actual responses to real questions and concerns raised by previous participants.

The Three Levels of Practice

Clearing the mind is an increasingly refined practice involving three levels of progressive attainment that unfold in their own time. These are:

- Creating a Clearing

- Resting in Clarity and Stillness

- Settling Naturally Into Present Moment Awareness

It is quite important to appreciate these increasingly subtle levels of practice. Why, because *in the West inner practice is usually taught as a relaxation technique.* We learn to quiet the mind and that is where we stop. Using practice as a method to relax is fine, but it only takes us so far. When you stop practicing, your mind will once again begin to chatter. That's because nothing has really changed. You have merely used a method to *temporarily* suppress your busy mind. But this is not the goal of practice. The goal of practice is to progressively, over time, mature inner development and gain the great treasures of life. That is our aim here as we carefully progress through these three levels of practice. Let's look at them one at a time.

Creating a Clearing

The first level of practice involves creating a clearing in the overactive mind. The aim of this level of practice is to tame the constant out-of-control mind chatter and clear a space through which we can experience the openness, clarity, and stillness of the undistracted mind. Clearing the mind is the necessary foundation for all levels of practice. It is in this clarity that we progressively discover the qualities of human flourishing. We have fully discussed this in the previous chapter.

Resting in Stillness

As we practice clearing the mind we occasionally gain glimpses of mental clarity and inner stillness. At first these may only be momentary gaps in a sea of mental chatter, like the gap between two thoughts. Nevertheless, these glimpses are of great importance. Even a quick peek lets you know with certainty that you, yes you, can calm and still your mind. To know this is possible, if even for a moment, is for many individuals a great discovery and relief. If we continue to practice we can be certain that these glimpses will expand over time.

We do not actually strive to attain mental stillness and an undistracted mind. This is an important point. It will unfold naturally at its own pace. *Do not set it up as a goal.* That will not help your practice. Just follow the instructions for clearing and taming the mind, nothing more. In the beginning, which may last for months, you may spend most if not all of your session trying to tame your mind through mindful breathing. That is just fine. That is how we train the mind.

However, if and when you progressively experience islands of clarity and stillness, slowly let go of your focus on the breath, progressively resting and relaxing into the calm mind. This is the second level of practice. It is dependent on the first level, taming and clearing the mind. You must be quite patient as this will take time and vary from session to session. That is how it develops.

Naturally Settled Present Moment Awareness

Naturally settled present moment awareness has been given many names. It has been called undistracted presence, pure being, pure awareness, open awareness, timeless awareness, naked awareness, truth, and has even been given the name of a creator. Although the direct personal experience of open awareness is unchanging over time and across diverse societies, it is characterized and labeled according to its cultural context. Even though it goes by many names, the experience is always the same. It is the natural result of study, reflection, and practice. This final step is the experience of our authentic self, a simple and effortless presence and being.

The basis for naturally settled present moment awareness is an undistracted and clear mind. That is why we begin by taming the mind. If we focus on taming and clearing the mind, this final stage of practice will naturally unfold over time.

We will now focus our attention on the first two levels of practice.

The Formal Daily Practice: Clearing the Mind.

Before you begin, identify a quiet and serene place that will support your daily sitting practice. It is best to have a special place that is clean, neat, and perhaps contains special and important objects and photos. A quiet, peaceful, and reverential space enhances the context and quality of practice. It is best that you use the same place with each session. It is also best that you practice, if you can, first thing in the morning when your mind is still from the night's rest. This is not so for everyone, so you must find what works best for you. Next, find a comfortable position—sitting in a chair or on a cushion that is comfortable yet allows you to maintain alertness. Try as best as possible to sit straight and maintain a "noble" posture.

One of the first questions individuals ask is, "How long should I practice?" The key point is not to take your practice to the point of frustration. I would like to offer three options.

(1) Begin with a 20-minute session, which you can consider extending to 30 minutes in the future. That is your first option.

(2) If your mind is overly active and you cannot practice for 20 minutes try this option. Break a single 20-minute session into four 5-minute sessions. Practice for five minutes and then open your eyes, move about and then return, resuming your practice for another 5 minutes. In this way you avoid getting overly frustrated during the 20-minute session.

(3) If this is also difficult try this next option. Practice in shorter sessions (5 to 10 minute sessions) at several fixed times throughout the day. Slowly you will build up to 20 minutes.

If your session becomes too overactive or dull you can always "refresh" your session. You do this by stopping, taking a deep breath and holding at the peak of inspiration. This will slow or stop mind chatter, creating a gap of relative stillness. You may do this several times in a row. Then return to your practice session.

You can also start by using the audio CD accompanying this book. For many this is an easier way to begin. I'll review this option below.

See what works best for you. However, once you set the time and duration of the session, stick to it. It is important to complete it, even if it is filled with chatter. However, if it is overly difficult, just drop that session. But please, do not make a habit of dropping sessions.

A Word on the Use of the CD Included in the Book

If you are, as I have suggested, first reading through the entire book, then you only need to read through the practices, returning to them later when you are ready to start.

If you are ready to begin the practices now you can do so by following the instructions below or using the accompanying CD. In either case read through the full set of instructions for the mindful breathing practice. If you wish to begin without the audio CD, jot down on an index card the key points from the summary of the practice that follows the instructions. You can glance at these key points during practice until you are familiar with the steps in the practice.

Alternatively you can begin with the CD. This is the same audio recording we use in our classes. There are three tracks. The first is a brief introduction, which you only need to listen to one time. The second track is our basic mindfulness breathing practice as described below. The third track is a loving-kindness practice which you will work with when you read chapter nine.

For some individuals it is a bit easier to quiet the mind using the guided practice. If this is you, you may want to stay with the audio recording until you are comfortable doing the practice on your own. Some individuals take a hybrid approach. They use the CD until their mind is a bit still, and then turn it off and continue on their own. Use what works best for you.

You are now ready to begin.

Step #1: Enhancing Your Motivation

We begin each session by strengthening our motivation. To do this we recall and reflect on the four thoughts which motivate practice. Eventually they become a mental habit. And that is important.

- Think of how *fortunate* you are. At this pivotal moment in my life I have the time, freedom, teachers, and teachings which enable me to move beyond ordinary existence toward the precious qualities of human flourishing. That conjunction of circumstances does not happen very often in life. It is infrequent. In fact, it is quite rare. I should not waste this opportunity. I can use it to shape a new and rich future.

- *There is not much time.* Each day I fail to move my life forward is another day which cannot be retrieved. If I subtract my childhood years, the time required to sustain my life, and the time needed for sleep there is little time left. I cannot wait until I am ill. That is not the time to practice. I must take advantage of the time I have now, this moment.

- *The practice session I am now going to begin is a step in this direction.* Each practice session assures my time will be well used and my life fully lived. Each practice session assures that I will move one step further toward developing the qualities of human flourishing, which will benefit myself as well as others. All that is necessary is for me to sit and do the practice as instructed. There is no better way to use my time.

- *If I do not practice I can be assured that my life will remain as it is.* I will have an ordinary life, ordinary disease, and an ordinary death. That is how it is.

It would be helpful for you to reflect on these points at the beginning of each session and recall them during the day.

Step #2: Mindful Breathing

Begin your practice by taking 10 deep breaths and counting each breathing cycle on the in-breath. Imagine you are taking in ease and peace with the in-breath, allowing it to move throughout your body, tissues, and cells, and that you are blowing out tension and stress with the out-breath. Peace and ease are riding the in-breath and stress and tension are riding the out-breath. Do this for the first 5 breaths. Then, for the next 5 deep breathes hold your breath for a few moments at the peak of inspiration. When holding the breath your mind quickly slows down. Feel the natural stillness that accompanies resting the breath. Then resume breathing, remembering the stillness that developed when you held your breath. The cycle is in-breath, hold and feel the stillness, out-breath, in-breath, hold and feel the stillness. Each time carry the stillness through the entire breathing cycle.

What we are doing with this deep breathing practice is slowly quieting the coarse activity of the mind. We are calming down the really loud noise. This is a transitional time. We are separating mind and body from day-to-day activities. We are setting off a special and sacred time and space for practice. It is like turning the inner volume from 10 to 5. Next we work on going from 5 to 0. If you feel you would benefit from another round of 10 deep breaths, that's OK. You can also do this part of the practice for a few moments anytime during the day. For some individuals visualizing tension going out and relaxation coming in may work better than holding the breath. Or, it may be the other way around. Work with what is best for you.

It is now time to pick a *focal point* for the main part of your practice. We will use the breath as our focal point. This is quite traditional. Decide where you can best "feel" your breath. You may chose the in and out movement of the breath at your nostrils or the rising and falling of your chest or abdomen with the breathing cycle. Choose what seems easiest and most natural for you.

Then, like a mother gently placing her hand on her child's face, place your attention gently on your focal point and observe the movement of your breath at that location. Don't examine or too tightly attach to the breath. Just observe it with a gentle "touch." Maintain enough attention to control your wandering mind, but not too much so that you are tense. It is a loose but effective attention. You may adjust and readjust this balance with each session, and even within a single session.

If your mind moves toward a thought, feeling, image, or sensory experience, which will occur many times, bring it back to your focal point as soon as you become aware of this movement. What is important here is to embrace mental activity as a friend, as a part of life. Thoughts, feelings, and images are not enemies to be pushed away, judged, or disliked. *The problem is our tendency to grasp and attach to them.* When they take over we simply greet them, remember to relax mind and body, and bring our attention back to the focal point.

Do not follow random mental activity into the past, project it into the future, preoccupy yourself with it, or further elaborate it in the present. Allow it to be like a cloud passing in the sky, a wave rising and falling into the sea or a reflection appearing and disappearing in a mirror. Here is where mindfulness is absolutely essential. Do not be concerned with the number of times you are distracted; just gently relax mind and body and bring yourself back to the breath. Continue until your mind begins to settle. This back and forth may occupy most of your practice, or even the entire session. That's fine. Just follow the instructions.

You may try a few additional ways to enhance the taming of your mind. For example, when we harmonize and regularize breathing, the mind will simultaneously calm down. So you may make an effort to slow and harmonize your in- and out-breaths. Regulating your breathing will regulate your mind as well. As previously mentioned, you may also try holding your breath at the end of inspiration for a short and comfortable few moments. You will notice the mind slows down. You will feel a gap in the noise. Carry this into the out-breath and remember it on the in-breath. Then, return to mindful breathing as before.

When your practice seems to be "out-of-control" it may be helpful to once again take a deep breath and hold your breath at the peak of inspiration. This is a way of refreshing your practice. If it helps, you can repeat this several times. However, only use this tool when you need it. Breathing normally and maintaining attention to your breath is the main practice.

It is also important to remind you that this is meant to be a pleasant and relaxing experience. Central to working with the mind is relaxation. So remember the importance of always relaxing and letting go of your mind and body. We want to maintain a good and sacred posture and attend to your practice, but always in an entirely relaxed manner.

Step #3: Observing Clarity and Stillness

Continue focusing on the breath throughout the practice session. However, if your mind on its own becomes progressively more still you can slowly and naturally release your focus on the breath and increasingly rest in the openness and spaciousness of the still mind. Remember, allow it to develop naturally and effortlessly. If your mind remains active, continue focusing on the breath.

If your mind clears, become aware of the stillness and clarity of this inner clearing—its openness, spaciousness, peace, and ease. The stillness will be your new focal point. Observe it with a relaxed mind and body. This does not mean that thoughts, feelings, and images won't continue to arise. They will. But they will diminish in intensity and "density." At this point the mindfulness is softer and less tight, as the mental movements are less insistent.

This part of the practice must be personalized. It will vary for each individual, within a session and session-to-session. You must learn to be guided by your own experience. If your mind is excessively distracted you should return to observing your breath. Know when to move towards stillness and relax your mindfulness and when to emphasize and tighten your focus on the breath. Find the right balance. Sometimes you may go back and forth in any one session. Do not judge yourself just practice at the level that works for each session. Tailor the practice by taking the measure of how your practice is going and what it requires.

As the mind stills so does the body. Our physiology follows the roller coaster of out-of-control mental activity as well as the harmony of stillness. Observe these changes in your body that accompany the shifts in practice. If your mind sustained a natural state of peace and ease, how would your body feel, in the moment and over the years?

When you complete the allotted time for your session, you may return to the time and space of the room.

A Brief Summary

The following is a brief summary of your basic practice which you can copy on an index card and refer to during practice until you are familiar with the sequence.

(1) Begin by taking 10 deep in- and out-breaths counting each cycle as 1 on the in-breath. For the first 5 cycles imagine you are breathing in peace and ease and breathing out tension and stress. For the second 5 cycles take a pause in breathing at the peak of inspiration, feel the stillness when the breath is still and carry that sense of stillness into the out-breath and the following in-breath.

(2) Next, return to normal breathing and bring your attention to the breathing cycle, to the in- and out-flow of your breath, at the nostrils or the rising and falling of the chest or abdomen with each breath. Tether your attention to your focal point with mindfulness and guard your attention with vigilance. Measure the "tightness" of your mindfulness according to the tendency of your mind to wander. Above all, relax. This is the main part of your practice.

(3) When your mind wanders, notice. Do not follow these mental movements into the past, project them into the future or elaborate them in the present. Gently, without judgment, bring your attention back to the breath.

(4) If your mind becomes increasingly still you can diminish the intensity of your focus on the breath, gradually allowing yourself to rest and relax into the mental clearing you have opened. If the stillness feels sufficiently stable you can let go of your focus on the breath and rest in the spaciousness and stillness of the mind. As mental movements occur you will still need to use mindfulness, but with far less intensity.

(5) It is unlikely that your moments of clarity and stillness will, in the beginning, be stable or prolonged. It is important to remember to return to mindful breathing when your mind becomes very active. Rest in stillness only when this naturally develops. Otherwise stay with your breath.

(6) When you think the time is up look at a clock (no alarm) and if you have finished your session return to the time and space of the room.

I have now described the main parts of your formal practice. Please remember that it is very important not to judge your practice as successful or unsuccessful, or compare one session to another. This is a mental trap. Just follow the practice and it will be perfect exactly as it is—no judgment, shame, striving, excess effort, or perfectionism.

Practicing in Daily Life: Mindfulness

The formal sitting practice is followed by our usual life activities. We call the latter, our "day-to-day life" or the post-practice period—the time in-between sessions. We support formal practice by extending it into daily activities. We accomplish this by practicing mindfulness in daily life. It is a bit strange that we call this a practice. Living attentively rather than mindlessly, distracted by mental chatter, should be our normal way of living. But right now it is not.

Here is the practice. Intermittently, during your normal daily activities, stop and remember to bring full attention to the activity you are doing. This could be working at the computer, washing dishes, tying your shoelaces, eating a meal, driving your car, or talking to a loved one or friend. In your formal practice you brought your attention to the breath and rested it there with mindfulness. Now, you similarly bring your attention to your present moment activity and mindfully maintain your focus. If your mind wanders notice it by being vigilant and return your attention to your activity. The aim here is to rest fully and attentively in what is actually happening in the moment. That experience becomes your focus. It substitutes for the breath.

It's quite simple. "Ah … I'm walking down the hallway. Let me bring my attention to this activity and let go of any other mental distractions. Now my mind has wandered. Let me bring it back again and hold it with mindfulness to the experience of walking. How do my feet move when I walk? How quickly do I walk? What am I passing as I walk?" When your mind wanders bring your attention back. It doesn't matter how often your mind wanders, just observe your mind and if it wanders return it to what you are doing in the moment. This is how we train ourselves to attend to what is happening in the present moment.

We want to experience each moment and each activity as if it was occurring for the very first time—and in actuality it is. We want to approach daily life like a child who looks with awe and wonder as the world is discovered anew each moment. We put aside our tendency to perform activities through routine and habit. We put aside our tendency to interpret, judge, or comment on our experience. We approach what we are doing with full attention and awareness. We are fully present in the moment. How else should it be?

What is it like to see the morning dawn? What is it like to experience the beauty and aliveness of life without commentary? What is it like to actually experience tying our shoe for the first time, taking a meal for the first time, going to work for the first time, looking at a tree for the first time? It is always the first time, isn't it? There are never two moments or experiences that are the same. We simply make them the same by replacing freshness with labels, comparisons, and automated patterns of thought. We categorize and assign meanings and interpretations. We are asleep to what we are actually experiencing. We falsely experience each moment as if it was the same as the previous moment.

So we want every moment and every "routine" experience to become a unique "event." Each experience is an opening to the great mystery of presence, an opening to the beauty and uniqueness of the moment. So transform each moment of your day into a special "event." Be fully with it as a unique occurrence that will never happen quite the same way again. When you fully experience each moment, you reconnect with a sense of awe and wonder.

By doing this repeatedly, much like in formal practice, we train the mind in mindfulness. As an important "side effect," focused attention during our daily activities will always still the mind, reveal an inner calmness, and enhance the quality of our experience.

Sometimes it is helpful to use a simple tool to remember to be mindful. Wearing a little bracelet around your wrist, pasting color-dots around the house and work, identifying one specific daily activity that you will attend to can help remind you to be mindful.

In this way we continue to train our mind in the post-practice period (our daily activities) by bringing mindfulness and awareness to daily life. This is a very powerful practice you can use throughout the day.

We have now covered the first two practices. We are on our way. Remember that our aim is to flourish into our greatest potential and rest assured these results will follow your practice. That is how it has been for others, and it will be for you as well—guaranteed!

chapter 5
Cultivating and Abandoning

When teaching this program in a class setting we begin each session by closing our eyes and sitting quietly for a few moments. It is a way of settling mind and body. I would like to suggest that you do the same before each chapter. Close your eyes, take 10 deep breaths, relax your mind and body, and then begin the reading.

The mindful breathing practice described in the previous chapter will enable you to progressively create a clearing in the dense thicket of mental chatter. Even though it may take time to stabilize the capacity to clear your mind, this will certainly occur if you persist. However, we cannot ignore the fact that our culture supports and encourages an overactive mental life linked to hectic lifestyles. That is a major reason why taming and clearing our mind can, at the beginning of practice, be quite a challenge.

Consider the following. We nourish and care for our body to protect it from harm. We learned to do this from a very young age. We use seat belts when driving, helmets when riding our bicycle, clothes to protect us from cold, vitamins to support our physiology, exercise to condition our body, and so on. But what about caring for and protecting our mind? Wouldn't it make sense to protect ourselves from mental wounds caused by an overactive mind and disturbing mental states? Wouldn't it make sense to encourage lifestyles that support mental well-being?

Let us use a simple metaphor here. Is it possible for a fish dropped into a cesspool to survive for very long? Similarly, is it possible for our mind dropped into a toxic environment to survive and flourish, even with diligent practice? It would certainly be a great challenge. Just look at the modern-day epidemics of anxiety, stress, mood disturbances, attention disorders, and chronic disease. The answer is clear. We need more than good intentions for our practice to flourish. We need a supportive lifestyle and environment.

Can we care for our mind by adopting habits and lifestyles that protect us from an overactive mind, support inner stillness, and optimize our mental capacities.? Do we see this as important as caring for our body? How strange it is to have to point out the importance of caring for our mental life. To care for our mind is intelligent, virtuous, and wholesome.

As we progress in practice, we recognize the need to support our practices with a supportive lifestyle. In the beginning we may think that if we practice regularly that will be enough, and of course this is essential. But when we begin to taste the ease of a still mind, diminished reactivity, and improved relationships, we naturally want more of these changes. That is when we decide to create the optimal conditions for the success of our efforts. We realize that our goal is to transform our lives, not merely to add another "healthy" activity.

There is an ancient word for cultivating and abandoning. That word is "purification." Its meaning is the same now as it was long ago. We purify our lives by encouraging mental attitudes and lifestyles that are wholesome, healthy, and virtuous, while abandoning those that have the opposite effect. Our ancestors sought to purify mind, body, and spirit through approaches such as fasting, ritual bathing, contemplative practice, vision quests, and devotion. Now, as in ancient times, this is an important and practical step towards a larger and healthier life. In a way suited to modern times we similarly create the context, or let us say the healthy soil, which will support and sustain our journey toward human flourishing.

The Wisdom to Know What to Cultivate and What to Abandon

Discerning wisdom is a form of wisdom that knows the difference between attitudes and behaviors that support a healthy mind and life and those that get in the way. Often this is quite obvious and requires no more than common sense. At other times this can be a very subtle process, requiring a wisdom that progressively develops and over time can make an increasingly accurate measurement of our choices. Without this ability we go through life largely unaware and unconcerned with the impact of our thoughts and actions on our life.

Transforming our life so that it supports inner development and human flourishing is not something we do all at once. What happens is that we slowly fine-tune our attitude, actions, and lifestyle as we discover what supports our mental life. So the process is not like a hard immediate monastic-like shift in our lives. Slowly, we gain a clear understanding of what contributes to developing our inner life in the short and long term. We will get accustomed to asking the question: Do these attitudes, words and behavior cultivate inner development or not? Then, we act accordingly.

Let us begin by considering a few important ways in which we cultivate and support our journey towards optimal well-being.

Letting Go of What Does Not Work

Let us start with what does not work by looking at attitudes and actions that obstruct the way to a larger health and life. We begin by examining two mistaken views—habitual ways of thinking which block our path to human flourishing. Why is this so important? Our view or belief system is the basis for our actions. When we hold a certain perspective we focus on it and strengthen it over time. We create habits out of these views. These habits become so familiar and automatic that we never question their accuracy or impact on our lives. We therefore act them out in daily life through our speech and actions, reinforcing them even further. And we don't even know that we are doing this.

When our view is incorrect our actions are misguided and incorrect, and incorrect actions lead to a cluttered mind and mental distress. On the other side correct views lead to correct actions, serenity, and happiness.

Abandon an Exclusively Physical Approach to Health

A major obstacle to a larger health and well-being is the limited perspective of modern medicine. Unfortunately, we have all adopted this as our personal perspective as well. We believe that a biological based medicine can provide us with the best opportunity for full health. This is a false, mistaken, and potentially fatal view. Our aim is not to abandon or reject medical science, but rather to realistically value and support its contributions while acknowledging the inherent limitations of a solely external approach to health and healing.

Medical science is concerned with the physical and material aspects of life. It devalues the impact of the mind on health. As a result, major contributing factors to disease—stress, emotional afflictions, psychological, and spiritual disturbances—are disregarded. Similarly, mental factors that contribute to health and well-being are also disregarded. Yet, regardless of this limitation of modern medicine we all tend to avoid this obvious problem, acting as if modern medicine can heal and whole all aspects of our life, when this is far from the truth. It is this incorrect view that we must abandon, or as the ancients would say, purify.

When you realize the limitations of an exclusively biological approach you will at the same time recognize that a comprehensive and far-reaching health and wellness requires that we also develop the *inner* dimensions of health and healing. Only a fully integrated outer and inner approach can be the basis of optimal health.

This is not easy as we have been well-trained in this viewpoint and are accustomed to assigning importance, time, and resources to physical health, resources that we are far less likely to apply toward inner health. Just consider the issue of setting aside time for practice each day. Many individuals find this very difficult. Many reasons are given. "I don't have enough time. I can't get up that early. The family was visiting, and so on." But if I wrote on a prescription pad, "take 20 minutes each day to sit quietly and calm your mind," it is likely you would follow this medical prescription, particularly if it were a prescription for a physical ailment. Isn't that strange!

The same is true with our allocation of money. We consider it essential to spend money on health insurance or medical services which treat physical ailments. But how willing are we to spend a fraction of these resources on inner development? So even if we agree in theory that inner development is important, our actions are largely determined by our culturally-encouraged focus on the physical and material. We must be very aware of this faulty perspective and progressively, supported by actions, cultivate a correct life-enhancing viewpoint that brings a balanced concern for body, mind, and spirit.

Abandon a Reliance on Outer Sources of Pleasure

Similar to our reliance on outer approaches to health, we have also learned to rely upon outer experiences, people, and objects for happiness and inner peace. These may bring moments of happiness and calm, but these moments will always degenerate into dissatisfaction and disturbance—a truth we will discuss more thoroughly in the next chapter. *Authentic and enduring happiness and serenity can only be found through inner development.*

We have wasted a great deal of time and life chasing external pleasures in the form of romance, success, fame, name, approval, and materialism only to discover that in time they become unhealthy attachments or addictions. These are temporary remedies for aloneness, dissatisfaction, and the soul's unmet longing for a larger life. They constantly need upgrading as their glitter will dim and eventually they will degrade into loss, distress, and suffering. Outer pleasures are not the same as authentic and sustained sources of happiness and peace which can only be achieved through a healthy inner life. To find the latter we must first abandon this second false belief, the belief that happiness, peace and wholeness can be reliably found in external pleasures. Again, we are purifying a false belief and replacing it with a correct and life-enhancing one.

Reflect on these two mistaken perspectives. How do they show up in your life? Remember that these faulty perspectives can be quite subtle and tenacious. You must guard and protect your mind from their negative influence. To do so is to support your desire for a larger life.

Abandon Harmful Attitudes, Speech, and Action

Finally, we must abandon all attitudes, speech and actions which cause suffering to ourselves or to others. It is not merely a matter of ethics or basic goodness. It is a practical issue as well. If we clutter our mind with negative thoughts and cultivate harmful speech and behavior, we leave little possibility that practice alone can enhance our life.

Just consider anger. One moment of anger can consume our mind and energy for a day, two, or even more. We are so taken over by this feeling that there is little more that we can do with such a disturbed mind. Once we are swayed by such strong emotions it is very hard to settle our mind and retrieve any level of inner clarity and stillness. So if we desire to grow our practice we must be careful to avoid and abandon destructive emotions, a topic we will address in chapter seven.

Knowing what causes suffering to ourselves and others can at times be difficult. It is not always easy to know the short and long-term consequences of our speech and actions. Sometimes we must undergo periods of distress that are necessary to insure long term happiness. Sometimes we must be firm with a loved one, an action which may be hard in the moment, but lead to positive change over time. That is where discerning wisdom is helpful. For now we avoid what will obviously cause distress and suffering for ourselves and others, and when possible we approach more subtle circumstances with the insights and wisdom we are developing through inner development.

In summary, we have discussed three basic things we must abandon in order to support our efforts to achieve a larger life and health:

- The false belief that an exclusively physical medicine can itself promote optimal health;

- The false belief that people, experiences or objects can bring us enduring happiness and inner peace; and

- All speech and actions that cause suffering to others or ourselves.

We cannot accomplish all this on the first day. It is a gradual process. Do not be discouraged by momentary fallbacks to old behavior. That is how it is. Habits are strong. But over the long term your intention, supported by mindfulness, will increasingly orient you towards a health mindstyle and lifestyle. Cultivating and abandoning, what our ancestors called purification, is a time-tested approach to the good life.

Cultivating What Works

Letting go of what does not work to support inner development goes hand-in-hand with establishing the mental attitudes and behaviors which do. In the first instance we are slowly letting go of entrenched habits that diminish our life and in the second instance we are establishing a new set of mental habits and behaviors that honor life. If the mind could not be trained, we could not accomplish this, but it can.

Refining and Cultivating Your Motivation for Practice

The motivation for applying your self to inner development matures over time. Cultivating a more expansive motivation will result in an increasingly stable foundation for your efforts.

In the beginning your motivation may be quite similar to what brings you to a doctor. You experience distress and suffering in its various forms. You want to be rid of these symptoms and enjoy life. You have heard something about working with the mind and hope that such an effort can resolve our problem. At this basic level of motivation you are pushed by coarse and overt suffering.

Fairly soon, perhaps in the first few weeks after beginning practice, you begin to have new experiences. You feel that your mind is calmer; you are less reactive, and more mindful. For some individuals this is the time at which the initial motivation diminishes and practice drops off. This shows up as procrastination, lack of discipline, or diminishing interest. It is as if practice was merely a remedy, a temporary form of first aid. Once the overt pain is gone the medicine is placed in the drawer.

However, with further examination you discover that even though overt suffering has diminished all is not well. Perhaps it is the persistence of low-levels of distress, unsatisfying relationships, recurring mood disturbances, or a subtle and persistent longing for more of life. Perhaps in the past these were covered over by more overt concerns or perhaps you simply considered these subtler forms of distress as normal, paying little attention to them. But now you see them for what they are. They exhaust life. Rather than dropping practice when overt suffering calms down, the recognition of these subtle disturbances can further motivate your efforts.

As you continue inner development, you will progressively experience positive changes in your life. Your motivation slowly becomes more proactive and less reactive—a desire to live a healthier and happier life rather than a response to distress and suffering—overt or subtle. You will feel sweet longing for more of the peace and happiness you are now experiencing. Instead of being pushed into practice by distress and dissatisfaction you will increasingly be pulled by the birth of new possibilities. You will experience a renewed burst of enthusiasm and energy. Practice becomes increasingly effortless and joyful as well.

Up to this point your motivation has been centered on your own life—finding relief from distress and suffering and promoting optimal well-being. That is a fine and appropriate motivation, but to go further you must begin to consider others as well. We do this by shifting from a focus on self to a focus on others. We now know that neither suffering nor distress is a requirement of life. We feel sadness for the needless and pointless distress and suffering of others. We wish and hope that they could find what we have found. We realize all individuals want to be free of suffering and to have a happy and healthy life. We have been fortunate to gain from our efforts. But can we really be fully healthy and well while others continue to needlessly suffer? Can we really flourish if our only concern is with our self?

We realize that only through our own development can we attain the understanding and skills that will be of the greatest help and value to others. When this understanding penetrates our mind and heart, our motivation will undergo its final transformation. It will reach toward the purest and most human motivation: to fully develop our humanity so that we can be of service to others. We exchange a focus on our self—a motivation based on our personal needs and desires—for a focus on others. This is a high, noble, and sacred intention. We are now inspired by selfless motivation that reflects the highest capacity of humanity. It is the most profound reason to pursue inner development through practice.

The transformation and maturation that occurs when we shift from a motivation based on personal suffering to a motivation based on the longing for a larger life, and finally to a motivation grounded in the wish to benefit others is a flowering of the human spirit. With each shift we expand our reach. With each shift there is an enhanced commitment to practice in and out of formal session. I have seen this occur with predictability in the many individuals I have worked with, individually and in classes. It is important to deepen your motivation for practice. This will be of great help to your practice.

Be patient. It is a progressive process and you will likely find that your motivation at any one time is a mixture of all of the above. However, over time your motivation will progressively become subtler, refined, sacred, and noble.

Cultivating Wholesome Motivations in Daily life

We have now spoken about the progressive refinement in the motivation that underlies our desire to practice. It is equally important to examine the motivations that underlie daily activities. Why, because our actual motivations are often very different than they appear to be at first glance. And a confused or improper motivation will lead to stress, distress, disturbed relationships, and suffering. On the contrary, a clear and proper motivation will lead to well-being, all of which will support our efforts toward a larger, wholesome life.

Let's look at two examples. We take an action that on the surface is caring and generous towards another, perhaps towards our lover or partner. In fact, we "give" to the other quite frequently. However, over time we notice that we are beginning to harbor a subtle and progressively more apparent resentment and anger towards this person. They have not returned what we have given. They have not shown us appreciation or reciprocity. Giving to him or her seems like a one-way street. That does not feel good. What is wrong with this person? We feel they are stingy and only know how to "take."

Perhaps we could learn more from examining our motivation for giving, rather than dissecting the other's personality. After all, we can only deal with our self. So let us take a deeper look at our motivation. What appears on the outside as "giving" may look the same irrespective of the underlying motivation. That is how we get fooled. There is "giving" that is motivated by the selfless desire that the other person be happy. There is "giving" that is subtly motivated by self-interest such as getting back approval, appreciation, self-satisfaction, or something else in return. It is difficult to see these distinctions by observing the behavior itself, as on the surface the behavior may look the same regardless of the motivation. But the results are far different.

When we give from a selfless motivation we seek and expect nothing in return. As a result, we are happy to give regardless of the response of the other. However, if we are deceiving our self and actually giving from a hidden self-interest we are silently making demands on the other. We are actually engaging in a business transaction in which we expect something back for what we give. But we neither inform the other of this expectation nor get their agreement to go along with our undisclosed bartering arrangement. This can be quite subtle. Seeking or expecting something in return for our giving may at first glance seem only fair and decent. But if unstated and not agreed to by the other it is actually self-centered and manipulative. Such actions will certainly end in distress for our self as well as others, as soon as our *unstated* expectations go unmet. Give this some reflection. Examine this in your own life. You will undoubtedly discover, with great dismay, that your "giving" is not as altruistic as you once thought.

From this example we can see how the courage to examine our motives, even when they seem wholesome on the surface, will enable us to identify and abandon unwholesome motivations and actions and replace them with motivations and actions that will lead to happiness rather than distress.

Let's look at a second example. Our friend or family member engages in an action that is clearly unwholesome and invariably leads to distress. We are concerned. We may even become angry that they are not taking proper care of themselves. This anger arises solely from compassion, from the desire that they be happy and free of suffering. However, if this individual does not alter their behavior, our anger may shift, turning into resentment, judgment, and condemnation. We may even act this out by striking out with anger towards the other.

If we look carefully we will discover that the anger that was initially motivated by selfless compassion is now increasingly about *my* distress. I want things to be how I want them to be. "Why can't this person change? Why won't they change? I'm unhappy and annoyed with him or her. This is making *me* upset." Can you notice the subtle change that has taken place? Selfless compassion for the other has taken a turn toward manipulation and condemnation.

Initially my feelings were about the other. Now they are about me—my helplessness in getting the other to change and my increasing resentment and inner distress. On the surface the anger may look the same, but the motivation is far different, and so is the result. Anger motivated by selfless compassion comes from an open heart. It is helpful to the other. Anger motivated by self-concern will be destructive to all involved. So here again we see how we must always look carefully and honestly at our motivation in daily life, cultivating wholesome motivations and abandoning unwholesome ones. And this may require ongoing evaluation and great wisdom, as our motivation may subtly shift from wholesome to unwholesome.

In daily life there are actions we take that are significant and others that are less so. When we take important actions we must carefully examine our motivations *before* taking action and *throughout* our action. By cultivating a wholesome motivation we progressively create a positive context for growing a larger life.

Cultivating Inner Calm

So how do we cultivate inner calm in a busy, extroverted world? How do we maintain and sustain mindfulness? We start by slowing down and cutting out unnecessary activities—for example, unnecessary entertainment, trivial conversations, needless phone calls, consuming relationships, and meaningless social engagements. This is a slow and progressive process of letting go of activities that squander our time and agitate our mind, while at the same time taking on activities that are protective, nourishing, and supportive of a healthy mental life.

This is not a forced process. Your interest in unessential outer pursuits will naturally diminish as you gain inside what you once sought outside. You will naturally let go. I often hear this from participants in our course. I hear comments like, "I don't turn on the television as much as I once did." "I am spending less time with friends that just want to talk and talk." "I'm finding myself staying in the house more and giving less time to activities that now seem less attractive to me." That is how our outer life begins to change as our mind slows down.

You will also feel the desire to create still and serene environments at home and at work which support inner development. This may involve creating a special place in your home where you can retreat for stillness and silence, adding natural beauty to your environment, turning off sources of extraneous noise, and so on. In this way we create and cultivate islands of solitude everywhere that we can. At times these islands may seem as if they are floating in a sea of turmoil. But slowly they begin to coalesce, providing your life with greater solitude and less needless stimulation that agitates your mind.

The point here is to become mindful of the unnecessary noise and stimulation in your life, abandoning the sources of these unwholesome experiences as best you can. Simultaneously, you make the effort to bring as much solitude and peace into your life as possible, cultivating the foundation for inner calm. We are purifying the toxins of unneeded agitation and stimulation and cultivating a wholesome space of quiet and ease.

Cultivating Loving-Kindness

Without exception all great healing and spiritual traditions inform us that cultivating loving-kindness toward others supports and accelerates the development of our inner life. Why do they speak of this with one voice, because they understood that focusing on others is a powerful way to diminish self-preoccupation and foster healthy inter-connection. Loving-kindness is the antidote for isolation, loneliness, and disconnection.

Loving-kindness is cherishing others the same way that we cherish ourselves. At first this may seem a bit odd, as we believe that cherishing our self is a natural instinct and caring for others is a luxury. But this does not make sense. Are others less valuable or deserving of love and care than we are? Isn't it true that others wish to be cherished just as we do? And on close examination isn't our need to be loved more fulfilled by loving others? Look around and you will see that the happiest people are those who love and care for others!

We cultivate two levels of loving-kindness: aspiration and engagement. In the first instance we aspire to be loving and kind to others. This initial step is what we call a "cushion" practice. Cultivating loving-kindness as a mental aspiration and intention will be of great help in stabilizing your mind and preparing it for inner work. In chapter nine we will describe this practice in further detail. In the second instance we translate this aspiration into speech and behavior. We substitute kindness, gentleness, patience, and affection for less wholesome behaviors. Every circumstance is unique and calls for a particular expression of loving-kindness. With a skillful wisdom we begin to discern the appropriate action.

Cultivating Simplicity

Consider the extent of your personal needs when your mind is still and serene. Perhaps you can observe this when you are in communion with nature, in a lover's embrace, playing joyfully with your children, or when in prayer or inner practice? Then observe how your needs escalate when you enter a shopping mall. All of a sudden you have a desire for things that previously were not even thought about, much less needed. How does this happen? Certainly it is no accident. The entire profession of advertising and marketing is designed to create new needs, and they are quite successful.

So think about the difference between authentic needs and momentary impulsive "wants." The more we chase after unnecessary and hyped-up wants, the more we have to work to pay for them, the less free time for inner development, and the more cluttered our mind. When is enough, enough? Is there an end to our wants? Is there an end to our mind being manipulated by clever advertising? Is there a point at which we can be satisfied?

If we consider those moments in which we feel few if any needs we will discover the secret to a simple life. *When our mind is still and peaceful we are relatively free of needs.* How amazing! Our needs are largely related to our mental state. They are fluid and change according to our state of mind. The formula is simple. A busy mind equals lots of needs and complexity. A quiet mind equals few needs and simplicity. Which would you choose? Which do you think will support your practice and a larger life?

By cultivating a simpler life there is less to occupy our mind, fewer things on our "to do" list and less financial demands. Cultivating a simple life, wherever we can, supports inner development.

Cultivating a Healthy Body

Our body is the container for our mind. Some would call it the temple in which our spirit resides. As such it deserves great care and honor. The preciousness in our body lies in its capacity to support our journey towards human flourishing, and its end result, selfless service to others. If we fail to care for our body we will undermine the circumstances that support inner development.

It is not my purpose here to review the many ways to cultivate a healthy body. You know them well. Proper nutrition and physical fitness are essential, but there are also other steps that each of us can take to optimize the well-being of our body. This is not to say that consciousness cannot develop in the presence of physical disability and illness, it can. But it is best that we cultivate as best a home as possible for our growing soul and spirit.

In summary, here are the changes we should cultivate in our life in order to support our efforts to achieve a larger life and health:

- Refining and upgrading our motivation for practice;

- Developing wholesome motivations in daily life;

- Encouraging inner stillness;

- Cultivating loving-kindness;

- Choosing voluntary simplicity; and

- Cultivating a healthy body

After this brief overview you may have some concern or fear that shifting your life towards wholesome attitudes, speech, and actions may be a bit colorless and take the fun out of life. At times this is raised as an issue in our classes. However, as I point out in class, nothing could be further from the truth. When we orient ourselves towards optimal well-being our relationships improve, work becomes more meaningful, our mind is progressively calmer, and life is easier and more delightful. This is a far better state of being than the usual stress and distress of an overactive mind and pointlessly busy life. Try it and you will surely discover this for yourself.

Slowly and with patience cultivate what is wholesome and abandon what is not. This is a gradual process that in time will encompass your entire life. In the beginning be mindful of how you want to shape your life and carefully assess what helps and what does not. Then, over time, begin the process of cultivating wholesome attitudes and behaviors and abandoning unwholesome ones. This is how we purify our lives as we progress on the path toward human flourishing. That is how the wise ones lived their wondrous lives, and it is no different for you.

The Art of Disappearing

I would like to conclude this section with a poem, *The Art of Disappearing*, by the poet Naomi Shahib Nye.

> When they say, "Don't I know you?"
> Say "no."
> When they invite you to the party
> Remember what parties are like
> Before answering.
> Someone telling you in a loud voice
> They once wrote a poem.
> Greasy sausage balls on a paper plate.
> Then reply.
> If they say we should get together
> Say "why?"
> It's not that you don't love them anymore.
> You're trying to remember something
> too important to forget.
> Trees.
> The monastery bell at twilight.
> Tell them you have a new project.
> It will never be finished.
> When someone recognizes you at the grocery store
> Nod briefly and become a cabbage.
> When someone you haven't seen in ten years
> Appears at the door,
> Don't start singing him all your new songs.
> You will never catch up.
> Walk around feeling like a leaf.
> Know you could tumble any second.
> Then decide what to do with your time.

This is not about whether or not you go to parties or what you eat or whom you talk to. It is about *you* deciding what to do with *your* time. Do not give that responsibility away to others. Know the difference between the activities and people that will help you achieve a larger life and the activities and people that will get in the way. Decide what is trivial and what is meaningful. Decide what is a good use of your time and what wastes your time. Decide what you want from this one precious life of yours. Decide as if you were on your deathbed looking back at your life. Decide, and then choose with clarity and strength how to best spend the moments you have.

* * *

Practice in Daily Life: Taking an Inventory

We are now going to add a second practice to daily life. The first was practicing mindfulness in daily activities. The second is the practice of taking an ongoing look at your day-to-day activities, noticing what experiences or people support your efforts to enhance your practice and well-being and those that do not. There is a simple question to ask of each activity. Does this help cultivate the conditions that allow for inner development, or does it get in the way?

I am suggesting that you relook at your day-to-day activities, even those which you highly cherish. Examine how they affect your mind and your time. Do these activities churn your mind, eat up your time, and distract you from developing a larger life? Is there too much idle chatter and meaningless entertainment? Even if these experiences are pleasant in the moment do they support your long-term goal of an enduring and profound health, happiness, and wholeness? I'm not suggesting you make any changes right now, but just take a close look at what cultivates a richer life and what is a distraction or detour, and with discernment know the difference.

You may naturally find that with ongoing practice you progressively let go of certain activities that no longer interest you. As you get quieter, less reactive, and more peaceful inside you will want more time for yourself and have less need to run from one activity and distraction to another.

So as you go through your day examine how you use your time, energy, and mind space. You might record these observations in a journal. Perhaps you will notice areas in which you can make some changes.

Tips for Sitting Practice

As we progress in practice I will offer some tips to overcome obstacles and enhance your practice. The point is to tailor your practice to your unique temperament and style. So when reading the "practice tips" in this and the following chapters, focus in on what works for you and move past what does not. That is the way you will slowly fine-tune your practice.

Remember that a mindful focus on the breath is a gentle attention and interest rather than a tight and tense holding. You are gently observing the breath. Relax into this.

Random thoughts, feelings and images are not adversaries to be pushed away or avoided. They are natural to the mind. As long as you have a mind and body you will have mental movements. The problem is not the mental movements, but your learned tendency to chase after them. Just note when they arise, leaving them alone in their own place where they will naturally dissolve and simultaneously, return to your focal point.

Once again we can summarize this in four points:

- Do not follow thoughts into the past.

- Do not elaborate and preoccupy yourself with thoughts in the present.

- Do not follow thoughts into the future.

- Relax into the natural stillness of your mind and body.

Remember, that if your practice becomes dull or agitated you can refresh it by taking in a deep breath and holding it. You can do this more than once. Catch the gap of stillness that opens up, stretch it as far as you can, and then return to your practice.

Once again, it is best to have a regular place to practice. Treat your regular practice spot as a special and sacred space. Keep it clean and organized. Perhaps add a plant, meaningful photos, or an object of special significance. This will bring the right mood and energy to your practice space and assist your movement into inner stillness. Instead of just starting your session without preparation, preparing your space will provide a smoother transition into practice.

chapter 6

The End of Suffering

To experience our greatest potential, we must first alleviate all forms of suffering, as these mental disturbances keep us from the treasures of human life. If the end of suffering was not a real possibility for each of us, there would be no need to go further. But it is. That is not my assertion alone, but the assertion of all the great traditions. However, this achievement does not spontaneously occur. You really have to want it. You have to want it with your whole being. It takes a devotion to your life that is backed-up by a strong and enthusiastic commitment to study, reflection, and practice. But you can do it. That is certain.

Suffering and happiness are mental experiences. They can only be approached through understanding and developing our mental capacities. Biological medicine has given us mastery of the physical aspects of life. It supports us in maintaining the health of our body, and a healthy body is an important resource in the movement towards human flourishing. But physical medicine alone cannot heal what is inner in nature. That is why this approach places so much emphasis on inner development.

Our mastery of biological medicine was the result of a progressive, detailed, and accurate understanding of biological structures and function, from the gross organ to subtle macromolecular genetics. Without this knowledge we could not have gained the capacity for diagnosis, treatment, risk reduction, or health promotion. It is no different with the mind and suffering. Unless we can gain a detailed, accurate, and comprehensive understanding of the nature of suffering and its causes, we cannot hope to move forward in our efforts to diminish or eliminate it.

Once we know the causes of stress, distress, and suffering we can apply the correct and effective remedy. Right now we simply know that suffering is unpleasant. That is equivalent to knowing that heart disease is unpleasant. In either instance such limited knowledge offers us few options but to bear it until it diminishes or comes to its natural end. *To overcome suffering, we must fully understand it.* We must understand it in a very detailed and comprehensive way. Fortunately, that is possible.

So we begin with an effort to understand suffering. Although an understanding of suffering is pivotal in achieving mental and physical well-being, it is rare to hear any real discussion about the nature of suffering. There was never such a discussion during my medical training. And it is quite difficult to find a discussion of this important life experience in the West, even though it has been thoroughly explored and taught in the East. Without this understanding we will continue to experience distress and suffering as part of our life, and a sustained happiness and health will remain forever elusive.

What follows is a detailed exploration of the causes of suffering. First, it is important for me to prepare you for this discussion. Some of what follows will be the precise opposite of what you have learned and pursued in your life. Your understanding, as well as your way of living, may be challenged and even uprooted. So please, take your time and be open to and patient with this precious information, which has been carefully transmitted to us from wise women and men. Skip over sections that are a bit too challenging at this time. Allow what you read to settle in. Reflect on it. Reread it as many times as you wish. It is very important. And finally, do not accept what does not feel right in your heart. Let's begin.

The Hidden Gift of Suffering

Stress, distress, and suffering are powerful holistic experiences involving body, mind, and spirit. They cast a black cloud over our relationships and experiences, shifting our attention from the routines of day-to-day life to suffering itself. It becomes the single focus of our attention. We either collapse into it in helplessness and hopelessness, or divert all our energy towards coping with and attempting to relieve it.

Yet suffering, unlike few other experiences, simultaneously offers us the extraordinary opportunity to gain our full humanity. Why, because suffering—emotional or physical—leads to an unusual level of openness and vulnerability. It stops our usual day-to-day life. Crowded schedules give way to a luxury of time, less important concerns drop away, the ego surrenders its useless attempt to control life, and long-held belief systems begin to crack. We become raw and naked.

Finally, we are ready and even compelled to focus on the profound issues of life. In this way suffering can be a doorway to the most teachable and potentially transformative moments in life. That is the hidden gift of suffering. If you ignore this opportunity, focusing instead on self-pity, blame, and fear, you will have the experience of suffering but *miss* its meaning and opportunity. And that is a tragic loss. That is "wasted" suffering. However, if you choose to "use" suffering, it can become a powerful gateway to human flourishing.

However, it is not only in moments of intense suffering and illness that we lose the opportunity to grow a larger health and life. We also lose this opportunity in the quiet and lonely despair of a troubled and unsatisfying daily life. These subtler forms of suffering show up as a persistent and aching dissatisfaction and discontent, a tender unhappiness which goes unspoken, and a persistent and nagging sense that there is "more to life." Because we have become anesthetized to these subtler forms of suffering, we simply accept them as a normal part of life. That is a tragic error.

Subtle suffering does not descend upon us with a suddenness that shocks our life. Nevertheless, from the perspective of a joyful and loving life it is correctly understood as profound and insidious sources of suffering, silently destroying the richness of life. When recognized and acknowledged, these subtler forms of suffering can become as powerful a motivation for change as overt suffering.

What is startling is that in the midst of suffering—more so than any other human experience—abides the ever-present possibility of human flourishing. In fact, that possibility is most available to us when we clearly and decisively understand and address the very life experience that would appear to be our greatest threat. *We can actually say that when seen at great depth and truth human flourishing is the hidden potential in all suffering.* It is the gold encased in dark ore.

So why do we miss this opportunity again and again? The problem is that we do not understand the nature of suffering. And in our desire to be rid of it as soon as possible, we miss its call to awakening. We want relief and we want it now. Of course relieving suffering in any manner is important. But in our urgency to address its most acute and overt symptoms, we fail to address its deeper sources and hidden potential. We remain unaware of the lost opportunity for a rebirth of soul and spirit. We have the experience of suffering, but lose its larger meaning and profound possibilities.

The Three Sources of Suffering

A very wise teacher once said, "You must know suffering." It took awhile for me to fully realize the double meaning of this statement. First, we must have the experience of personal suffering—physical, mental, and spiritual—in order to gain the motivation to be free of it. Second, to be free of suffering we must know the *real* causes of suffering. Understanding the true causes of suffering enables us to apply the *precise* remedies which will bring it to an end. If we eradicate the true causes of suffering we will eradicate suffering as well. That is how it is.

Gross and Overt Suffering

There are three forms of suffering: *gross or overt suffering, disguised suffering,* and the root cause of all suffering—*the suffering which occurs when we are in exile from our authentic self.*

We are all familiar with gross or overt suffering. It is obvious when it occurs. It is the physical, emotional, and spiritual distress that we have all experienced at one time or another. It is most often associated with anxiety, stress, mood disorders, afflictive and disturbing emotions, loss, disease, aging, and death. When overt suffering occurs, we are quite aware of its presence. We know we are suffering. It takes precedence over all other concerns.

We do not need to dive deeply into every pain and every experience of suffering, because some aspects of overt suffering are transient and easily resolved. This works fine for a laceration, abscess, sore throat, or minor headache. But persistent suffering, overt or subtle, requires an understanding that will enable us to address and undermine its deeper causes. In order to attain this understanding we must move below the surface of overt suffering to understand its more subtle causes.

Disguised Suffering

The second cause of suffering is far subtler. *The major difficulty with disguised suffering is that it is not recognized. Why, because it is disguised as ordinary pleasure.* I am certain that this sounds like a very radical and perhaps even a bizarre statement which likely goes against all you believe in, and in many instances the way you live your life. But be patient, as this is of utmost importance, and I am about to explore this with you in far greater detail. Then you can reflect on this and decide for yourself whether this statement is accurate or not.

Imagine chasing after pleasure and not realizing that you are actually chasing after suffering! That is why this is the most insidious and difficult form of suffering to work with. Because we do not see what is really happening, we cannot avoid disguised suffering. Until the connection between what we call "pleasure" and its deeper reality, suffering, is clearly seen, we cannot alleviate this subtle aspect of suffering and its effects on body, mind, and spirit.

There are several essential points to address. Let us look at these one at a time.

- **We mistakenly learn to look to the outer world for peace, happiness, and well-being.**

Early in life we learn to search outside of ourselves for pleasure and satisfaction—a search that consumes most of our life. This outer search for happiness and well-being is somewhat unique to modern Westerners. In traditional cultures children were raised within a community of parents, relatives, friends, and elders who were always available to provide the intimacy and guidance which is the proper and necessary foundation for a sane and well human life.

In modern times this has not been our fate. We are raised by one or two parents that are early on in their own process of maturation, often employed, over-extended, and unable to fully meet the emotional needs of their child or infant, even with the best intention and effort. As a consequence, few of us emerge from childhood with an inner ease, well-being, and emotional security. That is how it is in our time. Lacking inner wellness we are taught to turn outward, seeking to fill this unmet longing for security, peace, and happiness with experiences, people, and things, which, as we shall discover, cannot substitute for our lost childhood experience. This mistaken dependence on outer satisfactions leads to a lifestyle of constant striving, unrelenting ambition, busyness, and perfectionism.

But this is not simply a result of our individual upbringing. It is a collective problem that we all share. We live in a culture that supports and encourages the outer search for happiness and well-being. In fact, a large part of our economy and the entire field of advertising and marketing are based on encouraging this very behavior. So the inadequate childrearing of a nuclear family combined with the unhealthy influences of an outward-oriented culture point us in the wrong direction from early on in life. We learn to look outside for what can only be found within.

The wise psychologist Carl Jung stated it best when speaking about alcoholism. He remarked that the use of "spirits" was a misguided search for spirit. What Jung tells us is that our search for peace, happiness, and wholeness is really a search for our inner self—for our authentic soul and spirit. Alcohol and other outer attachments and addictions are misguided substitutes for the real thing. And as we shall see in a moment, this mistaken outer focus takes us towards an unseen suffering that is disguised as pleasure. The only cure, Jung suggested, was to return to our inner source. And Jung's vision became the founding vision of Alcoholics Anonymous.

To restate this point: *We mistakenly learn to look to the outer world for peace, happiness, and well-being.*

- **The quality of pleasure does not reside in an outer experience, object, or person.**

If outer objects, people, or experiences were a trustworthy and reliable source of well-being there would be no problem in looking outward to meet these life goals. In actuality, that would be the proper thing to do. The problem is that nothing outside of us actually contains, with any constancy, the quality of peace, happiness, and well-being. They are not built-in to other people, experiences, or material objects. They are only innate to our authentic self.

Consider a fan. In the summer we consider a fan pleasant and in the winter unpleasant. But the fan has not changed with the seasons! The same can be said about eating. A certain amount of food can be pleasurable, but if we continue eating this "pleasant" meal it soon becomes unpleasant. And how often do we discover that individuals who we initially experienced as pleasant in time we experienced as unpleasant, and the other way around.

So an outer or inner experience is neither intrinsically pleasant nor unpleasant in itself. If something were intrinsically or innately pleasant or unpleasant that characteristic would never change. The more food we ate the happier we would be. However, what is pleasurable in one context or in one set of circumstances can be quite unpleasant in another. Why is this so?

The answer is quite clear. At any one moment multiple factors come together to create an experience which, according to our personal taste, we will label as pleasant, neutral, or unpleasant. But this will change as circumstances change. That is why what we label pleasurable is so unstable. Pleasure does not reside in the particular experience but rather in the complexity of related factors, including our personal history, which together determine how we view the experience. As a result, no experience, object, or person is a trustworthy or reliable source of enduring happiness.

Consider the example of romantic passion. We generally attribute this to the attributes of the other person. But if this were so it would never change. It would always remain the same. But we know it does change. On closer examination we see that passion arises as a result of many factors: our personal sense of what is attractive, novelty, imagination, at times unavailability, a previous moment of loneliness, our tendency to exaggerate positive and minimize negative qualities at the onset of a relationship, and so on. If any one of these factors changes or drops away, the passion will shift, change, and perhaps disappear. So the sense of pleasure is dependent on multiple unstable factors, none of which truly reside in the other person. If the quality of passion merely resided in another individual it would never change.

To restate this point: *The quality of pleasure does not reside in an outer experience, object, or person. It arises from multiple interdependent and unstable factors that may change at any time.*

• **When we mistakenly think that pleasure innately resides in an experience, object, or person, we desire more of it. We grasp at it, crave it, and develop attachment and in certain instances an addiction to it. From this comes all of the afflictive and disturbing emotions that result in mental distress and suffering.**

What happens when we mistakenly think pleasure is an intrinsic property of outer experiences, objects, or people? Once we label an outer experience or object as pleasurable and mistakenly believe that pleasure is a stable quality of that experience we naturally want more of it. We crave and chase after it, whether it is a material possession, wealth, relationship, sexuality, praise, approval, name, or fame.

Our mistaken view that outer experiences, people, and objects contain an innate, intrinsic, and unchanging quality of pleasure is the cause of all disturbing and afflictive thoughts. We crave, defend, and protect what seems pleasurable and push away with anger anything or anybody that interferes with our need to possess our seeming object of pleasure. We get possessive, jealous, anxious, and fearful of not getting what we want or losing what we have.

Let's look at this more closely. We reach outside for peace, happiness, and well-being. In time, the momentary satisfaction of outer experiences lead to desire and craving for the perceived source of pleasure. As desire intensifies, it turns into attachment. It is like drinking salt water. We think we are satisfying our thirst, but actually we need to drink more and more. Over time, this insatiable hunger obsesses on these seemingly pleasurable experiences, people, and objects. We constantly need to upgrade the intensity of the experience to continue to feel its "high." Invariably, all strong desire and attachment leads to some level of addiction. So our pleasures become our attachments, emotional afflictions, addictions, and ultimately our suffering.

To restate this point: *When we mistakenly think pleasure innately resides in an experience, object, or person, we desire more of it. We, grasp at it, crave it, and develop attachment and in certain instances an addiction to it. From this comes all of the afflictive and disturbing emotions that result in mental distress and suffering.*

- **Why do people, objects, and experiences lack the stable qualities of peace, happiness, and well-being that we think we "get" from them? It is because all things are impermanent and subject to moment-to-moment change.**

Here is where our understanding of impermanence is essential. It is where the truth meets our confusion. All experiences are by nature impermanent. They arise as a result of specific and temporary combinations of causes and circumstances. A rainbow appears to us because of certain factors—sunlight, atmospheric moisture, refraction, and our organs of perception. When one of these factors changes the rainbow, dependent on a precise set of causes and circumstances, naturally dissipates. The label "rainbow" is the term we use to identify what appears as a result of this transitory collection of causes and circumstances. However, what appears, the rainbow, does not have a permanent identity or staying power of its own. It and its qualities are impermanent.

The same applies to our body. It appears to us as quite solid and substantial. Yet, on examination we know that it is composed of many constituents: water, air, solid material, and at a more subtle level cells, proteins, electrons, neutrons, and space. It functions as a "body" when all of these parts work harmoniously together in an interdependent way. However, it is constantly changing, moment to moment. As long as everything is working together in the right balance we call it a body. When this ceases, as it will, we call it a corpse.

Because the nature of all things is an unstable aggregate of parts, everything is subject to change, to appearance, and dissolution.

We usually see change only in its coarse appearance. We see it in our body at times of disease, aging, or death. We see it in objects at the time of gross deterioration—rotting wood on our house, leaves falling from the trees in fall, the crumbling of an old building. Such change is apparent to us. But things do not change all at once. Although change may appear to occur suddenly, it is really a process that goes on moment-to-moment. We call this unapparent change "subtle impermanence." How could it be otherwise? What changes in time must be undergoing change at all times. We simply cannot see subtle change with our senses. This is quite important to realize, as we are lulled into forgetting that change is an innate and continuous process in all experiences, people, and things that are made of parts. And that is everything!

How is this related to disguised suffering? Our mind makes another critical mistake in its inability to see subtle impermanence. It imagines things—experiences, people, and objects—as solid, fixed, and unchanging. As a result we neither confront directly nor experience the reality of impermanence. We tend to grasp at mental and physical phenomena and freeze them in place, mistakenly perceiving them as permanent when they are in actuality impermanent. We try with all our energy to keep things as they are. But that is not how things actually exist. Everything is subject to ongoing change. We hold a view that is in disregard of the truth of how things actually exist, and incorrect views invariably lead to suffering.

Consider the following 4 truths:

- Whatever is born will die.
- All meetings will end in separations.
- Whatever is accumulated will be consumed.
- Whatever is high will become low.

But it does not stop there! All separations end in meetings, everything that is used up re-accumulates, whatever is low becomes high. It is a continuous cycle of change. We cannot control this aspect of nature. As long as we reach outside of our self to attach to people, experiences, or objects, as if they were a reliable, stable and unchanging source of happiness, we are trapped in an illusion. *And that is a certain formula for suffering.*

We must recognize that loss and suffering is inevitable when we depend upon external stimuli to provide us with permanent happiness. We can only free ourselves from suffering and distress by realizing the truth of impermanence and ceasing to attach to outer phenomenon that are bound to change.

To restate this point: *All things are impermanent and subject to moment-to-moment change. Pleasure experienced in the context of outer experiences, objects, or people is unreliable and untrustworthy because all things change over time.*

- **What we experience as pleasure is actually suffering-in-disguise.**

So, in actuality pleasure does not turn into suffering. Suffering is already embedded in what we mistakenly perceive as pleasurable, much as a fully-grown plant is unseen but embedded in the seed. We cannot see it at first, but invariably it sprouts and blossoms. That is why we call this type of suffering "disguised suffering." It lies dormant in the outer search for pleasure. Once our experience of pleasure has run its course—desire, craving, attachment, addiction and loss—it reveals its true nature, suffering. It is like a sugar-coated poison pill. We think we are chasing pleasure but in truth we are chasing suffering.

This cycle may occur over minutes, days, years, or even decades. But rest assured it will occur. The cycle will run its course. In time all seemingly outer pleasures will bear their fruit of loss, mental distress, and suffering. *This does not mean that we cannot find joy in life's many offerings. It means we must first find joy within ourselves so we do not become reliant and attached to external sources of pleasure that cannot, because of their very nature, provide enduring happiness.*

So we have now discovered certain facts or truths about what we call pleasure. Let's summarize them here. Pleasure is not intrinsic to an outer experience, object, or person. What we call pleasure or happiness arises from an ever-changing aggregation of causes and

circumstances. The outer experiences we label as pleasure are impermanent and to one extent or another give rise to the cycle of desire,
craving, attachment, addiction and loss, which invariably ends in
distress and suffering. Reflect on these truths. Observe how they
play out in your own life. The more you can grasp them the closer
you will come to ending the cycle of pleasure/suffering and discovering the actual source and path to an authentic inner-generated happiness which is free of distress and suffering.

Due to the subtle nature of disguised suffering, we rarely deal
with it directly until at least one of three conditions are met: (1)
either you have recognized that your efforts to achieve happiness
through outer experiences, objects or people have and will recurrently fail, (2) unrelenting stress, anxiety, depression, or chronic disease *force* you into this recognition or, (3) you are fortunate to be
pushed to explore more deeply by the realization that there is more
to life than you have already experienced.

When disguised suffering loses its disguise and is seen for what it
is we can then begin to resolve it. We begin by gaining an intellectual
understanding of the nature of disguised suffering as discussed here.
We then reflect on our new understandings. At the same time we
begin to explore our inner life through contemplative practice which
slowly reveals an authentic and hardy health, happiness, peace, and
wholeness which is *truth-given rather than stimulus-driven.* As this
work progresses we slowly undermine the second cause of suffering
and come closer to the root cause of all suffering.

To restate this point: *When we recognize that mental distress arises
from our outer search for pleasure and happiness we will cease searching
in the wrong place and turn our life inwards towards the only authentic
source of happiness.*

Living in Exile From Our Natural Home

We live in exile from our authentic self. We have lost awareness of
our essence. There are many explanations for how this occurred. The
great traditions say it in various ways. We lost the knowledge of our
divine nature following a fall from faith and grace. We lost awareness
of our essential self when it became obscured by the disturbances of

an overactive mind. We lost awareness of our soul and spirit when we fell under the influence, an intoxication of sorts, of the outer world and its perceived pleasures. However we express it, what was once a source of luminous peace, happiness, and wholeness became increasingly dim, dimmer, and finally unseen.

Our mind suffers the emotional and mental distress that results from the loss of our authentic self. Our soul and spirit becomes lost in confusion and doubt. We are unable to find a genuine and stable meaning and purpose in life. The loss of our authentic self is a holistic experience that cannot be cured by any physical remedy or psychological fix. We live as refugees from life in exile from our deepest humanity. We are lost, as the poet Dante said in the opening lines of the *Divine Comedy*, "In a dark wood … for we have lost the path of truth that never strays." The subtlest form of distress and suffering, *the loss of our authentic self, is the root source of all suffering*

In response to this loss of our authentic self we mistakenly reach outside for remedies that only contain within themselves the seed of the second type of suffering—disguised suffering which we mistakenly label as pleasure. Unaware of that mistake we continue to court suffering, and as a result invariably end up with overt suffering—the only type of suffering we are usually aware of. The chain of suffering which begins with the forgotten Self ends up with pointless, unnecessary overt suffering.

To eradicate suffering at its root source is to return from exile to our natural home, to our inner life—a life of harmony and wholeness that transforms body, mind, and spirit—what we have called human flourishing. It is a second birth, from the womb of suffering into the joy of Self. And like a ripened fruit it cannot reverse course. Once accomplished, the return from exile is a final homecoming.

It is like meeting a beloved parent or lover after many years of separation. We feel the remembrance, the warmth, the sense of being, the assurance, and the joy. It is all very familiar. When we return home to our inner self, we become one with it. As the oracle of Apollo said so many generations ago:

Once you have touched it
There is no division:
No tearing your heart away
For it knows no separation.

In more modern times the poet Derek Walcott says it this way:

The time will come,
when, with elation,
you will greet yourself arriving
at your own door,
in your own mirror,
and each will smile at the others welcome,
and say, sit here. Eat.
You will love again the stranger who once was yourself.
Give wine. Give bread. Give back your heart
To itself, to the stranger who has loved you
all your life, whom you ignored
for another, who knows you by heart,

This essential self is not so far away. In the East they tell the story of a young child sitting on its mother's lap, facing away from her mother. The child is crying for its mother, looking forward and to the side in order to see her. But she cannot find her. Then, her brother points out to her that her mother is right there, and she is sitting on her lap. That is how it is with us. When we rediscover our authentic self we find it has always been right there. We have been sitting right in its lap. We have just been looking in the wrong direction, and someone has to point out to us where to look. And the place to look is within.

So here you have it, the causes of all distress and suffering. If you do not understand these causes you cannot apply the proper remedy. If you know the true causes, you can. But understanding without practice, without "working" and shaping your life, is insufficient. Both are necessary. That is why we are mixing knowledge and practice together in this book as a singular seamless process. Through study, reflection, and practice we progressively rediscover and re-experience our authentic self, eliminate the causes of distress and suffering, and gain the richness of human flourishing.

* * *

Practice in Daily Life: Mindful Listening

We have already discussed two daily life practices. The first is mindful living. This consists of reminding our self throughout the day to bring our attention to the task at hand. Whether cooking, working at the computer, doing paper work, driving, or any other life activity, we stop and bring our full attention to that task, stilling all unrelated mental chatter. By practicing mindfulness in day-to-day life we learn to actually be present in the moment, present to life as it is happening, rather than living in our mind. The second daily practice is taking an inventory of those aspects of your life that support your effort at inner development, as well as those which get in the way. We try to cultivate the former and abandon the latter. It is important to continue these two daily practices in the weeks ahead. We will now add another very important daily practice, *mindful listening*.

It is quite rare that we actually hear another person, or for that matter that we are fully heard when we speak. In general, the listener's mind, our mind, is filled with mental chatter and even when we think we are listening we are actually filtering what is coming from the other through our interpretations, judgments, fears, hopes, and previous life experiences. Said in another way, we may think we are listening to the other person, but in actuality we are listening to our personal "take" on what the other has said. *We are hearing our self.* What we hear and what was said are not the same. As a result the other individual rarely feels heard or acknowledged and our actions and reactions are inappropriate to what is actually being communicated. The result is misunderstanding, confusion, wasted time, and disconnection.

To be fully heard and "held" is profoundly acknowledging and healing. It is unusual for any individual to have more than a few scattered moments of being fully listened to in their lifetime. As was said before, this is not possible when our mind is filled with chatter, constantly evaluating, judging, and translating what the other has shared. Nor can we hear what is actually said when we filter it through a system of beliefs. For example, if we hear through a psychologically-oriented mind, we will interpret what is coming to us psychologically and filter everything else out. If we are listening through a medical mind, we will listen only to "relevant" biological information, filtering out anything else. When we listen through our usual mental framework we automatically delete vital parts of the communication. When we hear only part of what is said, we are missing the whole and not really "seeing" the other.

This practice will enable us to focus on listening to others when they are speaking. To listen fully and completely is to stop your ongoing random mental activity. Stop any interpretation, judgment, reactivity, or premature effort to formulate a response. Clear the mind and simply listen. Nothing else. No aim or goal. Just listen until the speaking is over, and then take a pause before responding.

If your mental chatter begins to "work" on the communication then note this and return to mindful listening. Stay in clarity and stillness, practicing listening from that inner space. At the end of the communication you will not only feel that you have fully and accurately heard the other, but you will also feel a sense of true empathy and connection. Simultaneously the other individual will feel completely heard, seen, cared for, and respected. Your actions and response will be appropriate and consistent with what was actually said to you. You will be a healing presence to yourself and to the speaker. A way to judge whether this has actually occurred is to note whether your mind is clear and calmer at the end of the communication process. If not, you have missed the opportunity.

Mindful listening is no different than your focused breathing practice. The only difference is that the object of your focus is now the other person's communication rather than your breath. Similar to your focused breathing practice, when your mind becomes distracted you immediately bring it back to your focal point, in this instance the other's speaking.

Mindful listening extends your sitting practice into daily life. This is quite important as you now have further opportunities to practice, and the more you practice the more quickly you will progress. Individuals who practice mindful listening are amazed at the quick improvements in the quality of their relationships, even difficult ones. Over the years I have discovered that the practice of mindful listening is a uniquely powerful way to enhance life, outer and inner.

Tips For Sitting Practice

Practice, like a physical workout, requires diligence and time to establish a new habit. But in time it will become an effortless pleasure.

We should continually remember and refresh our motivation. We are very fortunate to be able to meet these teachings and practices that will enable us to gain freedom from suffering and flourish into a larger, richer, and more meaningful life. To be reading and sharing this material, to learn and practice, and to have this possibility here and now is a special and precious opportunity, a gift which might not come again.

There is so much needless and pointless suffering in the world. It is everywhere we look, and it is you right now who are fortunate to be in this circumstance in which you have all of the necessary conditions and factors to enhance your life. And by healing your own life you not only benefit yourself, but others as well. Remembering our great fortune, here and now, motivates our efforts.

Keep in mind that it is best, within limits, to find your own style. First thing in the morning is easiest for many individuals as the mind is calmer (however, not for everyone) and it helps to "set" the day up—to prepare for activities and interactions with others. If this is not your best time then establish another time during the day. Try at least 20 minutes of practice in a single session. If this is not possible then try shorter periods of 5-10 minutes multiple times. Above all, be patient. Find your style and stick to it.

During practice session you may encounter a variety of experiences—pleasing colors or images, moments of great peace, intuitive insights, and so on. Experience these moments but do not chase or attach to them. Let them go. If you are afraid you might forget a specific insight, keep a writing pad next to you, jot down a few words, and then immediately return to practice. In this way you will not be distracted from your main goal of clearing the mind.

chapter 7

Transforming Afflictive and Disturbing Emotions

A s discussed in the last chapter there are two fundamental causes of suffering. The first is the afflictive and disturbing emotions that inevitably result from our pointless attachment to outer experiences, people, or things. We call this disguised suffering. The second is the loss of natural well-being that occurs when we live in exile from our authentic self. The absence of a stable inner sense of well-being is the fundamental source of distress and suffering This loss underlies and compels our misguided search for happiness in the outer world.

The effort to alleviate this root source of suffering proceeds in an ongoing way through inner development. Slowly, we tame our mind and progressively gain access to the clarity and stillness which lies below our usual mental chatter. This clearing of the mind reduces mental distress, allows for important insights, and points us toward our natural home and its innate well-being.

However, we cannot just wait until we are firmly settled in our natural self. We must simultaneously work on our afflictive emotions as they arise. This is a two-pronged strategy. These two approaches—working directly with disturbing emotions and simultaneously gaining access to our authentic home through practice—address both levels of suffering. In this way we have the synergism of both a short and long-term approach.

Afflictive Emotions

Afflictive emotions take over our mind and destroy our life. Whether it is anger, impatience, attachment, confusion, or similar negative mental states, we must really want to be through with them. And we must have faith that this is possible. It is like going to a doctor with a problem. He may offer us the remedy, but unless we really want to rid our self of the problem we will not take the medicine, or we will take it incompletely. So we must make the firm decision to turn away from afflictive and destructive emotions in order to heal body, mind, and spirit, and open the gateway to a larger life and health. Once we make this decision we can then apply the appropriate remedies to these mental disturbances.

The first step is to realize when you have been "tricked" and taken over by an afflictive emotion. It is as if you are in a trance-like state which you are unable to get out of. Your mind becomes intoxicated by the emotion. You feel the emotional intensity building within you. You feel yourself contracting and tightening, mind and body. You feel your inner juices and physiology getting ready for battle. You feel overwhelmed, and there seems to be no way out. These are some of the signs that tell you that you are being *captured* by an afflictive emotion.

Intense emotions are easier to notice. Subtler ones are more difficult to identify. Nevertheless, these less apparent afflictive emotions—doubt, confusion, irritability, fatigue, moodiness, dissatisfaction, anxiety, and others—insidiously deaden life over many years. If we do not realize that we are captured by an afflictive emotion, coarse or subtle, there is little we can do about it. So learn their early signs and identify them quickly, *before* they take over.

The next challenge is to develop skills that enable us to stand back from our entanglement with afflictive emotions. Once you are able to step back a bit you can then work with any of the seven approaches discussed below. Given the specific circumstance one of these approaches may be more appropriate than another. In the beginning it requires being honest with yourself about your level of skill. Then, you will know what approach will work best in any situation. The good news is that we are not helpless. We have lots of ways to address afflictive emotions and slowly eliminate their pull on mind and body.

There are seven basic approaches or "remedies" to afflictive emotions. The range from the most coarse, avoidance and distancing, to subtler approaches which focus on gaining insight and understanding, to the subtlest remedy, resting with stability in our authentic self. We start by discussing the coarser approaches and work up to the subtlest, most effective, and permanent ones.

Avoidance

The first rule is to stay away from people and circumstances that may provoke intense reactivity which you are unable to deal with. You would not voluntarily walk into a burning house or an otherwise dangerous situation, so why walk into a situation which may provoke emotions you are unprepared to deal with. You may say, "Well, I didn't know this would happen." But as much as we have learned to respect the signs or circumstances which indicate physical danger, we must similarly learn to identify emotional danger zones before we enter them. We must protect and guard ourselves from mental danger just as we do from physical danger.

At all times it is essential to know what we can handle and what will overwhelm us. It is intelligent and courageous to leave some situations for another day. There will come a time when our increasing skills and capacities will enable us to extend our boundaries, allowing us to be in circumstances that previously provoked intense and uncontrollable emotions. Then we will be able to handle them from a wiser and more skillful perspective. Rather than wasting our energy dealing with overwhelming emotions, it is far better to channel our efforts toward developing a more stable inner life which will serve us better in the future.

There is a certain level of judgment that is involved here. The question is: "What can I handle at this time and what would be best to avoid?" Cultivate the skill of knowing the difference between the two and acting accordingly. Remember, *avoiding what you cannot handle must be part of a simultaneous effort that enhances your skills and capacities.* To only withdraw is to respond with fear and perpetuate a habit of withdrawal. That makes you smaller, not larger.

Consider the words of Shantideva:

> When just as I am about to act,
> I see that my mind is tainted,
> At such time I should remain
> Unmovable, like a piece of wood.
>
> Whenever there is attachment in my mind
> And whenever there is the desire to be angry.
> I should not do anything nor say anything,
> But remain like a piece of wood.
>
> Whenever I have distracted thoughts, the wish to
>   verbally abuse others,
> Feelings of self-importance or self-satisfaction;
> When I have intention to describe the faults of others;
>
> Whenever I am eager for praise
> Or have the desire to blame others;
> Whenever I have the desire to speak harshly and cause
>   disputes;
> At such times I should remain like a piece of wood.
>
> Whenever I desire material gain, honor, or fame;
> Whenever I seek attendants or a circle of friends,
> And when in my mind I wish to be served;
> At these times I should remain like a piece of wood.
>
> Whenever I have the wish to decrease or to stop
>   working for others
> And the desire to pursue my welfare alone,
> If motivated by such thoughts a wish to say something
>   occurs,
> At these times I should remain like a piece of wood.
>
> Whenever I have impatience, laziness, cowardice,
> Shamelessness or the desire to talk nonsense;
> If thoughts of partiality arise,
> At these times too, I should remain like a piece of wood.

Shantideva urges us to be mindful at all times lest our mind be swept away by negative and destructive emotions, coarse or subtle. If we know we cannot handle the situation, avoidance is our first line of defense.

Distancing

There are times when we find ourselves caught in a very intense mental affliction—thought or emotion—and we can no longer avoid it nor can we call upon subtler approaches which are not yet fully developed. In this circumstance we make the effort to distance our self from the afflictive thought or emotion. We accomplish this by setting mental "boundaries" around it.

There are several techniques we can try. First, you may start by labeling the afflictive emotion—anger, attachment, jealousy, and so on. Labeling and naming it gives you some distance from the experience, as the moment you label it you are no longer fully enmeshed in it. There is now the mental affliction, the observer of the affliction, and the separation between the two. *You realize that you are not the afflictive thought or emotion.* To some extent that breaks the tight enmeshment.

If the disturbance is too intense this may be difficult. If so, try the following exercise:

> Close your eyes and sit as comfortably as possible. Create a mental image or picture of the disturbing thought or emotion—this can be an abstract or representational image. Next, place this image in front of your mental visual field. Observe it with detachment much as you observe the breath in your formal practice. Watch how the image shifts and turns. If your mind gets attached to the image, begins to analyze it, or you become otherwise distracted from this focal point, bring your mind back to observing it.
>
> You will discover that it is easier to create space and observe an afflictive thought or emotion when you experience it as a mental image placed in front of your mental "field." Keep watching the image as it changes. If your mind wanders, bring your attention back to the image. In time your

mind will calm down, experience greater spaciousness, and unexpected insights may arise. When your mind becomes sufficiently quiet, shift back to your usual breathing practice.

In this way you will have taken the steps that move you from a tight and disturbed mind to clarity and stillness. You will observe that nothing about the circumstance has changed, only your relationship to it. The enmeshment and suffering is gone. Quite an achievement!

An alternative is to sense where you most feel the emotion or feeling in your body. Then, make a mental image of that part of your body, place it in front of your mental field, and similarly observe the image as it shifts and changes. From here you can follow the directions given above. With either approach, if you maintain your focal point and the separation between yourself and the image your mind will calm down.

A third approach to gaining distance from the afflictive emotion is to "disown" it by realizing how much trouble it causes you. Realize that you have nothing to gain from it. So why not discard it? Insist that there can only be one king in your "castle," and that is you, not the afflictive thought or emotion. So let it go, insist it go, and allow it to dissolve like morning mist dissolves into space.

Each of these approaches will assist you in "disempowering" the afflictive emotion when you can no longer avoid it, until such time as you have developed the subtler capacities described below.

Antidotes

Reaching for a bit more subtlety, we can begin to develop mental attitudes that serve as long-term antidotes to afflictive emotions. This approach is based on the fact that two opposing thoughts or emotions cannot exist simultaneously in the mind. As we develop the attitude that opposes a specific afflictive emotion, we will discover an increasing immunity to its corrosive power.

Consider the following example. One cannot hold both loving-kindness and anger in the mind at the same time. As we develop the mental attitude of loving-kindness towards others, we simultaneously develop the antidote to anger. The idea is not to wait until we are in distress from anger. We do not wait until an automobile accident occurs to tighten our seat belt. We do it preventatively. An easy way to start developing loving-kindness is with the listening exercise described in the previous chapter. You can also use the loving-kindness practices described in chapter 9. If we practice now this mental attitude will be there when we need it as a stable inner experience and effective antidote to anger.

Let's look at other possible antidotes. For example, humility is the antidote to pride. What could be a more humbling experience than the recognition that we cannot control our own mind? What could be more humbling than to realize our lifelong perspectives and behaviors are conditioned through habit rather than arrived at through free will? Each day we confront the gap between where we are and where we would like to be. Instead of responding with frustration, impatience, or self-deprecation, it is best we take this as a lesson in humility. In this way humility becomes settled in our mind and serves as a constant antidote to excess pride.

Generosity is the antidote to miserliness and possessiveness. Generosity can take many forms. These include: helping a person to safety, providing for material needs, deep listening, caring, mentoring, and so on. As we slowly develop this mental attitude, it serves as an antidote to miserliness and possessiveness, and opens our heart.

In the same way rejoicing in the happiness of others is an antidote to jealousy, contentment is an antidote to desire, and wisdom is an antidote to confusion and ignorance.

When we cultivate these attitudes—loving-kindness, humility, generosity, rejoicing in the happiness of others, contentment, and wisdom—they will serve as both powerful antidotes to afflictive emotions and as life-enhancing qualities.

Insight

As we progress, we begin to achieve greater stability of inner clarity and stillness. That allows space for fresh insights and understandings to arise, insights which previously could not break through the dense thicket of our overactive mind. These spontaneous insights provide further understanding of the nature of afflictive emotions.

Consider the following. One of the most troubling and dangerous afflictive emotions is anger. "This person did this or that to me." Let us look at this statement. We can all agree that everyone wants happiness and no one wants suffering. Everyone wants to be liked and cared for and no one wants to be disliked and scorned. That is natural to all of us. When we act in a manner which brings suffering to others as well as to ourselves we are not acting voluntarily. Although it may in all ways appear voluntary, anger is *not* a voluntary act of free will. If we had a free choice, suffering is not what we would choose. Anger, projected outward like other negative emotions, is an involuntary repetition of fearful, protective, and defensive behaviors pushed by old hurts. Such individuals are at the moment under the influence of, or one could say, intoxicated by powerful old mental patterns. In their confusion they hurt themselves and others, and this is not what any sane person in control of their actions would choose.

It is possible that the angry person may seem pleased with their negative action. But upon closer examination, it is quite apparent that their actions, irrespective of a brief moment of perceived gratification, will in fact bring suffering to their own life. What is thrown out to others will always, in time, ricochet back. Such individuals find themselves hurt and isolated again and again. Their actions toward you are likely directed at others as well. Not only will they suffer from their disconnection and separation from you, but this will also occur in other relationships, and most often with their "loved ones." When you really understand the truth of what is happening, you will stop reacting. Your response will be heartfelt compassion for the unfortunate individual whose confused and compelled negative behavior is a cause of relentless personal suffering.

This does not necessarily imply saying or doing anything to or for the other. This is primarily about you—your clarity, inner peace, and heart. Perhaps you will choose to merely be silent, set boundaries where appropriate, or simply get out of the line of fire. In either case your heart and mental space will remain open and calm.

Let us look at the problem of anger in another way. There are many factors that combined together result in an angry outburst. Some can be traced back to what we learned from our family and educational system, to our sense of right or wrong, or to our unique sensitivities. Then there is the particular trigger which sets off these old patterns. Perhaps this trigger was primed by an earlier experience the same day, a previous interaction with you, or a physiological disturbance.

If you could carefully identify all of the cumulative factors which underlie a single experience of anger, you will find that they are too numerous to count. Which one of these factors should we blame—learned attitudes and behaviors, a cup of coffee spilled early in the morning which primed the anger, old fears, insecurities, sensitivities, or resentment? When you carefully analyze all the contributing factors to an outburst of anger it is difficult to know where to point a finger. You would not have enough fingers. So why bother? The truth is that there is not a single cause for anger. Anger results from a complexity of factors working together. When you exhaust your efforts to pin down anger to a single factor you will see the futility and meaninglessness of pointing your finger merely at the individual. It is far more complex than that!

And, further, it is even possible to say that there is no personal thought involved. Like the formation of the rainbow which depends on the aggregation of the necessary circumstances, anger arises spontaneously when its causes and circumstances come together. If, at the moment of anger, thought intervened, who would get angry? Nobody wants suffering. Everyone wants happiness. So any thoughtfulness at all would stop anger before it takes over. That is why we say that anger has no thought. So who is there to actually blame? Just consider this paradox, however strange it may seem.

These are examples of how the correct understanding of a destructive emotion can release you from years of reactivity. Just seeing the truth of *what is as is* can dissolve your reactivity. We are not looking for or expecting to find perfect people. We are seeking a perfect, clear, and accurate understanding of the actions of people we interact with. And what we have pointed out about anger is applicable to all afflictive emotions. Greater insight progressively frees you from misunderstandings, inner turmoil, and reactivity. Gaining insight and understanding through study, reflection, and practice diminishes susceptibility to afflictive emotions while substituting the more appropriate mental response of compassion. This is a fantastic achievement!

Further Insight

We will now discuss another way in which growing insight can assist in diminishing the pull of afflictive emotions. Here we will use as examples the afflictive emotions of intense desire and attachment and its opposite dislike and aversion. These are two sets of commonly misunderstood and disturbing emotions.

Desire and attachment result from an exaggeration of the positive qualities of a person or situation, and a simultaneous minimizing of the negative qualities.

Take the first few weeks of romance. Our partner is perfect. Everything is loving, delightful, and pleasing. There are no unpleasant qualities. We think, "How desirous and wonderful this person must be, or this new job, or this new car." So of course we like the good feeling and want more and more of it. So we unknowingly exaggerate these positive qualities and ignore the negative ones. We want to squeeze more pleasure out of the circumstance by mentally distorting how it actually is.

Our unwillingness to see this experience, object, or person accurately and in their entirety leads to the disillusionment and suffering which occurs when we are finally forced to see the entire picture as it actually is. Then we may point to the other and say, "Why did you change?" Or we may blame the circumstance, "But they didn't tell me all the facts." But alas, the fault is our own.

We only wanted to see what pleased us rather than the full and unblemished truth of the person or situation. We exaggerate what we like because we like it and want more of it. So we fantasize more than is actually there. Observe this in yourself and then observe the disappointment that occurs when your self-made delusion dissipates, as it must when the other appears in the full complexity of their positive and negative traits. What we choose to deny and not see in the other will eventually show up, and pleasure will become suffering. Is that familiar to you?

The same could be said for the negative emotions of aversion, anger, and hatred. Because we want to demonize this person we exaggerate their negative qualities and minimize or deny their positive ones. Again, in time, reality will break through. Everyone is a mixture of good and bad qualities. It might give us temporary pleasure to emphasize one or the other extreme, but in the end our delusion will dissipate as the truth asserts itself. It would be best for us to see the whole in a balanced way from the beginning. Illusions may be comforting in the moment but, as they are unreal, they are laced with future suffering.

What does this insight offer us? We can bring an end to the suffering related to desire and attachment, anger and aversion, by knowing our one-sided habit of falsely maximizing one set of qualities while minimizing the other. When we feel desire or aversion arise, we stop, recognize what we are doing, and balance our view. We seek a more equal view of the qualities of the other person. We develop a balanced view. We force our self to look truthfully at potentially unpleasant or negative qualities or, in the opposite case, pleasing ones. Surely loved ones are not perfect nor are enemies always bad. You can take it on face value that unless the other person is Jesus or Buddha, or you are living in a utopia, no one and no situation is all positive or all negative. We are a mixture of qualities.

By consciously balancing our perceptions—seeing all the qualities of a situation as they are—we diminish the afflictive emotions of desire and attachment and anger and aversion. We stop elaborating on reality and see it as it is. In the immediate moment this may not be as pleasing, but an accurate and truthful understanding will ultimately result in peace and happiness rather than suffering. That is the great value of continuously growing our insight through study, reflection, and practice.

Self-Liberation of Disturbing Emotions

We are now about to discuss the subtlest approaches to afflictive thoughts and emotions. These approaches will become available to you with further practice and insight. Because they are subtler, they take us closer to the source of the problem and therefore are the most effective approaches. It is like cutting a tree at the roots rather than taking it down one leaf at a time. But be patient, as these approaches will take time to mature.

Every thought, feeling, or image (afflictive or non-afflictive) is a mere mental movement, a brief neuro-electrical discharge which appears and dissolves if we neither grasp at them nor freeze them in place. Mental movements arise, abide, and dissipate very rapidly. We see this best in practice when we watch the mind at play, spontaneously displaying in awareness one thought or emotion after another. From this witnessing perspective we discover the truth that all mental movements are essentially brief appearances in awareness. They appear "substantial and continuous" only when we grab on to these otherwise brief mental blips and create a story around them. It is not the thought or emotion which is the problem, but rather our tendency to grasp at and elaborate them. It is in this way that a brief and neutral neuro-electrical discharge rises to the level of an afflictive thought or emotion.

As we become more comfortable with just watching the play and display of the mind they will quiet down on their own. We call this self-dissolving, self-evaporating, or self-liberation at their origin. What does this mean? It means that a thought, feeling, or image when left alone effortlessly dissolves and frees itself.

When compared to previously discussed approaches this is definitely a more subtle way of working with afflictive thoughts and emotions. It is actually not working with them directly, but rather working with our tendency to grasp, attach, and elaborate them. It is a far more difficult approach because it is subtler and requires more training and mental stability. A large barn fire is far more difficult to deal with than the first spark. If we can watch our mental movements as they form and let them be, they will naturally dissipate.

One further way to allow afflictive emotions to naturally dissolve is to view them as if they were dream-like. When we have a night dream it can be filled with disturbing emotions and thoughts. But when we awaken from the dream we realize that they were not real—they were only mind's imagination. They suddenly disappear. We feel relieved. Look carefully at your daytime mental afflictions. Are they really that different than those of the night dream? Aren't they also occurring in our mind? Aren't they simply our mind's imagination? What makes them different from a night dream? Are they more real, and if so, how?

When you realize that daytime mental activity is identical to the equally insubstantial thoughts and emotions experienced in a night dream they will similarly disappear. But be patient. This is a very subtle and developed capacity that only emerges through practice.

Remembering Home

The root cause of all afflictive emotions is the failure to remember and rest in our natural self. This is where we bring all disturbing emotions and all suffering to their final end. By returning home to our peaceful and natural self we no longer go searching in the outer world for what is already there in our natural state of well-being.

Our essential nature is a simple state of mere being. We are present to what is as is, allowing our awareness to unfold moment-to-moment. By returning home you will have cut the root cause of suffering at its source. Why is this so important? Because you now know that you have within yourself the formula for bringing all suffering and mental disturbances to an end. It takes only a brief recognition of your authentic self to know this. It is who you are and it is free of all forms of suffering.

It is no longer a question of whether you can live this way, but rather a question of stabilizing this experience so it becomes your ever-present home. That is the only difference between a master and yourself. That is why inner development is so important.

In Summary

Avoidance, distancing, antidotes, gaining insight, self-liberation of thoughts and emotions, and the cultivation of our natural state of being are the progressive set of methods which gradually take us towards permanently defeating disturbing and afflictive emotions.

The first step is the wisdom to know what to avoid when seeking a larger life, and asserting the discipline to do so. The second step, distancing, is helpful when we are already caught in an intense emotion and are not yet ready to apply the subtler approaches. It is emergency first aid. The third step is applying an antidote like loving-kindness, which counteracts anger. This is an ongoing practice. The fourth and fifth step, the progressive attainment of insight, arises as we develop and mature our understanding of afflictive emotions. The sixth step, self-liberation, arises from greater insight into how the mind works. Finally, we gain an experience of the natural settled nature of mind, the seventh step.

This slow but progressive accumulation of knowledge and experience will result in greater mastery and skill in applying the subtler approaches. It is then possible to maintain a stable and clear inner life, defeating mental afflictions at their root source. Afflictive thoughts and emotions no longer arise. We have cut through to the pure core of our being which is a simple, open, and unchanging peaceful awareness. You now know that *you* can alleviate and in time eradicate all afflictive thoughts and emotions. That is guaranteed!

* * *

Practicing in Daily Life: Turning Afflictive Emotions Into Practice

We have learned three practices that we are now integrating into daily life—cultivating mindfulness, mindful listening, and taking a life inventory to determine what attitudes and behaviors support our effort and which are obstacles. We are now going to add a fourth practice—letting go of reactivity and cultivating correct understanding and compassion in response to perceived negativity from others.

This practice is very courageous, powerful, and transforming for our self and for others. Instead of following the usual pattern of reacting to challenging individuals, we turn everything around. We use these challenges to enhance our practice and further our life. This opportunity is truly amazing. We take what is customarily disturbing and use it to grow a richer life. We are determined to turn dirt into gold.

Our new way of understanding and responding to afflictive thoughts and emotions—our own or others—will naturally evolve as we reflect on what we have learned through study and practice. So the sequence is stopping reactivity on the spot, remembering how afflictive behavior harms us, recalling the correct understanding of destructive emotions, and opening our heart to compassion.

With practice this new and life-sustaining way of transforming negative emotions and behaviors will become increasingly natural and automatic. At first it takes courage to turn the situation around, as we are trained to react. But we are only hurting our self and our opportunity for a larger life. So let your confused ego take what seems like a bit of a blow so that your life can move forward. Summon up the courage to step out of your usual reactions. If you do so you will diminish and defeat this very important cause of suffering. Turning adversity into a positive practice is the fourth way we use daily life as an opportunity for practice.

How about the other individual? This person will ultimately suffer the consequences of his/her behavior. You may or may not see this in the moment, but rest assured it will happen. Until they have suffered enough there is not much you can do. When they are ready they will take responsibility for their actions and get help. Meanwhile, your compassionate response will help to neutralize the problem. You will grow in health and heart and the circumstance will be largely defused.

So this week I request that you add this practice to your growing repertoire. Observe individuals and their behavior more deeply, penetrate your understanding into the core of their pain and suffering and see how *you* change within—from reactivity to compassion, peace, and ease.

We are now moving quickly in terms of practice. We have our formal practice session as well as four practices in daily life. If you approach these with discipline and intention you will find them life-changing. It cannot be otherwise. So I encourage you to continue your practices and move beyond moments of frustration or difficulty. However, be patient with yourself.

Tips for Sitting Practice

In previous chapters we have discussed the first two aspects of practice—clearing the mind and resting in stillness. Here I would like to emphasize the second aspect, resting in stillness.

In the early stages of practice we will occasionally touch mental stillness. With time this will expand and stabilize. The movement from focused attention to resting in stillness is a natural one. We do not establish it is an aim or goal. When the time is ready it unfolds on its own. This may or may not occur in any one session. Do not worry. Just patiently follow the practice instructions.

In certain practice sessions our mind quiets down more rapidly and we feel an increasing clarity and stillness. When this occurs we can diminish the intensity of our mindfulness. If our mind remains relatively still we can progressively drop the focus on the breath and simply "sit" or rest in stillness, observing its openness, ease, and spaciousness. When this is possible we can let go of the previous intensity of mindfulness, as the thoughts, feelings, and images are softer and subtler. Eventually our mindfulness can be so soft and subtle that practice appears increasingly effortless. At this point we are no longer focusing on our breath. We are resting in stillness. Relax into it.

When resting in stillness, you have to some extent pacified or stilled random mental chatter for the moment. At this stage of practice you can expect that mental activity will reassert itself here and there. When this occurs you gently observe the movements, allowing them to resolve and dissolve on their own. If mental chatter becomes more intense, return to mindful breathing until you once again clear and still your mind. Do not see this as some sort of failure. It definitely is not. Remember you are training your mind to be mindful. With time and experience you will have less need for this method. But for now it is important to continue to use it as your central practice tool.

When your mind is relatively clear and resting in stillness, a second problem may occur. Although your mind is clear and calm, it may become dull. This feels like sleepiness, nothingness, a void, or a "dropping off." That is an involuntary movement of the mind towards dullness. You have cleared your mind but you are having difficulty maintaining alertness and awareness. Both are necessary. A still and calm mind without clarity is only a simple relaxation technique. We are seeking a calm, clear, and alert mind that is neither disturbed by lingering mental chatter nor taken over by mental dullness.

When dullness or dropping off occurs there are several steps you can take. First, you can open your eyes and look forward. You can also raise your eyes upward until your mind is no longer dull or sleepy. You can move around a bit in your chair or cushion, or you can return to mindful breathing until the dullness dissipates.

Do not value either aspect of practice, focused breathing or stillness, over the other. At this point they are of equal value. Begin with mindful breathing and allow the natural unfolding of your session. Be patient with the back and forth that occurs over time, and even in a single session. With practice your skills will improve, your mind will become increasingly accustomed to clarity and stillness, and important insights will spontaneously burst forth.

chapter 8

Overcoming the Overactive Mind

If you have begun practicing you will have by now encountered the obstacles posed by the overactive mind, and perhaps experienced brief moments of mental clarity and stillness. It is likely that you have also experienced changes in your daily life. Perhaps your practice has not yet become a habit and your mind continues to be quite active, nevertheless you have taken the important first steps. You have established your *intention* to practice and you are slowly backing up this intention with the discipline of a daily sitting practice and practices in daily life. That is a good beginning. Do not underestimate the importance of your intention and early steps. Remember that a child learns to walk by getting up each time he or she falls. It is the same way for us when beginning practice.

At first, practice can feel like a battle. You are not sure that you can overcome the power of an overactive mind or your learned tendency *to do* rather than simply *sit and be* in practice. You may not be able to quiet the mind for more than brief moments, if at all. But it is a learning process, like any other. As you progress with your practices it is guaranteed that one step at a time you will slowly master the capacity to calm and still your mind. You will progressively become the author of your life, from the inside out.

In this chapter we will explore the increasingly subtle under standings that enable you to permanently undermine the overactive mind. Our particular concern will be developing a more detailed understanding of random mental activity. Although it will not be possible for you to access or use all of these understandings and skills at this time, it is important for you to understand as much as you can.

I have intentionally waited until this point to introduce these understandings and skills. I wanted to allow you to first gain some experience and stability in your basic mindful breathing meditation.

That is a necessary first step. But to progress further we need to gain a more expansive understanding of the moving mind.

It is important to note here, as we move ahead with this discussion, that when I use the phrase "mental movements," "the moving mind," or just the word "thoughts," I am referring to all aspects of automatic mental activity—thoughts, feelings, mental images, and sensory impressions.

Random Mental Activity

For the sake of comprehensiveness let us once again start where the problem begins. We have already spoken about the continuous proliferation of random mental activity which seems "normal" in usual day-to-day life. Because we are so accustomed to an overactive mind it is difficult to imagine it being any other way. At home and in our school system we are continuously trained and rewarded for a hyperactive and dysfunctional mind.

How does this all begin? Let us just say that the mind itself goes astray early in life. It wanders from its natural innermost home of clarity, stillness, openness, and ease, and becomes entranced with mental and sensory experiences which naturally arise in the stream of consciousness. Perhaps we can compare this to a lover who forgets his own life when bewitched by his beloved. That is how it is. Unlike romance, which loses some of its luster over time, the bewitchment with mental activity becomes more tenacious with time. The moving mind is a persistent and hardy lover.

Straying from our natural home begins what for many is a lifelong enmeshment with mental activity. The mind's movements assume an illusory identity, solidity, and continuity that they do not actually have. We mistake mental activity for life itself. Like our evening dream, it seems quite real. We live in and are imprisoned by an abstract imaginary mental life. We are unaware that we are missing life itself.

It is like we are trapped in a daydream or movie. Although we always *awaken* from our night dream to discover its imaginary nature, we rarely *awaken* from our daydream, which similarly takes place in mental imagination. The false mental self and day-to-day kingdom constructed in our mind is an unseen disaster for body, mind, and spirit. That is where we find our self at the beginning of the journey to human flourishing, and that is if we are fortunate enough to realize our dilemma.

Suppressing the Overactive Mind

We all long for the experience of inner peace. We want a respite from stress, anxiety, and fear. We have had enough of confusion, exhaustion, worry, and mental busyness. We have each cultivated techniques that can help us quiet down.

We reach out for relationships, sexuality, material comforts, fame, name, endless mind-diverting activities, alcohol and other drugs, hoping one or another of these will help calm our mind and provide a moment of relief. When we take a careful and thoughtful look we discover the disheartening truth, much of our lifelong quest in the outer world is motivated by the desire to calm our mind, relieve aloneness, and experience mental ease.

These external fixes do not last very long because they do not actually fix anything. They just suppress mental activity for a few moments, providing a brief respite in an otherwise unchanged mind and life. As a result we always need another fix. So we crave and cling to the "agents" of this relief—people, experiences, and things. Some forms of relief, like the extremes of athletic activity or a good yoga session, are innocuous, but most are harmful to body, mind, and spirit. When looked at deeply they are all harmful as they cover over the real problem and keep us from moving beyond external fixes, to address the overactive mind at its source, which is the only place that it can be permanently healed and made whole again.

Whatever our preferred method, when we *suppress* mental activity, we cover over the real problem and thus lose the opportunity to gain control of our life.

Mindfulness Training

When we begin mindfulness training we choose to directly address the problem of the overactive mind, rather than temporarily covering

it over with a relaxation technique or soothing experience. We recognize that our previous efforts to still the mind are temporary at
best, and we have heard somewhere of a training process which may
permanently end the problem of an out-of-control mind.

Mindfulness practice works on a basic principle: by learning to
focus our attention and diminish the proliferation and distraction
of mental movements, we can progressively achieve a calm, still, and
stable mind. That is a very old practice which can be found in most
religious and philosophic traditions. It is time-tested. That is why
we have used this practice as our primary training exercise. In the
beginning, maintaining our attention is difficult, and mental distractions seem quite persistent and powerful. However, with practice
we begin to experience moments of clarity and stillness, which over
time result in greater mental stability.

We not only experience the effects of mindfulness training in
sitting sessions, but there is also an overflow into our daily life, even
for beginners. As a result we are less reactive, more patient, and life
seems increasingly easeful. But our sitting sessions are not enough.
There is much more we can do to accelerate this process. We extend
and further stabilize mindfulness when we integrate it into daily life
by repeatedly focusing attention on the activity of the moment.

Mindfulness training is a positive approach to working with mental movements. We are gaining new skills and useful understandings
rather than merely attempting to suppress unwanted mental activity. We are shifting our reliance from an outer experience to inner
behavior. We are maturing our response to the wandering mind.

Undermining Grasping, Attachment, Fixation and Elaboration

The next step is to directly address mental movements. Our purpose is to gain an understanding of how we become entangled with
random mental activity. We need to know this if we wish to reverse
this dysfunctional process. Fortunately, as we increasingly clear our
mind, new insights and understandings emerge and we begin to see
with increasing precision how the mind actually works. The more we

understand what is happening, the more freedom and capacity we gain.

One of the first things we notice is that our mind has developed a faulty habit of moving toward and investing in mental movements. A random thought, feeling, image, or sensory impression arises in the mind and our attention jumps towards it. Next, we quickly grasp, attach, and identify with this mental movement. Random mental activity is like a magnet. It seduces the confused mind and grabs its attention.

As soon as we are enmeshed in mental activity we further elaborate it by superimposing upon it old perspectives and stories stored in memory. In this way we turn simple, unadorned, and brief mental movements into complex mental events which are largely imaginary, and more old then new. What was once a momentary neurological blip appears to assume a life of its own. And at the same time we unknowingly move away from clarity and stillness that is the innermost essence of our self.

Once we elaborate a mental movement we then add feelings and emotions to this cancerous growth. That leads to a proliferation of further mental activity which includes fear, anxiety, anger, desire, aversion, and so on. Then, we act out this personalized and imaginary story in the outer world through our speech and actions. A small mental blip, which would naturally come and go, becomes our life, and the life that is actually happening in the moment is lost.

The next step in this sequence is *fixation*. Once we are attached, enmeshed, and identified with a mental movement we *fix* this movement in time. The natural life cycle of a mental movement is arising, abiding, and falling, all of which takes place in a quarter of a second, almost too quick for us to notice. But once we attach to a mental movement we extend its duration. It may last for a few minutes, a few hours, or even an entire day. We contract our attention down to a single mental event that preoccupies our mind. When we do that we stop the natural flow of our mind, as we become tightly absorbed and preoccupied with it.

When our mind is functioning in its natural state we experience life moment to moment. An experience arises in the mind, we notice it and it automatically drops away. There is an ongoing uninterrupted flow of awareness that experiences *what is as is* when it is happening. Once we attach to a mental movement we fix and freeze it in place, taking it into the next moment as if it were still occurring in life, when it is actually now only occurring in our mind. That is how mental movements persist and shut off the natural flow of experience.

Once we become aware of the habitual process of grasping, attaching, elaborating, fixing, and freezing mental movements, we shed a light on what is actually occurring. By understanding this process we can begin to observe it during sitting practice, as well as in daily life. Most of the time we will miss it completely, as it occurs so quickly. At other times we will notice it while it is ongoing.

The more we understand this dysfunctional sequence of events the better equipped we will be to address and undermine it. When it is no longer unconscious, it progressively loses its power. When we know what is happening our mind cannot be easily tricked into this dysfunctional and faulty process. That is a major shift in our relationship to the moving mind.

We no longer have to rely on effort to suppress or control the overactivity and intrusiveness of random thoughts, feelings and images. We realize that they are not the actual problem. The problem is our habitual tendency to attach, identify, elaborate, and fix mental activity. With this understanding we can now come closer to the true source of the problem and become aware of this destructive cycle of mental events far earlier in the process, before it gets out-of-control. Progressively, we will be able to reverse the tendency of the mind to automatically engage with mental appearances. That will stop the entire dysfunctional sequence of events, before it even starts. That is the value of this new understanding and capacity.

Isn't it amazing that we can actually discover how our mind works? Isn't it amazing that we can see the individual steps that lead to the overactive mind? We have now come a long way from our initial and futile efforts at suppressing mental movements. We can now more clearly understand the dynamics of the mind.

Self-Liberation on Arising

To understand self-liberation on arising let us now consider the metaphor of a mirror. A mirror allows whatever arises on its surface to come and go on its own. In this metaphor the mirror represents our naturally settled open awareness. Similar to the mirror surface, the resting bare state of the mind, our natural open awareness allows whatever mental activity arises within its expanse to appear and dissolve on its own. It is a passive observer of mental movements. The mirror provides the surface for reflections, but does not grasp, attach, or elaborate them. Our open resting awareness is much the same. It is not attached or absorbed in anything. All mental movements appear in the expanse of awareness, but in the settled state the mind does not in any way concern itself with them. That is how our mind naturally operates. Life happens and we are present and experience it just as it is.

If you watch your mind during practice, when it is relatively still, you will notice that left alone mental activity appears and rapidly dissipates on its own. Your awareness remains steady and ever present as thoughts, feelings, and mental images come and go. Unlike the agitated overactive mind which grasps at everything that arises, the settled mind just watches and *allows* in ease and spaciousness.

We call this natural arising and falling "self-liberation." What this means is that all mental activity that appears in awareness will naturally arise and quickly dissipate when left alone. It comes and goes like morning dew, waves rising and falling in the ocean, or a rainbow appearing and disappearing in the sky. That is how the natural mind is.

As our understanding of mental activity matures, we slowly realize that we can solve the entire problem of an overactive mind by simply allowing mental movements to arise and dissipate *on their own*, while remaining at rest in our natural state of awareness. There is nothing we have to do. We just have to *let go and allow*. As a result of this understanding, we progressively reverse our habitual tendency to become enmeshed in mental appearances. The mind itself is stabilized in its natural state, automatically reversing the entire faulty sequence of events that leads to an overactive mind.

The term "self-liberate" is not exactly accurate, but that is how we experience it at first. Without any effort of our own, mental activity appears to quickly subside by itself. So what is it being *liberated from* if it is already free to come and go of its own accord? It is liberated from our tendency to attach and elaborate it, and in this way imprison what is by nature free. Spontaneous mental movements are no longer subject to the distortions of our mental life. But in reality they have always been free. So in actuality we discover that our mental movements are just as they have always been, the natural unfettered activity of the mind which spontaneously arises and dissipates on its own. It is our faulty mental habits which makes this seem otherwise.

Understanding and experiencing the natural life cycle of mental movements and their inherent tendency to self-dissipate or self-liberate is subtle and sophisticated. It takes time to untangle the mind and know this with clarity and conviction, an experience that is gained only in practice.

Resting in the Vast Expanse of Natural, Still, Open Awareness

Our natural open state of awareness and presence is and has always been our supreme and irreducible authentic self. That authentic self becomes increasingly apparent and stable as we mature our understanding of mental movements and allow them to self-liberate. We progressively return to the natural peace and stillness which is the basic essence of our mind, experiencing all that appears in awareness as mind's energetic play and display, while remaining alert, clear, calm, expansive, and open. In the midst of mind's movements we remain at the center of our being.

There is no more need for suppression, mindfulness, or concern with the endless process of attachment and elaboration. The mind has given up its mistaken and faulty ways. We can simply rest with ease in the continuous and natural flow of life. We are in life itself. Once we do this all will be well—the spontaneous and fleeting play and display of appearances will be of no further concern.

I have provided you with this overview as a comprehensive guide to the progressive understanding of your mind and its mental activity. As mentioned before, *we are not aiming at mere relaxation.* That is why we must increasingly refine our understanding of the workings of the mind, an understanding which at first is intellectual and then directly experienced through practice. That understanding will result in an effortless and far-reaching remedy to the overactive mind. It will cease on its own, and never again will it infect your life and betray your possibilities. Be patient, study, reflect, and practice and the result will unfold on its own.

* * *

Practicing in Daily Life: Observing the Moving Mind

We are fortunate. We want to learn about the mind, and it is right there for us to examine at all times. That is the point of practice. It's like examining a material object with a microscope. In a similar way we can use our increasingly finely tuned practice and observational skills to understand and overcome the moving mind.

There are two important opportunities to observe your moving mind and verify for yourself the sequence of events that leads from an innocuous electrical bleep to an emotional affliction and overactive mind. The first is in formal practice and the second is in your daily life.

Let us first look at our next daily practice. Once or twice during your usual daily activities stop, turn your attention inside, and watch the movements in your mind. Instead of allowing them to run your mind, begin observing them. First, notice that they *are* in *your* mind. Next, in order to undermine their seeming solidity and duration, pick a specific thought or feeling and ask the following questions. "Does this mental movement have any color? Does it have any shape? Does it have any form? Does it have any contour? Does it have a specific location? Does it have a taste, texture, or smell?" Take your time with each question, carefully observing the mental movement you are working with.

By the time you finish asking even a few of these questions it will likely disappear. That will be a successful inquiry. Because mental movements have no substance, they cannot stand up to analysis. Once you really look at them and wake up to their real nature, they dissolve into awareness. You will have reversed the cycle that solidifies a mental movement. Slowly, you will come to know the dreamlike nature of a mental movement, a dreamlike nature that we make real and turn into our lives. So take a pause here and there during your day, sit quietly, and study the movements of your mind.

The second opportunity occurs during your formal sitting practice. When your mind is still you can turn your attention for a few moments to mental movements. Create a thought or feeling if one does not naturally arise. Observe that the mind expresses itself in three ways: thoughts, feelings, and mental images. Watch your mind and its activity like a journalist. Without becoming involved, observe how the mind moves from one thought to another to another. Notice your tendency to become involved with and identify with these thoughts. You will observe that when this happens you simultaneously lose your position as an impartial observer. You become "stuck" in mental activity. When you notice this, you will return to being an observer.

Next, try to notice the natural life cycle of a thought, feeling, or image that arises in the mind. If you can watch it from beginning to end you will notice that it appears, abides, and falls much like a wave rises and falls back into the sea. When allowed to unfold its natural sequence, this process occurs quite rapidly. The dissolution or evaporation of a mental movement occurs almost simultaneously with its appearance. So, left alone, thoughts, feelings, and images, which collectively constitute the mind's activities, simply dissipate by themselves.

If you have a particularly "sticky" mental movement observe it and ask the same sequence of questions as before. "Does this mental movement have any color? Does it have any shape? Does it have any form? Does it have any contour? Does it have a specific location? Does it have a taste, texture, or smell?" Once again observe the mental movement dissipate.

The purpose of this exercise, both as an aspect of your formal sitting practice and as a practice in daily life, is to provide you with a direct experience of the natural life cycle of a mental movement. As you get more familiar with its dream-like insubstantiality your mind will progressively quiet down and moments of stillness will expand.

chapter 9

The Noble Heart

It is now time to shift our discussion from mind to heart. Why? Because mind and heart are seamlessly interwoven and we can move towards human flourishing from either direction. We can even accelerate our progress by working on both at the same time.

In the Eastern tradition there is a single word for mind and heart, because they are as indivisible as wetness and water. They work as one. When the *heart* is open it is not possible to have an overactive mind. It is not possible to experience mental afflictions and distress. So when we practice opening our heart we are simultaneously clearing and stilling the mind. Similarly, when the *mind* is open and clear, mental afflictions, defenses, and fears that bind the heart are absent. The heart, freed from these restraints, opens in an unconditional embrace. That is why we work on mind and heart at the same time from either, or better, from both directions. The result is a quicker path to human flourishing.

An ordinary heart is exclusively focused on self-concerns. A noble heart is focused on others. The shift from self-centered love to other-centered love is reflected in a growing capacity for selfless intimacy and unconditional love, a love which progressively expands to embrace the entire community of beings.

In a sense, the most "intelligent" form of self-centeredness is developing loving kindness for others. When we primarily care for ourselves we court a host of disturbing emotions. We become defensive, protective, jealous, attached to what pleases us, and annoyed with what does not. That results in isolation and disconnection rather than happiness. However, when we are focused on the happiness of others we become more patient, generous, kind, and compassionate. Our relationships improve, others are kind in return, and the result is happiness for ourselves, as well as others. And that is smart!

The Challenge of Authentic Love

We presume that we naturally know how to grow healthy relationships. That is a foolish and ultimately costly assumption. The shift from a focus on "I" to a focus on others does not, for most of us, come naturally. It requires educating mind and heart. We would not be expected to design a bridge without an education in engineering. Yet, we expect to grow and develop healthy and meaningful relationships, which are arguably more difficult than building a bridge, with little or no advice and training. We do not learn about relationships in our customary education, and we are fortunate if we have an opportunity to observe healthy relationships in our family.

The poet Rainer Maria Rilke speaks to the challenge and opportunity of relationships with the following words:

> For one human being to love another human being: that is perhaps the most difficult task given to us, the ultimate, the final problem and proof, the work for which all other work is mere preparation ....

The work of inner development, which precedes the capacity to create healthy relationships, depends on teachers. In the East it is said that we have two groups of teachers available to us for this purpose—the wise ones and all others. They further tell us that it is the ordinary individual who we meet in day-to-day life that is our most valuable teacher. More provocatively, they say that the individuals who we find most difficult can potentially be our greatest teachers. This may seem outlandish at first, but nevertheless we are told to cherish such individuals, as they are important catalysts for further growth. They offer the challenge and opportunity for "hands on" learning.

These individuals force us to see everything we never wanted to see in ourselves. In their presence we confront reactivity, prejudices, and mental patterns which may otherwise be deeply buried in our unconscious mind. We can continue to repeat these reactions or avoid them by avoiding "difficult" people, or we can confront these challenges and free ourselves of old patterns by gaining greater understanding. It is our choice.

I recall sitting at a teaching in a large open courtyard in India. The teacher is well known to all of us as one of the great wise men of our time. He was speaking about compassion. At the same time a group of individuals sitting on cushions in front of my friends and I began moving around, talking amongst themselves, and creating quite a distraction. Friends, who had come across these individuals at previous teachings, had forewarned me about their disruptive behavior. Regardless of this warning, I was getting increasingly angry. I could feel it in my body, mind, and heart. I was no longer able to focus on the teaching, but only on these individuals and their behavior. I shared this with a friend sitting next to me.

Her response was, "Who do you think is now your most important teacher on compassion—the speaker or the folks in front of us?" How true. I realized it was far easier to listen to the teachings than confront the immediate situation, which was right there in front of me at that very moment. I began to think of their circumstance, the roots of their disruptive behavior, and how they were missing the valuable teachings they had come to hear. I realized they had a positive intention in attending the teachings but their inner circumstance was keeping them from what they actually wanted. My anger changed to understanding and concern, and even a bit of compassion. Slowly, my heart began to open and my mind became clear and still. I learned a very important first-hand lesson from these unexpected teachers. I learned that people, often those that are the greatest challenge to us, could be our most important teachers. And then, I kindly asked them if they could be a bit quieter.

That is why Rilke calls authentic love the most difficult task given to us. It is easy to feel love for our "lover" of the moment. But it is not so easy to love individuals that are not satisfying to us. Opening our heart by cutting through the barriers of old patterns, judgments, and reactivity is not easy. And it is only in fully and impartially opening our heart, irrespective of the circumstance or person, that we touch one of the greatest gifts given to us—the gift of an expansive and joyful love. In this way, all of our relationships, particularly those we avoid, can help us to undertake this great human challenge. It is finding the opportunity in each experience. Rilke was not speaking about the small momentary love based on pleasure, but rather, about an encompassing love that is freely given.

With commitment, effort, and proper guidance our relationships, comfortable and difficult, can evolve and flourish, from a preoccupation with ourselves and our needs to an increasing concern for the other. The focus on another is then progressively expanded into a universal embrace that includes all individuals, whether we know them or not or like them or not. We grow from ego-centered dependent relationships to genuine intimacy, to an expansive interconnectedness—from "I" to "You" to "Us" to "All of Us" to "ONE."

It's All About "I"

Our first relationship is entirely focused on our own needs. It is instinctive rather than conscious. Infants and young children do not concern themselves with the needs of their parents, nor should they. The early parent-child relationship is a one-sided dependent relationship, which is age appropriate and necessary for survival, physical development, and emotional growth.

However, remnants of this self-centered relationship often linger into adult life. What was an appropriate self-centered focus for the infant and young child becomes a dysfunctional relationship for the adult. What was valuable for the child destroys the adult. In adulthood, dependency invariably leads to excessive attachment, manipulation, and fear. We reach outside and cling to others as a means of satisfying our unmet emotional needs, and we dress this up in nice words and call it "love." In truth, we have a relationship with our own needs rather than a meaningful relationship with another. It is a concealed love for our self rather than an authentic love for someone else.

Pleasures derived from such relationships are like candles which invariably burn themselves out one after another. The truth is that we cannot find outside of ourselves what we must first find inside. Without a genuine inner life, one that meets our basic needs from the inside out, authentic intimacy with another is not possible. The movement towards an open and rich love begins with growing our inner self and overcoming self-centeredness. The aim is to attain a basic well-being first, which then serves as the foundation for a self-less love of others.

Basic Well-Being

When Eastern teachers began to travel to the West they made an important observation. They observed that Westerners appear to suffer from a fundamental dis-ease—an absence of a sense of basic well-being. To them, it was as if our lives—mind and body—were like engines which are always in gear, never resting in neutral, filled with ceaseless striving and driving.

In seeking to understand the source of such restlessness and discontent, Eastern scholars found themselves in accord with Western psychologists. In traditional societies children are raised by large extended families. There is always someone to help, lend an ear, provide affection, demonstrate cooperation, speak words of wisdom, and provide compassionate care for a child's needs. But modern society has assigned this responsibility to one or two parents. It is impossible for a busy young person or couple to substitute for an extended family, including elders. In this understanding East and West are in agreement. The absence of a fully nourishing childhood experience results in an underlying restlessness and anxiety that persists into adulthood.

When we enter the educational system we sustain a second blow to our capacity to experience basic inner well-being. Our educational system, a product of the industrial revolution, is designed to prepare us for an occupation. That preparation focuses on developing our intellect. As a result we know how to deal with complex problems requiring language, logic, and reason. We are active and successful doers. We have educated the intellect but have failed to provide the education which is necessary for a healthy emotional life, a loving, kind, and connected heart. Too often our educational system, like the nuclear family, has failed to teach and cultivate values that support basic wellness. Until we can experience a basic wellness, we cannot truly concern ourselves with others. We cannot mature our personal relationships.

How do we address this? A very important approach is the practice of inner development. From the earliest stages of practice we begin to experience moments of mental peace and ease. At first it may be only a fleeting glimpse. But when you touch this special peace and ease, for that moment you have directly experienced basic wellness as an adult. The great news is that we can re-establish basic well-being in adulthood, not by reaching backwards to relive the past or outwards seeking false substitutes, but by reaching inward and re-parenting our self through inner practice.

Time and time again I have had the opportunity to observe this in my classes or counseling practice. I learned that with proper guidance every individual can re-experience basic wellness. When it arises during a practice session I immediately point it out. I point out that this *is* the precise experience missed in childhood. It is basic well-being. "There it is! It is in you. No one injected you with calmness and mental ease. It is there, waiting for you." That is how I emphatically point it out.

I follow this with a clear statement reaffirming once more that this natural experience of well-being arose from within through practice—nothing changed externally, nothing changed in ones past history. The mind quiets and stillness and well-being arise together. Think of how this has happened during some of your practice sessions. Everything becomes still and all is peaceful and well. That is how, through practice and inner development, we re-experience a lost basic well-being.

As our practice progresses and stabilizes, we simultaneously stabilize and strengthen this new-found basic wellness. It is a prerequisite for the growth of our personal life and relationships. At peace in our self we are then ready to shift our focus from self to others.

From Self to Others

The shift of focus from self to others starts with basic well-being and then progresses to what we can call "equalizing." Equalizing is the process by which we begin to wish for others what we previously sought only for ourselves—happiness and peace. Once our own needs are met we realize that others are equally deserving of such a life. Their desire to be happy and well is as worthy and meaningful as our own. Why should we be concerned about our happiness and suffering and not the happiness and well-being of others, particularly our "loved" ones? Are we more deserving than others, more special than others? Is happiness and well-being scarce? Is there not enough for everyone?

The awakening concern for others is a monumental shift from selfness to otherness, from loneliness to connection, from sorrow to happiness. It is a shift from a childlike focus on how others "make us happy" to a focus on how we can assist others in gaining happiness.

When we begin to act on the realization that others equally deserve happiness and well-being, equalizing progressively upgrades to "exchanging." Exchanging is giving to the other what we previously sought exclusively for our self. We give kindness, understanding, care, support, and an open heart. We sincerely wish for the other, as we do for ourselves, a life of happiness free of suffering.

We ask our self, "What can I do to help another achieve this goal?" It is this intention, this altruistic opening of the heart uncontaminated by self-interest, that we call *authentic love*. First the other becomes as important as our self and then we give to the other what we wish for our self. We move from selfness to otherness, from loving our own needs to a concern with the other's needs.

Love and care begets love and care. What we give out is naturally returned to us. When we are truly concerned for others the natural consequence is their heartfelt appreciation and concern for us. It takes time and effort to shift from selfness to otherness. At first it is a learned skill. Over time it becomes quite effortless.

From "Other" to "All of Us"

The following thoughts summarize and expand on what we have discussed above and will further assist you in extending to *all* others the good wishes we too often extend only to our family and loved ones.

- All individuals without exception want to be happy, healthy, and free of suffering. What is so special and deserving about my suffering and the suffering of my loved ones? In wanting happiness and freedom from suffering we are all equal—family, lovers, strangers, and even enemies.

- What we consider pleasant or unpleasant in another individual is largely the result of personal or cultural preferences. If you ask ten people to comment on one individual you will get ten different opinions. The individual is not different. Our opinions and biases are largely what makes one individual likable and another unlikable. At the core of our being—our authentic self—we are all precisely the same and basically good. Look deeper and you will surely see that human beings are more similar than different. So why should we limit our affection to a small group of individuals simply because of our superficial and learned biases?

- No individual is all bad or all good. All individuals have some of each quality. One aspect or another may show itself today and another tomorrow, but they are both there. No permanent statement can be made about the benefit or harm caused to us from a particular person. This can change over time. We must be willing to see that we are all equal in containing a mixture of qualities.

- Individuals who are friends today may lose affection and become enemies tomorrow. Our enemies may become friends tomorrow. The ordinary emotions of love, hatred, affection, and rejection are impermanent and fickle. So why place so much emphasis on the emotion of the moment? What is unchanging is the universal desire to be happy and free of suffering.

- We are interconnected in many ways. Our survival and flourishing is a result of this interconnectedness. We are not solitary islands. We are dependent on the kindness of many people. And we never know who will be there when we need someone. It may be a loved one, a stranger, or even someone we consider an enemy.

- Health, happiness, and wholeness arise from learning to love and care for others rather than seeking and demanding love for ourselves. The more we love, and the greater the reach of our love, the more we will experience love. The more love we experience the more open our heart. The more open our heart the more clear and still is our mind. And an open heart and clear and still mind are quickest ways to a richer life and human flourishing.

Each of these points deserves considerable reflection. With practice, the boundaries that define some as friends and others as strangers and enemies will soften and collapse. We will see deeper, through the surface to the basic goodness of all people. As these understandings progress our heart will open in a more universal embrace.

In time we discover a great wisdom: to give to another, to all others, is to give to our self. To heal another is to heal our self. Consider the wise words of Shantideva:

Whatever joy there is in this world
All comes from desiring others to be happy.
And whatever suffering there is in this world
All comes from my desiring to be happy.

What need is there to know more?
The childish work for their own benefit,
The wise sage works for the benefit of others.
Take a look at the difference between them.

To see another, acknowledge another, hear another, be present with another and feel connected with another—a lover, partner, child, friend, stranger, and even an enemy—is a profoundly healing gift for oneself and the world. The development of a far-reaching loving-kindness is the final step in interpersonal development.

Oneness

Until this point we have focused on "otherness" in the context of interpersonal relationships. However, we are no more separate from our physical environment than we are from other individuals. We are seamlessly interwoven into the life of our planet. First we soften the distinction between our self and others and then we soften the distinction between our self and our environment. Our aim is to realize a profound truth, the truth of the inter-relatedness and interdependence of all life. With this wisdom we realize that all life either heals together or deteriorates together.

Consider for a moment what it would be like to relate to our environment as if it were your beloved, your precious other. With joyful anticipation you would do all you could to care for and be kind to her. You would see her as close and dear, and a joyful smile would stretch across your face whenever you knew you were doing something to please your lover. You would give thanks for the special nurturing and embrace that is given to you. You would feel the warmth of her hold. You would experience sadness upon seeing the suffering of your beloved. That is how it should be, isn't it? You might for a moment close your eyes and imagine our wonderful planet as your lover. Feel her in your heart. Cultivate the aspiration that she be happy, whole, and free of suffering. That is caring for the other when the other is our beloved planet.

By cultivating a pervasive and all-inclusive mental attitude of otherness we diminish and slowly eradicate the dominance of our self-centered "I" which is the cause of so much of our distress—body, mind, and spirit. In exchange we gain a noble heart and a community of others. By growing our heart we decisively move forward on the path to human flourishing.

* * *

A Second Sitting Practice: Giving and Taking

Now that we have gained some experience with our mindful breathing practice it is an appropriate time to add another sitting practice, "cultivating loving-kindness." This new practice will support our mindful breathing practice. Remember that by cultivating an open heart we are simultaneously cultivating a clear and still mind. At first cultivating loving-kindness is a sitting practice. That is to say we use this practice to cultivate the attitude of otherness in our mind stream. As our mind and heart progressively open, our speech and actions will follow and the sitting process will be integrated into daily life. Let us begin with this simple yet profound practice.

A Note About Your Practice CD

The loving-kindness meditation is the third track on your CD. It may be helpful to use the audio recording the first few times you do this meditation. This will enable you to become familiar with the practice itself. You may wish to stop the practice at the end of step #3 as suggested below. That is sufficient for our purposes here. If you feel you gain from the further steps, that is okay as well.

Step #1: Calm Abiding

Begin with your usual breathing practice. Complete 5-10 deep breaths to clear away coarse mental activity and then settle into mindful breathing. Maintain this practice until you naturally transition into moments of stillness and clarity. These may only be short glimpses, but you can nevertheless proceed with the next step in this exercise.

Step #2: Basic Well-Being

Notice the qualities of these moments of stillness: ease, peace, restfulness and well-being. Even if your experience is brief be aware of the sense of wellness which characterizes the still mind. Notice that the resting mind lacks the usual wants and desires. There is no sense of stress, restlessness, and unsettledness. You feel content, whole, and well. Nothing is missing and nothing is needed. We call this feeling "basic well-being."

Step #3: Equalizing and Exchanging with a Loved One

Next, create an image of a loved one and place this image in front of your visual field. If a specific individual does not come to mind then create one in your imagination. Observe the image of this individual and become aware of the goodness and loving-kindness of this dear person. Dwell on this for a few moments. Let this feeling settle into your heart.

You are now ready to start the practice of giving and taking. With each out-breath give from your heart to your dear one all of the well-being you have found in your inner life. You can imagine and enhance the intensity of this well-being. Simultaneously repeat the phrase, "may you have happiness—may you have happiness."

With each in-breath imagine yourself taking in the confusion, mental afflictions, misunderstandings, and reactivity which known or unknown to this person may be a current or future source of distress and suffering. Simultaneously repeat the phrase, "may you be free of suffering and the causes of suffering—may you be free of suffering and the causes of suffering."

Riding the out-breath send out happiness and well-being. Riding the in-breath take in distress and suffering, allowing these negativities to dissolve in your open heart. Practice this for five minutes. Observe the quality of your heart. If you get distracted return to the practice.

Although I am going to now shift to steps #4 and #5, for the first several weeks of this practice you may want to stop here and stabilize this part of the practice before the practice becomes a bit more challenging. If this is the case, merely extend giving and taking to a loved one for a total of 10 minutes. Then, return to your regular practice to end the session.

Step #4: Equalizing and Exchanging with Strangers

Next, shift your image. Imagine yourself in a bus, movie theater, or other public place where you are amongst strangers. With the image of these individuals in mind, repeat the giving and taking as you did with your loved one. That should be quite easy, as you have no strong feelings about these individuals, in any direction. Remember, like the previous practice this is only a sitting practice that we do to further open our heart.

On the out-breath give out the basic wellness you feel within and repeat the affirmation, "May you each have happiness—may you each have happiness." On the in-breath take in negativity and repeat the affirmation, "May all of you be free of suffering and the causes of suffering—may all of you be free of suffering and the causes of suffering." We can do this because we can assume that all individuals struggle with emotional afflictions and an overactive mind as much as we do. Continue this for five minutes observing in your mental image the strangers around you, as well as your own heart. How do they change? How do you change?

Step #5: Equalizing and Exchanging with Someone You Dislike

Now bring to mind someone you dislike, someone you might consider an enemy. Place an image of that person in front of you. Because of the strength of the animosity, we must take a preliminary step before this section of the giving and taking practice.

Look at this person and see through their outer behaviors. Penetrate deep enough to see that this person is powerless over his or her negative behavior. See the hurt and pain which is the source of their unfortunate reactive behavior. Know that he or she wants happiness and freedom from suffering the same as you. Know that this person is neither all good nor all bad. Know that at the core this individual has an innate basic goodness that is now covered over by hurt and confusion. Like a wise person, see deeply. See the truth of this other individual's circumstance until some understanding and compassion begins to awaken within you. Rise above your conditioned antipathy. Become larger. Remember this is an inner practice. There is nothing you are actively doing with this person. The work is within yourself.

Next, begin the giving and taking part of the exercise. On the out-breath give out the wish that he or she gain greater understanding of their life and behaviors, and in this way gain an enduring happiness. You sincerely wish they could have the happiness which comes with the end of confusion and afflictive behavior. With each in-breath take in the confusion and hurt which you wisely know is the cause of his or her afflictive behaviors and distress. You really want this for the other. You really want him or her to be free of suffering. In this way you extend the reach of your loving-kindness even to those you dislike. We learn, grow, and our heart opens even wider. What we give is returned in full measure. This is an extraordinary gesture. Continue this part of the practice for 5 minutes.

Step #6: Equalizing and Exchanging as a Universal Embrace

Now, imagine yourself in a vast field. You are facing an endless sea of faces in front of you. Your loved ones are in front and all other beings are behind. It is here that you engage in the noble act of giving and taking to everyone, equally. Giving and taking to an immeasurable number of people means an immeasurable capacity for love—love that is immeasurable for others as well as for yourself. Here you will repeat the following four lines three times as you breathe in and out:

> May all beings be free of suffering and the causes of suffering.
> May all beings find authentic and enduring happiness.
> May all beings never be separated from happiness.
> May all beings live in peace.

With each repetition further open your heart and enhance the sincerity of your aspirations. Feel the sense of this open and expansive universal embrace. Continue this for 5 minutes.

Step # 7: Returning Home to Basic Well-Being

Release the imagery and return to inner stillness. Remain there for 5-minutes. When you have completed the session you may open your eyes and return to the time and space of the room. Give your self a few minutes to reflect on this experience.

It is worthwhile to practice this exercise once or twice weekly, substituting it for your regular mindful breathing exercise. Another alternative is adding an abbreviated version of this practice to the end of your usual practice session. You can do this by limiting the practice to your loved ones and extending the session by 10 minutes. However, some participants in the class gravitate towards this heart-centered practice and make it their daily practice. Each of us has a unique way of approaching inner development and reaching towards human flourishing.

Practicing Loving-Kindness in Daily Life

We have just reviewed the loving-kindness practice. It assists in training our mind and heart to develop the attitude of otherness.

It is important to complement this inner practice with small acts of kindness to others during the day—a smile, a word of affirmation, patience, open listening, tenderness, and generosity. You may also find that you can silently repeat the four aspirations at any time during the day. Consider this an important addition to your daily practice. It serves to continue our effort to use all life experiences as opportunities for practice. In this way we practice loving-kindness in session and in daily life

We have now introduced five daily practices: mindfulness, open listening, taking an inventory of what to cultivate and what to abandon, working with negative emotions in self and other, and loving-kindness. You might think this will keep you quite busy during the day. However, the point here is to transform your day-to-day life rather than to merely add to it. Implementing these daily practices will at first require effort and discipline, but in time they will become a natural and effortless part of day life, bringing ease, lightness, improved relationships, and greater efficacy. Relationships can become powerful opportunities for practice, and our practice can become a powerful way to transform our relationships.

One Final Word Here— Do not Confuse Love and Relationship

If we see love as the wish that others be happy and free of suffering there are no boundaries or limits to the openness and fullness of our love. Love such as this is given from the heart. It does not require romantic involvement with another person. The basis of an open heart is merely our intention and good will—nothing else.

Love is essential for a healthy intimate relationship, but it is not sufficient. Relationships require other qualities and capacities that are shared between partners. You can love another with all you have and this may not be enough for an intimate relationship to develop and flourish. If you get confused about the difference between love and relationship you might find yourself wondering why love alone cannot create or grow intimate relationships. You will end up disappointed, disillusioned, and perhaps even abused. So love fully all the time and, if you wish, consider a personal intimate relationship when it is appropriate for you.

Practice Tips

At this stage in practice the focus is often on renewing our effort to stabilize our formal practice sessions. It becomes important to renew our commitment to settle on the time, place, and a regular daily schedule.

I often make the comparison between a daily physical workout and a mental workout. We are more familiar with establishing a regular gym schedule. However, we find it difficult to apply the same discipline to a mental workout. Of course, that is not a surprise, as we live in a physically-oriented culture. We learn to take care of our body, but not our mind.

This is particularly evident when individuals come to class sharing that they missed practice because they were traveling or had guests, both of which altered their normal routine. I then ask: "Did you brush your teeth each day? Did you take a shower each day? Of course the answer is yes. We are accustomed to habits which care for our body. We have time for them. We even have a special room set aside for them. We do not allow changes in routine to alter these daily habits. We would not even consider that. So whether in your daily routine, on vacation, or entertaining guests, treat the care of your mind each morning as you do the care of your body.

It is necessary to develop the same attitude toward caring for and protecting our mind. That is what practice accomplishes. If it is important to clean our teeth each day it is certainly important to purify our mind each day.

chapter 10

Work as Practice

In this chapter we will focus on another major life activity: your work life. We will examine how ordinary work can be transformed into a profound practice. Does this sound plausible to you? Perhaps you might think that this is true for someone else's work, but not your work. But that is not the case. I can assure you of that. Through a series of simple steps you can take charge of your work and transform your experience without any changes in the circumstances of your work. This is not a new age gimmick. It is age old wisdom!

The Wisdom of the Sages

Let us turn once again to the great healers and listen to their advice as it specifically applies to work. We can then explore how to translate their wisdom into the realities of contemporary work life.

The advice we are given is simple and direct, and at the same time difficult to accomplish. Although our process will be gradual, I am not going to dilute the pure essence and truth of their advice. *The great teachers tell us to commit ourselves fully to our work without regard to its outcome in terms of personal gain or loss to ourselves.* Regardless of the nature of our individual work, they instruct us to let go of personal ambition and striving and focus only on the character and quality of the work we are doing at the moment. We are encouraged to work with *attention, selflessness, care, diligence, presence, and heart.* Stated another way, turn work into a practice.

This does not mean that we disregard income level, working conditions, and other factors when choosing our work. What it means is that once we are in the midst of our work experience we fully engage ourselves in the work-at-hand. We are fully present to what we are doing. We are fully mindful and devoted to our work.

We are further advised, and this is their central point, to work for the good of others—to use our work, whatever it may be, to serve others. This, they inform us, is the highest possible human motivation. And paradoxically, to work for the good of others is perhaps the fastest way to enhance our personal development, as well as our joy at work. Service to others accelerates the path to optimal well-being. It is how we turn ordinary work into noble work.

"Surrender your smaller self," we are told. Cease looking for what is right for you and ask how you can serve others exactly where you are now, today. If you can do this you can flourish in your work, irrespective of what is placed in front of you. Of course, selfless service is not simple to accomplish, that is why it is a *practice*.

From Survival to Service

Unfortunately, a sincere concern for service to others often seems to have no place at the work site. The wishes of our supervisor or the needs of the corporation and its profit line take precedence over any other values. We may not feel in control, work relationships may be harsh and difficult, and at times we may even feel victimized. That can set up a cycle of resentment, anger, and work-related stress. That is reflected in our effectiveness at work, mind/body disturbances, and, as research demonstrates, an increased susceptibility to degenerative disease. If we could, irrespective of our work setting, adopt the attitude of service, we could reverse these life-destroying consequences of an unsatisfying work life.

Some of us are more fortunate. Our work lives are more satisfying, and that is good. We feel content. Our work is creative and meaningful. That may take us toward a good life, but not toward human flourishing, not toward the most precious and enduring qualities of life. For that we also need to progressively transform our work into service.

Viewing our work as service—the desire to be of benefit to others and society—does not mean that we abandon the need to meet our material requirements or our desire for creativity and meaning in work. What we are seeking, whether our work life is unsatisfying or satisfying is a way to create something more out of what we already have. We are seeking to use work to grow and deepen our lives. We are seeking a way to reach for the higher ground that is the basis for human flourishing. I know that feels like a large order. But as we shall see, it can definitely be accomplished in small steps.

Transforming Work One Step at a Time

We transform work by first learning to *own* our work. Owning our work is the key point. This means taking charge of how we relate to and carry out our daily work, irrespective of the many complexities and difficulties which may be part of our work setting. If we can take charge of how we relate to work we can turn any form of work into an experience which benefits both ourselves and others. There are many givens for any of us at work, but none of them defines how we come to our work. What follows is a series of steps each of us can take to assume ownership over our work and progressively transform it into a life-enhancing practice.

Preparing the Mind for Work

We are accustomed to preparing for many of our life activities. For example: scheduling activities, cooking, vacation planning, and so on. In fact, we are experts at planning. However, if we look closely at our planning skills they are generally related to logistics—how and when we do this or that, arrive here or there, meet with this or that person, or arrange this or that activity. That is what we have learned.

But do we ever prepare our mind for our daily activities, specifically work? Isn't it strange that we are never taught to do so, even though the condition of our mind—our emotions, mood, attention, and attitude toward work—has a profound effect on what we do and how we do it? When we bring our unfocused chattering mind to work, what do we expect to happen? How can we take charge of work when our mind is out of control?

Here is a suggestion on how to prepare your mind for work. Practice this experiment for a week. At the conclusion of your morning sitting practice reflect on this variation of the affirmations discussed in the previous chapter, repeating them three times to yourself. You may remind yourself of these during the work day as well.

- May all individuals I meet today be free of suffering and the causes of suffering.

- May all individuals I meet today find enduring happiness.

- May all individuals I meet today never be separated from happiness.

- May all individuals I meet today live in peace.

- May I be the instrument that brings well-being to others.

These affirmations establish an intention to serve others. In this way, bringing a new mental attitude to work may change the very nature and experience of your work. Try it, and see what happens.

I would like to share with you two "prayers" that are written by healers to be used in preparation for the day's work. The first is from the West. It is ascribed to the great physician Maimonides who lived in the twelfth century. The second is from the East and was written by the Buddhist scholar Shantideva in the ninth century.

Maimonides Daily Prayer of the Physician

Almighty God, Thou has created the human body with infinite wisdom, ten thousand times the thousand organs hast Thou combined in it that act unceasingly and harmoniously to preserve the whole in all its beauty—the body which is the envelope of the immortal soul.

. . . .

Inspire me with love for my art and for Thy creatures … Preserve the strength of my body and of my soul that they may ever cheerfully help and support rich and poor, good and bad, enemy as well as friend. In the sufferer let me see only the human being. Illumine my mind that it recognizes what presents itself and that it may comprehend what is absent or hidden ... delicate and infinite are the bounds of the great art of caring for the lives and health of Thy creatures. Let me never be absent minded. May no strange thoughts divert my attention at the bedside of the sick, or disturb my mind in its silent labors. Great and sacred are the thoughtful deliberations required to preserve the life and health of Thy creatures.

Almighty God! Thou hast chosen me in Thy mercy to watch over the life and death of Thy creatures. I now apply myself to my profession.

Shantideva's Prayer

May I become food and drink
For those who are poor and famished.
May I remain in their presence
A source of all they might need.

May I protect those who are without protection
And be a guide for those who journey on the road.
May I become a vessel, a bridge, and a ship
For those who wish to cross the water.

May I be an isle for those who yearn for landfall
And a lamp for those who yearn for light.
May I become a bed for those who are weary
For all that need a servant, may I become their slave.

For all those ailing in the world,
Until their every sickness has been healed,
May I myself become for them
The doctor, the nurse, the medicine itself.

Can we each compose a "prayer" or a series of affirmations which prepare our mind and heart for daily work? I think you will agree that this small step, irrespective of your work or work conditions, can have a significant impact on how you experience your work day, and on how others who interact with you experience theirs.

Living the Personal Connections

Consider the following. For many years I have worked with physicians and other healers who are disturbed by the lack of personal relationship with their patients. They no longer experience a heart connection or a sense of soul and spirit in their work. They experience medical practice as an empty chore. There are many reasons for this. Foremost are the many life-denying aspects of our current medical care system. Yet I always remind my fellow practitioners that the moment they close their office door, the moment they are face-to-face with another individual, there is always a precious opportunity for open-heartedness, loving-kindness, empathic listening, and presence. That is a moment that soul and spirit can flourish.

In that moment of direct contact there is always the possibility of an intimate human connection, regardless of the difficulty or complexity of outer circumstances. If we open to this human connection, value it, and consciously try to create it, these few moments are worth far more than an hour spent exchanging information.

To those physicians who feel they are too busy, I suggest they stay late one night a week or leave a couple of hours open one day each week to sit with a single patient as long as it takes to fully listen and tend to the other in a spirit of communion and care. What I am suggesting is that healers take this time to practice their work as service, bringing to it their highest wisdom, loving-kindness, compassion, and integrity. I ask them to "spiritualize" their work at least once a week, and experience what comes back to them from this shift in intention.

Irrespective of the nature of your job or profession you can definitely try this approach as well. As an experiment, take just one of your daily work interactions and infuse it with kindness, care, and presence. This merely requires a stable intention. Then, evaluate the result of this experiment. Observe what happens to you, as well as to the other person. I think you will agree this is a small but potentially important step in bringing meaning and fulfillment to work by offering loving-kindness and service to another.

Drop Into Inner Stillness

Here is another suggestion. During a lunch break, stop what you are doing for a moment and allow your breath to take you inward to a calm inner state. Drop into the ease of a relaxed body and mind. Try this for a few minutes several times a day. Observe the moments following this "inner break." Has anything changed in your work experience? Have things slowed down a bit? Are you more mindful and present? Has your sense of well-being changed?

The mind is accustomed to quickly returning to its familiar chatter. However, if you use this quick moment to upgrade your clarity and mindfulness and apply this to the work at hand, you may discover that you bring more ease and delight to your work. If you discover that you can change your work experience by calming your mind and upgrading mindfulness, you can be assured that not only will your work change, but your coworkers will change as well!

Understanding Interconnection

Here is another way to look at work. All work, whether it is the construction of a house, sales, marketing, plumbing, or police work is, at its core, service to others. All work is a cooperative venture that supports each of us. Writing at my computer requires support from the woodcutter, mill worker, carpenter, and construction team that built the cottage where I live and the furniture on which my computer rests. Then there is the plumber and electrician who made this home livable, the farmer and store owner who provide the food that sustains me, and let us not forget the computer people who created the machine I write on, and the people who taught me how to type. All these individuals are part of what you are now reading.

If we continue this line of reasoning we soon realize that our current life is sustained through the efforts of many people. Although the ultimate impact of your work on another person's life cannot always be seen at first glance, it is definitely there. Each contribution is an essential piece of the whole. Without this interdependence and cooperation none of us could meet our daily needs in the complex society we live in. Consider the role of a single neuron in the brain. It does not realize that it is part of a complex web of brain cells which together create a fully integrated mental activity. Although it cannot see its part in the whole, without it nothing would happen. Your role in life is far larger than you imagine.

Close your eyes for a few moments and consider the links that connect you to others. Consider how your work might have meaning for others, how it might serve others, and how it is part of the larger whole. Can you see how your efforts are essential and irreplaceable, without which things would fall apart? Can you see the purpose and connection in all you do? Unlike the single neuron, we can comprehend our relationship to the whole. If you do so, that will be another way to understand how your work serves the whole.

The Healer at Work

When we bring a sweet loving-kindness to our work, coworkers and clients, we emanate a healing presence. Every kind of work and every moment of work done with care and kindness can be healing to others as well as to ourselves. We can become a teacher of patience, care, generosity, loving-kindness, and compassion. Can you recall an individual like this, an individual that lit up the room? Perhaps this *is* your actual work. Perhaps you are a healer-in-disguise, and the office is your healing space. We can each be carriers of spirit and healers at work regardless of our occupation.

This is particularly important with co-workers whom we find difficult, or perhaps even abusive. There are times that the best choice is to simply get out of the way. However, we might see these individuals as important teachers and opportunities for practice. They point out the further inner development that awaits us. They do not need to know they are teachers for us, but we do! If we can include them in our experiment we may see how the shift in our attitude is a cause for a shift in theirs as well.

"Difficult" individuals are also suffering and like us want happiness.

They are confused and do not know how to go about it. The result of their confused understanding and behavior is suffering for themselves and for others. How can we transform this seemingly hopeless situation? We can listen deeply without comment, understand their needs and fears, and respond in a skillful manner. By stabilizing your own mind, moving beyond your immediate reaction to this person, seeing deeply and acting skillfully, you can take charge, own, and transform the most difficult of circumstances. That is the high road.

If you continue inner practice and add one or more of these other practices, your relationship to work can undergo unexpected change. You may see a surprising shift that turns a chore into joy and a difficult relationship into a teaching opportunity. Nothing that you can see with your senses changes, yet everything begins to change from the inside out. Work can become a source of creative expression, meaning, fulfillment, and selfless service. I assure you that I have seen this time and again in the work lives of participants in this course who follow one or more of these simple steps.

Discovering Your Deepest Calling

As your inner life grows you will progressively discover your deepest calling—a calling that best expresses your temperament, disposition, and innate talents. And this calling will be your soul's longing which naturally expresses itself as effortless and selfless service. For some this may come early and easily, while for others it may take time. I recall the advice of the poet Rainer Maria Rilke in his *Letters to a Young Poet*:

> ...I want to beg you, as much as I can, dear sir, to be patient toward all that is unsolved in your heart and try to love the questions themselves like locked rooms and like books that are written in a foreign tongue. Do not seek the answers which cannot be given you because you cannot live them. And the point is, to live everything. Live the questions now. Perhaps you will then gradually, without noticing it, live along some distant day into the answer.

And that is our direction, to live our work *today,* whatever it may be, with integrity, spirit, and loving-kindness toward others. As we develop our inner life, our most authentic calling will naturally arise in its own time.

Work as Love Made Manifest

The poet Kahlil Gibran speaks to work in his masterpiece, *The Prophet.* He asks us, "What is it to work with love?" and then he responds:

> It is to weave the cloth with threads drawn from your heart, even as if your beloved were to wear that cloth. It is to build a house with affection even as if your beloved were to dwell in that house. It is to sow seeds with tenderness and reap harvest with joy as if your beloved were to eat the fruit.

Gibran asks us to work as if we were working for the beloved. But who is the beloved? In an ordinary sense the beloved is a person for whom we have feelings of deep tenderness and affection—a friend, a family member, a spouse, or a special lover. Imagine what it would be like to work each moment for the benefit and happiness of that person. How would it feel if work were a gift we were tenderly preparing with elegance, skill, and heart for our lover? What devotion and delight we would feel in our work. Work would assume the sacredness, beauty, and connectedness of a lover meeting his or her beloved.

But what the poet is actually speaking of is the larger Beloved. He is speaking about the sacred—about the love and connection that has no boundaries, no name, no center, and includes all. If we can see that your work, regardless of its specific character, becomes a work of love and service to this universal Beloved, then your work will magically be transformed from mundane to the sacred.

Gibran sums this up in his parting advice:

> And if you cannot work with love but only with distaste, it is better that you should leave your work and sit at the gate of the temple and take alms of those who work with joy.

If you wish to use work as a spiritual practice you will use every challenge it presents as an opportunity for practice. So the immediate task is not finding the "right" job as much as taking on the challenge of where you are at the moment, owning your work, and regardless of the difficulties bringing to it care, love, and the attitude of service. In this spirit and understanding you will discover that work, one step-at-a-time, can become a great support for inner development, placing you firmly on the path to human flourishing. That is the great potential of work.

Learning from a Woodcarver

The story is told in the East about a woodcarver who was commanded by his king to create a bell stand. The woodcarver did not have much choice. Perhaps he had other plans, in which case he could have become angry and resentful, feeling victimized by the king's demand. But that was not the course he chose. The woodcarver accepted what was required and began preparing himself. He fasted for three days and then intensified his contemplative practices, taming his mind so that it was completely emptied of negative emotions, of ambition, greed, pride, and any thought of the king. When he was finally ready, the woodcarver skillfully brought his mind to stillness, and with complete focus on his work he went into the forest, saw the bell stand already completed in the perfect tree, and then merely cut away the excess wood.

The king was amazed at the beauty of his creation and could not understand how he had done it. "Was it the work of the spirits?" he asked. No, not at all, it was the work of a wise and skilled master. The woodcutter had transformed the king's demand into an act of personal choice, discipline, and reverence. He took the king's demand as an opportunity to master spiritual practice. He owned his destined work and infused it with meaning. An outer order became, through the alchemy of his wisdom, an inner opportunity to engage his mind, heart, and spirit in the perfection of his work and life. He spiritualized the entire process, transforming a simple demand into a great treasure. This is the miracle of transforming work into inner practice.

Do not think this inner miracle, this inner wisdom and skillfulness, is only possible for a mythical woodcarver. It is a possibility for every one of us. It is in everything we touch even though we may not yet have the vision needed to see the hidden gold or all of the skills required to transform the challenges of work into spiritual practice. But as we grow more skilled and see the opportunities in front of us, we can embrace and shape our work as we wish. We can gracefully and wisely mine the possibilities present in what is given to or asked of us. In this way we flourish, not because our job or our world is perfect, but because we bring beauty and spirit to it, just as it is. We perfect the world through the force of our own inner development.

Here is the full story of the woodcarver—a modern day story first told many years ago.

The Wood Carver

> Khing, the master carver, made a bell stand
> Of precious wood. When it was finished,
> All who saw it were astounded. They said it must
> Be the work of spirits.
> The Prince of Lu said to the master carver:
> What is your secret?
> Khing replied: "I am only a workman;
> I have no secret.
>
> "There is only this:
> When I began to think about the work you commanded
> I guarded my spirit, did not expend it
> On trifles, that were not to the point.
> I fasted in order to set
> My heart at rest.
> After three days fasting,
> I had forgotten gain and success.
> After five days
> I had forgotten praise or criticism.

After seven days
I had forgotten my body with all its limbs.

"By this time all the thought of your Highness
And of the court had faded away.
All that might distract me from the work
Had Vanished.
I was collected in the single thought
Of the bell stand.

"Then I went to the forest
To see the trees in their own natural state.
When the right tree appeared before my eyes,
The bell stand also appeared in it, clearly, beyond doubt.
All I had to do was to put forth my hand
And begin.

"If I had not met this particular tree
There would have been
no bell stand at all.
What happened?
My own collected thought
Encountered the hidden potential in the wood;
From this live encounter came the work
Which you ascribe to the spirits."

* * *

Practice in Daily Life: Becoming a Healer-at-Work

My suggestion is that you choose one workday before the next class
and use your morning practice as preparation for work. Repeat the
four affirmations included in this chapter three times at the end of
your session. Remember them during the day. Consider them your
intention to practice being a healer at work.

It is best that you practice this without the knowledge of your coworkers. Bring serenity into your interactions with others. This may

mean stopping for a few moments during the day in order to refresh your innerness. Remember the words—"Calm inside even when it is complex outside." Use your capacity for open, non-judgmental listening. Have no agenda while listening, except being fully present. Practice loving-kindness by emphasizing patience, generosity, and care. Overcome your tendency to react to your coworkers. Replace reactivity with insight and compassion. Take charge of the circumstance. In summary, practice otherness—the wish that others be free of suffering and gain happiness. And further, that you, through your presence, be the instrument that aids others in achieving this.

Just remember you are exploring whether you can actually be a healer to others through your presence, intentions and actions. Do not judge yourself. Do the best that you can and see how it feels at the end of the day. Do you feel more balanced and at ease? Do you feel more connected to others? Was work a more pleasant and meaningful experience? Did this practice help you see others in a different way? Can you have a role in determining the quality of your workday? I think you will find that your intentions and actions can shape the character and quality of your experience, as well as the experience of others.

Tips for Sitting Practice

I would now like to discuss a problem which often emerges in practice. We begin to turn what is a restful and easeful exploration of the mind into a strenuous goal-oriented project. When we do this we get enmeshed in all the aspects of doing: the strenuous effort, the orientation towards success, perfectionism, frustration, and feelings of failure, disappointment, and self-deprecation. These feelings may actually lead to a dropping off of practice.

There is much to learn here. First, we automatically bring to practice our entire personality—helpful and unhelpful. We begin to treat practice as another form of "doing," as another chore. We bring to it all of the habits related to doing. This is a major obstacle to practice. Clearing the mind is not about doing. It is about clearing a space for being.

If you notice this tendency, become aware of this aspect of your personality and how it has followed you into practice. Let it go and relax. Your practice should not have an aim, a goal, a direction, a target, or a preferred endpoint. Just relax into it and follow the instructions. If any of the feelings mentioned above arise, just consider them mental movements. Do not attach to or empower them.

Another practice tip. Remember that your focus on the breath is a gentle attention and interest rather than a tight holding. Relax into this. Random thoughts, feelings, and images are not adversaries to be pushed away or avoided. They are natural to the mind and body. As long as you have a mind and body you will have mental movements. The problem is not the mental movements, but as we have said before, the problem is your mind's habitual tendency to chase after them. Be gentle. Just note them when they arise, leave them alone in their own place and return to observing your focal point.

Patience is an important virtue in practice. It has taken a lifetime for your mind to become habituated to chasing after and becoming invested and enmeshed in thoughts, feelings, and images. It will take time to reverse this. The amount of time is not of significance. The fact that you are committed to practice and are progressively gaining control of your mind and life *is* what is important. Just focus on your breath and return to it whenever you notice your mind has wandered. Turn discouragement into a source of inspiration and attend to your practice with greater regularity and diligence.

chapter 11
The Alchemy of Adversity

As you spend time with the understandings and practices we are exploring, you will certainly notice progressive change occurring in your life. At times this may seem so gradual that you barely notice it, but change is definitely happening. When the foundation of your life is a chaotic and uncontrollable mind, the invariable result is mental and physical distress. When the foundation of your life is inner clarity, correct understanding, and loving-kindness, your life will obviously be very different. What initially began as an effort to calm your overactive mind, over time becomes life changing.

In previous chapters we have discussed how to use the challenges of relationship and work as opportunities for practice. Now we will address another challenge, how to transform adversity into a life-enhancing practice. We will discover how we can take life's difficulties and use them for inner development.

What I am suggesting is that unexpected adversity can be an opportunity for change rather than a seemingly insurmountable and unbearable catastrophe. That is what the wise ones have told us. Creating a healthy inner life prepares us for adversity when it arrives. The cumulative effect of ongoing inner development assures that we can move through difficult circumstances with greater ease and clarity. Rather than collapsing into anger, resentment, or despair, we can rise to the challenge. We do not seek adversity, but when it arrives on our doorstep we are ready for it.

But is it really possible to turn life's difficult challenges into opportunities for further growth and development? Can adversity motivate us to reach for our largest self? Consider Viktor Frankl whose time as a prisoner in a concentration camp led him to develop the field of Logotherapy, a psychological approach described in his book *Man's Search for Meaning*. And then there is Gandhi, sitting in a jail cell and changing the course of a great nation. The same could be said of Nelson Mandela. These individuals were not preoccupied with desperation and fear. They saw opportunity in their challenging circumstances. They used what they were given in the moment. They are each well-known examples of what is possible. However, there are many individuals who have done the same in their own lives. Perhaps you can think of someone you know who has turned adversity into opportunity, or perhaps you can remember a time when you accomplished this yourself. It is not so uncommon. It can be done. Adversity can become a practice by turning it into a call to awaken or by using it as a master teacher.

Adversity As a Call to Awaken

Adversity, particularly major adversity, interrupts our lives. It may arrive in the form of illness, the unavoidable changes of aging, loss of a job or a loved one, or failure to achieve an important life goal. Or, it may be the growing sense that things are not right and that there is more to life. These moments can be sources of great distress. They can also herald a long-awaited *call to awaken* to a new and richer life. If we can stop, place anxiety and despair aside, and listen carefully, we may hear a quiet yet persistent message from our depths, a fateful call for change, an opportunity to reexamine our life and awaken to the preciousness of each moment, to the goodness and beauty of life. The timing may be inconvenient, but in retrospect it usually proves to be quite precise.

Where does this call come from? What is its source? The call to awaken comes from within. This inner call, amplified by adversity, is the voice of our soul and spirit subtly beckoning us towards a larger, more authentic life. It can be foolishly put aside for a moment in our futile effort to resolve adversity by covering it over, but ultimately our inner voice cannot be stilled. It tells us about the state of our being. It tells us about our true needs, our deepest yearnings, and our unique destiny. It insists that we live a genuine life of meaning, wisdom, and passion.

Consider the heartfelt words of the writer Anais Nin.

And then the day came,
when the risk
to remain tight
in a bud
was more painful
than the risk
it took
to Blossom

That is how it is. You cannot feel, touch or measure this inner call as you can a material object, but nevertheless it is present and compelling.

At times of great adversity we must listen carefully. If we fail to pay attention to the language of our deepest self we will merely collapse into adversity, bear it, and insure a stale and stagnant life, repeating old patterns over and over until the end of life. If we do not sense the possibilities we cannot transform adversity into opportunity. We are at a dead end. Yet, the wise ones knew that the very experience, which is so unwanted and intrusive, is in fact the very experience which can awaken us to a larger life, offering us a second birth, a spiritual birth.

But there is no guarantee that this will occur. When confronting adversity we have two choices: to refuse the call to awaken and collapse into our difficulties, or confront our circumstance and awaken to a larger life. There are many ways we can refuse the call to awaken—"Not now, maybe next year, after the kids are grown, I'm too busy, when life is a bit more stable, after I finish this project, not enough time, not enough money, I can't find 20 minutes to practice- -and on and on."

The alternative is it to take this opportunity and turn inward. If you have done so already, through your investment in inner development, you are prepared. You have a heads up on adversity. As a result, there is less upheaval. You will not react to life's turbulence quite like you may have. You will not be dragged here and there by unstable emotions. You stop, respond to the immediate needs of the circumstance, and remember that there is a deeper meaning and purpose to adversity. And then, you turn inside with greater intensity and motivation.

If you have waited until adversity strikes and you are hearing your inner call for the first time, then this is your opportunity to turn inward. This will require that you find skillful assistance and resources which will assist you in moving forward on the journey ahead. That is the healing choice. That is the life-giving choice. With a wise tweak you can transform adversity into a call to awaken.

Adversity as Teacher

Adversity can also be a catalyst which leads to important and life-changing insights. I would like to share with you three examples of what can be achieved when adversity becomes a teacher.

Complexity on the Outside and Stillness on the Inside

Occasionally an opportunity arises in class to demonstrate this first teaching. This occurs when an individual chooses to share with the group a recent personal experience which has caused great distress. I recall one such situation when a participant spoke about her dearly loved pet that had died earlier in the day. She was inconsolable. I asked if I could work with her in the class setting. She said yes.

I followed the instructions in chapter seven on emotional afflictions, specifically the instructions on how to work with negative emotions by separating from them through the creation of a mental image. As you may recall, this image then becomes the focal point of practice, similar to mindful breathing. The class member created, on my instruction, an image of her pet. I helped her to maintain her focus on this image. After working with the process for a period of time, her demeanor shifted. It was apparent that she was calmer and more peaceful, and in time this shifted into stillness. When we finished the process I asked her what she had discovered. She said, "The experience of loss, and the sadness that accompanies it, does not require suffering. The suffering came from my past losses. I was suffering the past rather than the present. *I still feel the loss and sadness, but not the suffering.* I feel calm." Those were her words—the words of a beginning student! It sounds like a paradox but that is how it can actually be experienced.

It is important to note that we deliberately and skillfully leaned into the suffering. We did not suppress, avoid, or become enmeshed in it. We worked with it. We transformed it into a practice experience, and further, we used loss as a tool to invoke inner stillness. This personal loss became an opportunity to gain valuable insights and understandings. At the time of this exercise the individual I worked with was only 5 weeks into the course!

The first of these insights was the recognition that adversity is not bound to suffering. Suffering is a superimposition from past experience. It is not a requirement of adversity. Suffering is neither inherent nor innate to adverse circumstances. In fact, we can feel and experience difficult events with greater clarity and fullness once we let go of the add-on of suffering.

The second insight was the startling discovery that adversity can be used to invoke sitting practice, to invoke a calm interior. She discovered, through her own experience, that it is possible to be calm on the inside while experiencing and feeling adversity on the surface. That is rather extraordinary. But as we can see, it is quite possible with skillful guidance, even for a beginner.

If this participant had sufficient practice experience the exercise would not have been necessary. She would have built up a reservoir of stability and understanding which could have "held" the loss and related emotions in the context of inner calm. That is why we continuously prepare ourselves so that when necessary we may have the depth and stability to hold adversity without suffering.

With a wise tweak this individual transformed the suffering of loss into a teaching opportunity that led to greater insight and understanding. The sadness of loss became an invaluable teacher.

Realizing Impermanence

This second and third teaching is encapsulated in a story told and re-told in the East. It is about a mother who lost her child and, in great grief, visited a master teacher asking him for advice and assistance.

He requested that she first visit all the homes in her community to see whether there was a single home in which there had been no loss. Two months later she returned to the teacher, in a very different mood. She said to him, "I have not found a single home which has not experienced loss, and many have experienced far more loss than I have. My heart has opened. I am touched by what I have seen and heard. I feel compassion for my neighbors. And, I am at peace." The teacher replied, "You have received my advice." Adversity, the loss of a child, resulted in two very important teachings—a teaching on impermanence and another on compassion.

If we actually understood and integrated the reality of impermanence we would know that everything comes and goes. We would not attach to people, experiences, and objects as we now do. We would realize that disease, aging, death and all change is inherent in human existence. As humans, of course, we would feel the emotions related to loss. But we would be amply prepared. The loss would occur within a greater context of understanding. Adversity forces us to accept the reality of impermanence. That prepares us to move through loss and change with greater ease and wisdom. The grieving mother in our story learned this directly and profoundly by following her teacher's wise instructions.

Compassion at the Center of Adversity

Not only can adversity awaken the mind to the reality of impermanence, but it can also awaken the heart to compassion, just as it did for the mother in our story. The compassionate heart is a powerful antidote to the suffering of adversity. Instead of a contracted absorption in our own circumstance we focus on others. We transcend our situation to see how others are similarly suffering. We are touched by their suffering and extend our love, kindness, and support. Our heart connects to others. We are no longer isolated in our own distress.

We break through self-rumination and self-pity, expand rather than contract, and become larger rather than smaller. Our distress evaporates in the presence of an authentic loving-kindness towards others. It is replaced by peace and joy. Perhaps you do not think you can do this. But much like our grieving mother, you can. Many have risen from personal loss and suffering to devote themselves to eradicating suffering in others. It is possible for anyone to create this life-enhancing shift. In this way, the suffering of adversity transforms into compassion and connection.

The essential point we are making is that adversity, however difficult, can be a great teacher and an important cause for a rich and profound life. It can be experienced as opportunity, serve as a call to awaken to a larger life, catalyze the realization of new insights, and awaken the heart to compassion and love. What other experience can teach us so much! This is how we turn adversity into practice and experience its many gifts.

* * *

Daily Life Practice: Turning Adversity Into Practice

We have many opportunities to practice what we have learned in this chapter in daily life. There are always challenges confronting us: physical distress, loss, difficult individuals, and so on. Take one of these circumstances each day, a less challenging one at first, and rather than react with annoyance or irritation or even feel victimized, consider how this circumstance can be turned into an opportunity. How can you see this circumstance in a way that can grow your life, open your heart, or cultivate new skills? How can you use this situation in a positive way? How can you turn it around irrespective of the circumstance?

You might want to jot down the possibilities discussed in this chapter: adversity as a call to awaken, an opportunity to gain insight, a teaching in impermanence, or as a catalyst for compassion.

In this daily experiment you can refuse to see this situation as adverse. Wipe that label from your mind. Insist you go deeper into it and use it rather than react to it. I think you will find that adversity can be your teacher, perhaps one of your best teachers. Alchemy is the art of transforming base metals into gold, or said another way, turning dirt into gold. That is what we seek to do when confronting adversity.

Tips for Sitting Practice

Mindfulness—attention to the practice process—is essential to our efforts to develop a still, clear, moment-to-moment awareness. However, becoming fixated on the use of a tight mindfulness when your practice has succeeded in calming the mind can halt further progress. What do I mean by this? Once the mind is still, a "tight" mind can hinder you from fully experiencing it. So loosen up the mindfulness. Yet, it is essential to once again strengthen mindfulness when the mind starts to wander again.

Learn to measure the intensity of mindfulness according to the stage of practice. An active chattering mind or a dull mind calls for steady mindfulness. When you are resting in stillness just a bit of mindfulness is helpful. The reappearance of mental agitation or dullness would indicate the need for greater mindfulness. Tailor your use of mindfulness to your stage of practice, which can shift even within one session.

Once you begin to have moments of stillness it is easy to replace the distraction of mental agitation with the dullness of "falling off" into drowsiness, a trance-like state, or even sleep. That is not practice. That is your mind once again dragging you around. When this happens you can open your eyes, move around a bit, or both, and then resume your practice maintaining alertness.

By now you can see how important it is to develop a regular stable practice, even if there is a lot of inner distraction. Just do it. Only through the direct experience of practice can you take what is learned through study and reflection and make it you own. When you have an "aha" and "get it" through a practice insight it will never leave you. There will be a certainty and decisiveness. That is why each aspect of inner development is necessary—study, reflection, and practice. Be patient and persistent.

chapter 12

The Lightness of Being

We began our discussion of practice by identifying its three sequential steps: taming the mind with mindful breathing, resting in stillness and clarity, and relaxing into our naturally settled presence and beingness. Taming the mind with mindful breathing is our basic practice. It will continue to be our starting point and most important practice for overcoming and stabilizing the overactive mind.

As your mind progressively quiets down you will increasingly find yourself resting in periods of stillness and clarity. In chapter 8 we discussed how to extend and stabilize these moments of stillness and clarity by further developing and maturing your understanding of mental activity. As we gain greater understanding of the mind and enhance our skills, the proliferation of mental activity will diminish. We will be less and less disturbed by the natural flow of thoughts, feelings, and mental images.

When the second phase of practice, resting in stillness, becomes increasingly stable, it is then possible to explore the third phase of practice, open awareness. At first we will catch very brief glances of this natural state. However, in time we become more accustomed to it. The problem is that we have been lost for so long in the overactive mind that it is difficult to recognize and settle into it. That may seem odd, as it is our authentic nature. However, our learned and faulty mental patterns are quite powerful and it takes time to move beyond these tenacious and obscuring habits.

I think you can see by now that our aim goes far beyond the use of techniques to relax the mind into a state of temporary and pleasant dullness. Through study, reflection, and practice we have learned a great deal about how our mind works. It is this knowledge and practice experience which will progressively enable you to access and once again rest in your natural state of being.

The poet, T.S. Eliot, speaking about this return, says in his Four Quartets, we will "… arrive where *we* started. And *know* the place for the *first time.*" What is the meaning the poet wishes to convey with these words? The authentic self we return to is a home we lived in as a young child. It is not new. But unknowingly we have wandered away from it. In youth we could not have known its value, so we became enmeshed in worldly life, forgetting the pristine experience of our natural self which was covered over by day-to-day concerns.

When we return once again to our innermost self and supreme identity we will, as a result of our inner education, consciously *know* it as our essential self and this time cherish its great value. The wisdom we have gained on the return journey home assures us that we will not again forsake the core of our being and its life-bestowing qualities.

Why is this return to our supreme, natural, and innermost self so important? Because it is here that the qualities of human flourishing innately reside. These qualities come in a single package. They are who we are. They are our authentic self. The rediscovery of our innermost home and its innate qualities guarantees a permanent end to dissatisfaction, distress, and suffering. It guarantees a progressive attainment of our full human potential. When accomplished and stabilized there will be no further need for study, reflection, and practice. There will be an imperturbable lightness of being which is unknown in ordinary life. That is why we choose to progress through the levels of practice rather than satisfy ourselves with the temporary calming effect of a relaxation technique.

When living from our innermost self we experience life as a continuous unfolding of moment-to-moment experience—nothing is held and nothing is fixed. Each moment of experience that arises out of our awareness and being is a fresh creation all its own. Each moment has never occurred before and will never again. Each moment is alive. Each moment is free of the past. Life unfolds, we are present, and everything is as it is without being manipulated, fabricated, mentally constructed, or elaborated by our cognitive mind.

One of the most interesting characteristics of this third phase of practice is that it is not an actual practice. It is more precisely termed a "non-practice." This is a very important point. Unlike the practices of mindful breathing and resting in stillness, relaxing into our natural presence and being is effortless. It is who we are. It is simply there waiting for us. There is nothing to do and no place to go. All we have to do is to let go and let be. Unfortunately that is not so easy, which is why we have to first master the earlier practices in order to overcome the obstacles created by our learned mental habits.

As we begin our discussion of the third level of practice it is at first quite important to distinguish it from the second level, resting in stillness. The distinctions are quite subtle. However, if we are to progress to this final level of practice it is essential to understand these differences. Part of the problem in describing them is that our natural home of being and presence is neither cognitive nor mental in the usual sense. It goes beyond our usual thinking process. As a result, it defies the use of language. It lends itself far better to the poetic realm. Here is an example of how this experience is described by the poet Willam Wordsworth in *Tintern Abbey*:

> ... a sense sublime
> Of something far more deeply interfused,
> Whose dwelling is the light of setting suns,
> And the round ocean and the living air,
> And the blue sky and in the mind of man;
> A motion and a spirit which impels
> All thinking things, all objects of all thought,
> And rolls through all things.

As mentioned previously there are many ways we can briefly and temporarily touch into this experience of our deepest self. There are rare individuals who, through an act of Grace, touch this experience of self and never leave it again. But this is not the case for most of us. We are on the gradual path. The way we get to know, realize, and stabilize this sublime experience of our authentic self is through the progressive development of practice. In order to accomplish this we first need to master the earlier stages of practice and then gain as much intellectual understanding of this final accomplishment as is possible. So let us begin by distinguishing resting in stillness from our innermost home of presence and being.

Cultivated vs. Spontaneous Arising

When I use the term "cultivated" I am describing the mental effort of practice that results in the inner experience of stillness. Resting in stillness is brought about through the use of methods to tame and still the mind. These methods "manipulate" the overactive mind into calming down. They include: intention, attention, mindfulness, and vigilance. These techniques are necessary to "create" the relatively undistracted mind of stillness and clarity.

You may even feel a bit exhausted just thinking about it. That is what I mean by manipulating the mind through mental methods to create moments of inner stillness. It does not happen on its own. Yet, the capacity to rest in stillness *is* a very major accomplishment which can be life-changing in itself. Beyond this it is also the launching pad for our final return trip home. So it is essential that we master the first two levels of practice in order to progress further.

The third level of practice, resting in our natural innermost home, *spontaneously reveals itself* when we remove the obscurations of mental misunderstandings and mental afflictions. Let us be clear here. The effort is in removing the obstacles to recognizing and experiencing our authentic self. We do not have to create this natural presence and being. In fact, we cannot create it. There is no cause for it. *Our innermost self of open awareness, presence, and being is always and already there.* However, we cannot recognize or experience it because it is hidden from view by our overactive mind. Once we remove these veils, there it is. No further effort is required. We simply experience it.

"Spontaneously arising" may not be the most precise term we can use to describe how this natural state reveals itself. Perhaps this metaphor will help. We can say that the sun spontaneously appears when the clouds move away. But we know the sun is always there whether obscured by clouds or not. It is the same with our natural presence and being. It is always there whether it is obscured or not.

We do not have to create it in any way. We just need to get out of the way and there it will be, spontaneously *present*. I suspect you are getting a sense of the distinction between the effort to create the undisturbed mind of stillness and the spontaneous and effortless experience of our innermost self. In the latter instance you just relax body and mind and let yourself be. It is that simple.

What could be easier? No practice, no practitioner, no attention, no mindfulness, no vigilance, and no concern about the natural flow of mental activity. Just a simple and ordinary presence and being in life—fully wakeful, vividly brilliant, and profoundly easeful.

That is the difference between the cultivated mental state of stillness that is dependent on techniques and methods and the spontaneous presence of our essential and easeful self that is *self-existent and self-arising*.

Effort vs. Effortless

In the early months of practice you will experience moments of mental stillness. With ongoing practice these moments will expand and stabilize. Less effort will be required as mental chatter and the proliferation of mental activity diminishes and becomes less dense. We respond to increasing mental calm by diminishing the intensity of mindfulness and vigilance. You rest into stillness when you can. This lesser level of effort may seem effortless, but it is not. You are still mindful and vigilant in watching for the reappearance of mental agitation or a new problem, dropping off into mental dullness—a trance-like state that is neither alert nor completely present. When this occurs you must reinvigorate your use of the mental techniques as we have already mentioned.

In contrast, the third level of practice, relaxing into your natural innermost self, is effortless. Why, because we do not have to create this experience. It is already there once the obscurations of an overactive mind are removed through the earlier practices. It is the easiest thing to experience.

When we first experience our innermost nature the immediate response is to say, "there it is." The moment we label or in any other way attempt to categorize or interpret this direct and natural experience we will lose it. Any effort to understand this experience when it is occurring will superimpose obscuring mental activity. Effort gets in the way. Effort keeps us from this naturally-occurring experience. The final phase of "practice" is easeful and effortless.

Temporary vs. Permanent

Mental stillness is dependent on the use of mindfulness, attention, and vigilance. We can neither achieve nor rest in stillness without them. That is why resting in stillness is not a natural mental state. It is cultivated. It is created by practice. As a result, it is temporary. It comes to an end when we cease being mindful and vigilant. That is why it comes and goes depending on practice.

When we diminish our efforts we will once again fall back into an overactive mind. There is definitely a growing stability of inner calm which is gained over time through practice. This often remains with us even when we drop off of practice for a few days. But if we stop for a longer period of time, our achievements will diminish. So be assured that the first two levels of practice will enhance your life, but many of the benefits that are specific to practice will diminish if your practice drops off.

In a way this is like a physical workout. After a period of regular workouts we achieve more and more conditioning, flexibility, and strength. However, if we stop our workout for extended periods, physical conditioning will reverse itself. Here the comparison drops off. With study, reflection, and practice there are changes that occur in our lifestyle and our awareness which remain even if we take a break from practice. But future growth and development will be lost and the power of the tenacious overactive mind may reassert itself at any time. The specific mental state of resting in stillness is temporary. It is largely dependent on ongoing practice.

Your innermost self is permanent and always present. It is independent of any other factors. It self-exists. Once you recognize and experience this innermost home you will be amazed at how simple and ordinary it seems. You will ask yourself, "Where have you been?"

Of course, it has been there all the time. A better question would be, "Where have I been?" The answer of course is, "Enmeshed in my overactive mind."

When individuals first drop into this experience while practicing they are surprised that bells and whistles do not go off. Suddenly the mind is still. Mental movements are still appearing, but you are no longer disturbed by them. "Why do I have to exert so much effort when it is right there," is the question I most often hear. The answer I give is the answer I have given throughout this book. "The problem isn't with your natural self; it is with the learned mental habits that led to your dense overactive mind. If you deal with your runaway mind, your natural self will simply shine through."

There are further distinctions that distinguish the second level of practice from the third level. Over time we will discover that our natural innermost state of awareness is steadfast, reliable, indestructible, and whole. It is immune to and cannot be tainted or destroyed by outer adversities, including aging, disease, and death. These characteristics are specific to our natural presence. These are the qualities of human flourishing that are inseparable from our essential self, like fire is from heat. We will review these qualities in more detail in Chapters 14-19.

It is now time for us to discuss how we can access and experience our innermost self.

Recognizing Your Innermost Self

To recognize your innermost self there is nothing you have to do. You just have to let go and let be. Then it is there in all its purity, nakedness, wisdom, and simplicity.

However, there are steps you can take that will facilitate and quicken the process of touching into your essential self. If you prepare yourself by cultivating the proper conditions you will markedly increase the possibility of "falling" into your true nature.

The first and major preparation is studying and reflecting upon the information in this book, over and over. The second is persistent disciplined practice both in sitting sessions and in daily life.

Without taming the mind, opening the heart, cultivating a conducive lifestyle, and clearing a space in the mind we do not stand much chance of gaining access to our innermost home. That is why I have emphasized the importance of the information and practices in this book. They are the foundation and basis for recognizing our supreme identity. Without practice we are merely engaged in an intellectual exercise that will never bear the full fruit of human flourishing.

It is important to repeat here that it is essential that you have a stable practice for at least six months to a year before you can begin the transition to the third level of practice. Be patient. Allow yourself the necessary practice time that is required to gain skill in taming your mind and resting in stillness. Create this strong and stable foundation. It will serve you well in attaining this final level of development.

The gradual approach that we will use builds directly upon the second aspect of practice, resting in stillness. That is the best place to start. The instructions that follow will assist you in shifting from stillness to the experience of your innermost home.

The Gradual Shift

We begin with our usual practice, taming the mind and resting in stillness. Then, we gradually shift into the third level of practice, open awareness. If you attempt this before gaining some level of mental stability you will likely be frustrated in your efforts. Here are the instructions.

- Begin this practice with your usual method of mindful breathing. If there is a natural movement towards stillness then rest in stillness whenever possible for as long as possible. However, do not turn it into a strained effort.

- When you have reached a stable level of stillness you can move to the next stage of this practice. However, this will not occur in each practice session. If you are experiencing a session in which your mind is persistently active, just continue your session practicing mindful breathing.

- Progressively refine your level of stillness. When you have reached an easeful and effortless stillness, there is a small tweak that will allow you to shift into the third phase of meditation. Merely let go of any remaining effort and practice, and *allow* yourself to just "be."

- The ancient master Tilopa, who lived around 1000 A.D., gave us the instructions below. They can serve as your instructions.

> To realize this inexpressible truth,
> Do not manipulate mind or body
> But simply open into transparency
> With relaxed, natural grace—
> Intellect at ease in silence,
> Limbs at rest in stillness
> Like hollow bamboos.
> Neither breathing in nor breathing out
> With the breath of habitual thinking,
> Allow the mind to experience peace
> In brilliant wakefulness.

- Let us look at these words one at a time. The first two lines tell us to let go of all mental effort or activity. Then, you will realize the "inexpressible truth" which is your essential nature and supreme identity. It is who you are. The third and fourth lines tell us to be simple in our efforts. Relax with the grace of authenticity and simplicity. We are then instructed again to relax everything into its natural harmonious state of ease, letting go of all intellectual activity, mental habits, and perspectives and allowing the spontaneous appearance of the glorious and expansive moment of being which is wakeful and vivid.

- Tilopa's words should be used as your instructions. Repeat them before practice and remember them during the day. These instructions given by a master are quite subtle, very special, and have many levels of meaning.

- When your mind is ready, let go of the idea of practice and the idea of you as a practitioner. There is nothing to do and no place to be. There is no practice, no practitioner, and no "I." Awareness is the "experiencer" of life rather than your mental "I." Just let go and be present. This is extremely simple. You do not have to do anything but relax into a completely wakeful and natural state of ease.

- *Recognize* the nature of the essence of mind and self as open, serene, and whole. The word "recognize" is important here. We must directly experience the essence of our mind in order to know it.

- When we relax into our natural state of being all mental movements will appear as naked or unadorned. Our mind does not elaborate or act on anything. A sensory impression is a mere sensory impression. A thought or feeling is a mere thought or feeling. All mental movements are free to come and go as they naturally will. Like a bird in flight they leaves no trace. It is so simple and ordinary. Just relax and experience.

- It is unlikely that this state will last for more than a few brief moments, as your ordinary mind will jump in with its usual habits and try to label and think about it. Perhaps it will say, "I've got it." "I recognize the nature of my innermost self." I am sorry to say that once this occurs your mental activity has resumed and you have lost this momentary experience.

- However, the important thing is that you have recognized this innermost home, if even for a brief moment. For that moment the veils have lifted and you have seen it. Remember, the key is to relax into it rather than label or think about it. That is the key to sustaining it as long as possible.

- When you lose this moment be grateful for this glimpse. Do not seek it again. Return to resting in stillness. If your mind becomes too active you should then return to mindful breathing. With this gradual approach we drop into open awareness when the mind is resting in increasingly subtle levels of stillness. Otherwise we stay with our basic practice.

That is the approach to recognizing and experiencing moments of this third level of practice. The main strategy is to take advantage of increasingly more subtle and refined levels of stillness which gives way to a simple, pure, and unaltered presence and awareness. It is a small but important tweak to your existing practice. Try it whenever the conditions are correct. However, be patient. It will unfold over time.

You may have realized by now that relaxing into your natural self is simply living life as it actually is moment-to-moment. That is why we call it a non-practice. Presence and being is natural whether we are in a sitting session, talking to another person, or working on a project. Life goes on in its daily complexities but we experience it all from an easeful, open, presence and being.

Of course this will be quite new at first. However, brief moments of recognition will progressively coalesce into more sustained moments. We have strayed away from home a long time ago and have become quite accustomed and foolishly enchanted with the familiar complex world we live in. But that is not how it needs to be. That is not who we are. Consider the words of the wise teacher Shabkar:

> Not knowing that this state is within oneself,
> How amazing that one searches for it elsewhere!
> Although it is clearly manifest, like the radiant disc of the
>   sun,
> How amazing that so few people see it!

How amazing that without being fabricated,
This mind, which is unborn and primordially pure,
Is spontaneously present from the beginning!
This self-awareness is naturally free from the very first,
How amazing that it is liberated by just resting –
At ease in whatever happens!

The Lightness of Being

When the mind is unburdened of its ceaseless mental activity there is a lightness of being that pervades body, mind, and spirit. You have all touched this for brief moments in ways we have already discussed. But these are only brief moments with a definable beginning and end. But imagine what it would be like if these moments were to become your life.

These moments of presence and being are your life. It is just that your mind has foolishly mistaken your mental experience for life itself. Remove this heavy knapsack of mistaken perspectives, fixed mental attitudes, fabricated identities, and emotional afflictions and you will discover that an incredible lightness of being will naturally reveal itself. You can forget it once again, but you can never lose it. And this lightness of being is your permanent and unchanging nature that is filled with the qualities of human flourishing. It is the fruition of study, reflection, and practice. It is who you are and have always been. Now you know it. Grace.

chapter 13

The Essential Points

We have now completed our journey through the basic elements of the path which takes us from a runaway mind to human flourishing. If we correctly follow the steps, we will invariably arrive at our destination.

However, a book is merely the written word. To be of maximum value, the knowledge and practices covered in the preceding chapters must become part of your life, not an add-on—but part of your life. You must bring them to life each day through study, reflection, and practice. The goal is to reshape your life so that your practice becomes your life and your life becomes your practice.

It is very difficult to pursue inner development in a culture that neither values nor supports it. So we need support from others. That comes in the form of supportive friends and skilled teachers. Fortunately, these are now far easier to find in the West than only a few decades ago.

There are many that teach but few who know the depths involved. So this can be a bit difficult. My suggestion is that you look carefully at the teacher. Does she or he come from a strong and time-tested tradition? Does he live his values? Does she exude peace, joy, and an open heart? Is he or she humble and kind? Do you know his teachers? How have his students progressed? You must explore this and more. Take your time.

And always remember: the most important teacher is within you. The more you clear your mind and gain access to your authentic self the more you will know and trust your inner teacher. However, allow me to warn you to be cautious at first, as deeply embedded beliefs can often be disguised as intuitive insights. Then it is once again the past in new clothes. With time you will come to know the truth found in the wisdom-filled state of natural awareness and being, and then, with certainty, you will be able to distinguish truth from camouflaged mental perspectives.

Let us now take a final look at the essential elements of the path which we have discussed in detail in the preceding chapters. I hope you will find a certain beauty and elegance, as do I, in the simple, precise, and profound knowledge distilled from years of study by our wise elders.

- We have learned about the preciousness of human life. Our capacities and potential are unlike any other species. By understanding our unique nature we are motivated to seek the highest within us. Through study, reflection, and practice we can progressively reveal our authentic self and the magnificent qualities of human flourishing. We can arrive at the truth of life and live in peace and happiness.

- We are accustomed to living yesterday today. Most often, our day-to-day life is predetermined by past experience. But we can change that. We can choose to shape our future from the present rather than from the past. How do we do this? We decide what we want in the future and begin to act that way in the present. Fortunately, wise men and women throughout time have shown us how to live in the present in a way that shapes a larger tomorrow.

- The path to human flourishing begins with an inward turn to explore the last unexplored frontier—our mind. Through an understanding of mind and heart we gain control over our destiny.

- Study and reflection provide us with an intellectual understanding. Sitting practice allows us to directly observe our mind and gain a direct experience of what we have learned through reading and study. It is like studying biology in a text and then looking at the actual specimen under a microscope, and seeing it for yourself.

- Through practices such as mindfulness, open listening, and loving-kindness we integrate what we learn into day-to-day life. These daily practices allow us to use all of the activities of life as potential sources of practice. In this way we dramatically increase the time we have for practice.

- The first step is creating a clearing in our overactive mind. Unless we can open a clearing in the dense thicket of thoughts, feelings, and mental images, there is little we can do. We create an oasis of clarity and stillness through practice. From this clearing we can observe the mind and see what is actually happening.

- We must be patient with practice. It takes time to stabilize a mental clearing. It takes time to reverse the faulty habits of our mind. But the process will begin as soon as you start practice. You will definitely progress from there. At first this will require commitment and discipline. Even if your sessions are more distracted than you might wish, be sure to practice

- We are seeking to undo the sequence of events that begins when the mind mistakenly strays from its natural home and attaches to and elaborates random thoughts and feelings. The natural life cycle of a thought, feeling or image *left alone* is actually quite brief. They are neuro-electrical discharges that appear and dissipate in the mind in less than 200 milliseconds. So we learn to let them go. We stop identifying with them. We are not our mental movements.

- A fish dropped in a cesspool cannot survive. The same applies to study and practice. We have learned to guard our body. We must learn to guard and protect our mind as well. So we look at how and where we spend our time. We cultivate those attitudes and actions which support inner development and abandon those that are obstacles.

- We are now ready to address the most difficult aspect of the human condition, suffering. There are three basic forms of suffering. The first is overt suffering. That is the immediate experience of suffering. In this instance we do not know much about the nature of our suffering, and as a result there is little we can do beyond applying temporary remedies.

- The second aspect of suffering is subtler and less apparent. It can be traced to afflictive and disturbing thoughts and emotions that arise when we chase after temporary pleasures which invariably degrade into attachment, loss, and mental unrest. Reaching outside for temporary pleasures cannot substitute for what is authentically and permanently available only within.

- When we look beneath afflictive thoughts and emotions we discover the root cause of all distress. The central problem is that our mind has inadvertently strayed from its natural home. We have become lost in the abyss of mental imagination. We live in mind rather than in life.

- The remedy for suffering is to understand and eliminate its causes. To accomplish this we use the seven approaches previously discussed to alleviate afflictive thoughts and emotions. Simultaneously, we continue to stabilize our sitting practice which takes us closer to our authentic self. If we apply these remedies—clearing the mind, gaining insight, reducing and eliminating afflictive emotions, and settling into our authentic self—we will experience the progressive end to suffering. That is guaranteed.

- We use all of our daily life as opportunities for practice, in order to accelerate our inner development and integrate what we have learned into our lives. This is particularly true in regards to our day-to-day relationships, our work experience, and even adversity.

- Finally, we move toward the final level of practice which is really a "non-practice." When our mind has become sufficiently still we let go of all techniques and methods and simply rest in an easeful and effortless openness and awareness. We experience and enjoy life in all of its "suchness" and perfection exactly the way it is, moment-to-moment. When we stabilize this experience there is no further need for learning and no further need for practice. We live life in its truth, goodness, and beauty.

- Could it be that simple? The answer is yes. That is its elegance and beauty. If we use our intelligence to examine our lives we will find that the answers to distress and suffering are actually quite obvious. And with a bit of effort each day we can move beyond these lifelong problems and find that "something more" we have been searching for.

We are now at the end of the practice chapters. This "manual for human flourishing" can serve as a lifetime guide. Any one of these chapters can be a course of study in itself. They can be returned to again and again. I have previously encouraged you to first read through these chapters and then complete your reading of the book before you return to "work" the program. If that is what you have chosen to do, we will now share the delight of exploring the qualities of human flourishing that are the invariable result of this journey.

Part III

The Fruition

Our *vision* establishes our goal, human flourishing. The *path* takes us there. The *fruition* is the result.

Human flourishing is characterized by specific qualities. These include: a natural serenity and ease, a profound and penetrating wisdom, enduring happiness, genuine compassion and love, boundless freedom, and the perfection of health—body, mind, and spirit.

At first, we will touch these treasures in small ways. We notice that our mind is calmer and less reactive. Our relationships become more heart-felt and enriching. Work seems more meaningful and joyful. Progressively, we gain insight into our own lives, and the universal human condition. In this way we slowly but decisively experience the unfolding of our full humanity. That is the future we intentionally create through day-to-day study, reflection, and practice.

During my studies in the East my teachers suggested that I resist the temptation to focus on the "mountaintops." They insisted that I "work" in the valleys. Their advice was good, and consistent with tradition. Why? Because *if we apply ourselves to the step-by-step process we have discussed in this book, the results of our efforts will unfold by themselves.* That is why it is unusual to hear teachings that focus on the final results.

However, I believe that it is important to have an intellectual understanding of the entire process from beginning to
end. That is why I am including the section on *fruition* in
this book. It is to provide you with the full scope of human
flourishing, even though we may not realize all of it at once,
or perhaps even in our lifetime.

Let us now look more closely at the development and flowering of each of these uniquely human possibilities.

chapter 14

Serenity

The unique qualities of human flourishing unfold sequentially like the petals of a flower. They are the result and ultimate reward of a well-lived life. The emergence of these qualities is like the spontaneous scent of perfume emanating from a mature flower. Once a seed is planted and cultivated and the greenery and flower unfold, the aroma of perfume is spontaneously and naturally present. It is the same for the qualities of human flourishing. We do not have to concern ourselves with the fruits of our efforts. If we properly cultivate the field of our life these sweet fruits will arise naturally and effortlessly.

The Unfolding Qualities of Human Flourishing

The first quality that we experience is an *all-encompassing serenity*—the calm easeful mind. Free of ceaseless mind chatter and mental afflictions, we effortlessly rest in our natural state of being and presence which is spacious and serene. All is well. All things are well. We are well. What was once, at the beginning of practice, a small clearing in a dense forest is now our life, moment-to-moment and day-to-day. The basis of a serene mind is overcoming, through study, reflection, and practice, the power of the overactive afflictive mind.

The second quality to unfold is *insight and wisdom*. This deeper "knowing" arises from the clear and still mind. This is not an intellectual knowledge. It does not rely on thought. It is not an accumulation of past information. It is fresh. It is new. It is unconditioned by prior experience. It is a precise and accurate intuitive knowing of the truth of life and living. It is a direct and clear experience of life as it is. The basis of this profound wisdom is the clear and serene mind.

The third quality to unfold is enduring *happiness*. A serene mind is the basis for a penetrating and precise wisdom. That wisdom provides a full and complete understanding of the causes of all forms of suffering, allowing them to come to a progressive end. As suffering progressively dissipates, we discover an ever-present, boundless, and permanent reservoir of happiness that is immune to all of life's adversities. The basis of this inner-generated and enduring happiness is a wisdom that knows the true nature of life and living.

The fourth quality to unfold is a natural self-arising *compassion*. The basis of compassion is wisdom and happiness. Wisdom reveals with decisiveness that suffering can come to an end. We witness and realize this in our personal life and simultaneously realize the full tragedy of the unnecessary suffering of others. Our own authentic happiness informs us what is possible for everyone. Wisdom and happiness touch our heart and move us to action. We wish for others what we have accomplished in our own life. We have pulled our hand out of the fire and wish to help others do the same. That realization and heartfelt desire gives rise to a spontaneously arising compassion accompanied by an expansive non-referential love. Boundless compassion and authentic love go hand in hand.

The fifth quality to arise is *freedom*. All the preceding qualities serve as its basis. What are we free from? We are free from suffering, fabricated intellectual beliefs, habitual patterns of behavior, mental afflictions, the overactive mind, and the pull of outer pleasures. What remains is who we are and what we have always been. We are finally free to just *be*. That is a vast freedom.

The sixth and final quality to unfold is the *perfection of health*—body, mind, and spirit. Its basis is an awakened, wise, loving, and well-lived life. We are no longer bound by conventional views of health, which equate health to the presence or absence of physical disease. The perfection of health is the experience of optimal well-being. It is complete, whole, and permanent. It is sustained throughout all of life's adversities including disease, aging, and death. Authentic living and optimal well-being come in a single inseparable package. When we live in our essential self we *simultaneously* achieve the perfection of health.

The amazing discovery is that our natural state of being, with all of its remarkable qualities, is so incredibly simple, ordinary, and easeful. That is why this level of achievement is called the "ordinary" mind in the East, a term that we usually reserve for our overactive and disturbed mind. In truth it is the latter that is complex and difficult, our authentic self is rather simple, easy, and ordinary.

It is rather extraordinary to experience our authentic self, to flourish and prosper into the truth of what we have always been. The first thought that arises is, "Where have you been all these years?" This is followed by, "Why haven't I seen you, as you have been there all of the time, right there in front of me?" One does not know whether to cry with joy, feel sad at the tragedy of years wasted in suffering, struggling, and searching, or laugh at the folly of the human condition. In any case there is not much to say. That is the dual mask of tragedy and comedy.

Recovering Serenity

Although the qualities of human flourishing reveal themselves sequentially, that is not quite how it actually happens. Life is not so orderly. Although they seem to appear sequentially, with each quality dependent on the preceding one, they actually overlap as they unfold. In a sense each quality contains all of the others. For example, serenity contains wisdom and compassion. Compassion is wise, calm, joyful, and loving. So, as we progressively achieve one we simultaneously attain aspects of each of the others. Even though they reveal themselves together, for ease and convenience we will look at them one at a time, beginning with serenity.

I could have as easily titled this chapter on serenity "recovering sanity." Although we call it normal, our usual state of mind is wild and out of control. But you know that by now, as we have fully discussed this dilemma in preceding chapters. And you certainly know it from your personal experience. So recovering inner serenity is akin to recovering sanity. There is not much we can change in our life without this first essential step.

Relaxing the Mind

The coarsest form of serenity is relaxation. Our culture offers many opportunities for relaxation. These include: mini-vacations, spa treatments, massages, sexuality, athletic activities, entertainment of all sorts, yoga, and many other relaxing activities. On the less healthy side are alcohol, illicit drugs, prescription medications, out-of-control consumerism, and a range of trivial activities which numb life. None of these "remedies" for the overactive mind have long-term value. They only temporarily relax and rest the mind. They only work when we use them.

That is why we consider relaxation techniques to be a very *coarse* approach. Relaxation does not help us overcome deeply ingrained habitual tendencies or mental confusion which are the source of the problem. As a result, relaxation techniques do not lead to inner peace or serenity. In fact, they actually delude us into a false sense of mental calm that keeps us from the actual effort of inner development. For the moment we feel better. However, the underlying problem remains untouched, and human flourishing remains a distant possibility, if that.

So we need to be thoughtful and careful when we invest in relaxation techniques. First, we must assure ourselves that they are neither harmful nor addictive, like drugs and alcohol. Second, we must also be certain that our effort to temporarily relax mind and body does not distract us from pursuing inner development. If we take relaxation techniques as a taste of what is possible we can move beyond them to pursue approaches which are both effective and long lasting. Seen from this perspective relaxation techniques are not ends in themselves. It is best that we consider them temporary first aid.

Inner Peace

Inner peace results from an alleviation of emotional afflictions and overcoming the overactive mind. Through inner development we can move beyond a dependency on relaxation techniques towards a more stable and peaceful inner life. This requires that we want sustained *inner peace* rather than momentary relaxation.

Perhaps you can now better understand why we addressed afflictive thoughts and emotions in the preceding chapters. Addressing them directly and decisively is an essential step in stabilizing a peaceful mind.

This progressive return to a naturally-settled, calm, and peaceful mind, achieved through understanding and practice, is not temporary. It is not an outer fix. It is an inner change. At first, perhaps for a year or more, there will be back and forths. But as we progress, inner peace will become a more constant quality in our life and our need for relaxation techniques will diminish and end.

All-Encompassing Serenity

In its full and complete form, all-encompassing serenity is a transcendent quality. What does it transcend? It fully embraces yet simultaneously goes beyond all previous and lesser levels of development. It embraces the relaxation arrived at through relaxation techniques as well as the inner peace and calm that result from inner development. Its all-encompassing and permanent nature transcends these prior accomplishments. It does not require any doing. It is a state of being.

To fully grasp all-encompassing serenity we must know it from experience, as it is difficult to place into words. It reveals itself when the mind has permanently abandoned its fascination and attachment to an overactive mental life. When we are able to let go and settle into our natural state of being, it is right there waiting for us, as it has always been.

Yes, we can catch glimpses of this "peace that surpasses understanding." As mentioned previously, we can catch it in a moment of communion with nature, at the peak of athletic activity, at the climax of sexual union, during the stillness of sitting practice, and in other instances as well. But these are just facsimiles of the real thing. They are temporary, fleeting, and dependent on causes and circumstances. The authentic and long-lasting experience of all-encompassing serenity can only be gained through progress on the path. Its basis is inner development.

The Characteristics of All-Encompassing Serenity

Let us now look at the characteristics of all-encompassing serenity. We will soon see that its characteristics are similar to the characteristics of each of the other qualities of human flourishing. Each of these qualities is a different aspect of the same gem.

Permanent and Indestructible

All-encompassing serenity is *permanent and indestructible*. What do I mean by this? The mental state of relaxation is achieved through the use of techniques. It is dependent on these techniques. When we cease the technique, relaxation dissipates. Inner peace and calm is dependent on alleviating mental misunderstandings and afflictions. These efforts are far more durable than relaxation techniques and will progressively stabilize your mind. However, it is only when we take the final leap into a naturally-settled state of being, the third level of practice, that we experience an effortless, stable, and irreversible serenity.

Our usual life experiences are dependent on a variety of causes, circumstances, and conditions. They are thus dependent and reliant on the stability of these factors. That is why our body, a car, and rainbows are impermanent. But this does not apply to the qualities of human flourishing which spontaneously arise when we experience our authentic self. These qualities are independent of any other factors, because all-encompassing serenity does not rely on anything else for its existence, it is permanent, indestructible, steadfast, and reliable.

Individuals often get small glimpses of this possibility early in practice. Participants in our program express this in the following way, "Something happened today that I would normally react to but instead, I remained calm. I don't know why. I was aware of the circumstance but irrespective of it I was calm inside, and it made quite a difference." That is a glimpse of how it is possible to maintain a steadfast and reliable serenity in the presence of adversity. With practice this capacity grows and flowers.

Until we have fully and stably settled into our natural state difficult circumstances can continue to give rise to fear, anxiety, and other mental afflictions. But when we have fully attained an all-encompassing serenity it does not move or change, regardless of life's ebb and flow. We are certainly aware of the difficulties and challenges of life, but our inner experience remains one of complete serenity. We are able to work with complexity on the outside while at all times remaining calm, peaceful, and serene on the inside.

Pervasive

All-encompassing serenity is *pervasive*. There is nothing untouched by it.

Consider the ordinary mind. When we are agitated, anxious, and restless, these mental disturbances touch everything and everybody in sight. We communicate mental agitation through our presence, speech, and actions. So our disturbed mental state affects others as well as ourselves. It is contagious.

When we experience a stable serenity, our presence, speech, and actions similarly emanate to everyone and everything we touch. Have you ever had the experience of being in the presence of a calm and serene person? How did that affect you? When you are settled in your natural home of all-encompassing serenity your calm inner life will have a settling effect on all that it touches.

Spontaneously Arising

All-encompassing serenity *spontaneously arises*. As with all of the qualities of human flourishing it is inseparable from our inner home. Once we rest and relax into our essential nature, serenity will naturally be there as well. All-encompassing serenity is self-arising and self-existent.

What do I mean by the terms "spontaneously arising, self-arising, and self-existing"? When we are stabilized in our natural self we will notice the sudden appearance of serenity. We cannot identify where it came from. All we can observe is that it spontaneously appears.

We cannot make or create all-encompassing serenity. It is revealed to us when the obscuring clouds of mental misunderstandings and mental afflictions dissipate. All we can do is engage in study, reflection, and practice that will undermine and alleviate the overactive mind. Then it will naturally and spontaneously appear, where it already is and has always been.

Free of Contaminants

All-encompassing serenity is *free of all contaminants*. What do I mean by that? The mental states of relaxation, and to a far lesser extent inner peace, are always contaminated by underlying and subtle mental misunderstandings and afflictions. In the case of relaxation they merely go underground for a short period of time. In the case of inner peace these obscurations are significantly diminished, but not fully eliminated. Until we experience our natural state of being, afflictive *propensities* remain. However, when we have achieved all-encompassing serenity these residual mental contaminants are permanently gone.

That is what we mean when we say that all-encompassing serenity is free of contaminants. We have finally abandoned the habitual tendency of the mind to attach, elaborate, and fix mental movements. We have abandoned our mistaken investment in outer pleasures, and with it the source of mental afflictions. All of these root causes of a disturbed mind are gone. What is left is our essential self. It is free of all contaminants and pollutants. It is pure and authentic.

All-encompassing serenity cannot be seen, as it is not visible. It cannot be touched, as it is not material. It cannot be studied, as it is an experience rather than an object of knowledge. It cannot be created, as it is already there. It is free of thought as it is not mental. It is pure and uncontaminated, as all contaminants have been abandoned. It is free from and resistant to all adversity, as it is steadfast, reliable, and indestructible. As a result it is virtuous and good. It is who we are.

chapter 15

Full-Knowing Wisdom

H uman life is the pinnacle of evolutionary development. We alone are blessed with the biology and brain development which is the basis for a highly-developed intellect. It is this capacity which offers us the opportunity to bring stress, distress, and suffering to an end, and to flourish into our full potential.

There is a range of knowledge available to each of us starting with the mere assimilation of information, progressing to a more comprehensive knowledge gained through intellectual analysis and reflection, and finally maturing into a profound and far-reaching wisdom that realizes the ultimate nature of existence. This final leap is not merely meant for great sages. It is available to each of us as well. However, its attainment is not possible in an unexamined life. Full-knowing wisdom only arises from an investment in inner development. It is the sign of an extraordinary life, a well-lived life, a noble life.

In its most complete and perfected form it provides us with a penetrating, precise, and full understanding of our lives. Its grasp of reality releases us from the mental misunderstandings and afflictions of ordinary life. Courageous men and women across time and diverse cultures have undertaken the journey from confusion to transcendent wisdom, from the surface to the depths. We can do this as well.

Although there is no guarantee that we will mature towards great wisdom, we do have a choice. The capacity for wisdom is encoded into every human life. It is present in its unripe state even in an infant. If you rub charcoal you will never find gold. If you chip away ore from gold ore you will find gold. That is how it is with the qualities of human flourishing. If they were not there to begin with we could not create them. That is why a full-knowing wisdom is possible for each of us.

Informational Knowledge

Informational knowledge results from the simple transmission of basic facts regarding a person, object, or experience through speech, writing, or other means of communication. This may be as simple as reading an instruction manual or attending a course on software programming. Informational knowledge is about how we do this or that. It is largely factual and practical. There is no insight or understanding involved, and only a superficial level of reflection.

Informational knowledge helps us live life. In fact, throughout our lifetimes we accumulate a great deal of information which enables us to successfully navigate the outer world. We can even achieve worldly success. Yet such knowledge offers no guarantee that we will attain the wisdom which characterizes human flourishing. It does not guarantee or offer us an in-depth understanding of our life, satisfying intimacy, or the capacity to skillfully and peacefully move through life's adversities. That requires greater understanding and knowledge.

Intellectual Knowledge

Intellectual or analytical knowledge penetrates deeper than mere information. It is acquired from the analysis of an object. A good example of this is medical science. Our understanding of the human body results from the development of theories and the analysis of anatomical and physiological processes. Intellectual knowledge draws upon valuable capacities of the cognitive mind—attention, abstract thinking, analysis, and reasoning.

Our intellect teaches us about the material world. It expands our understanding and capacities, providing us with a richer and more meaningful life. Although mastery of our intellectual capacities is an important foundation for higher understanding, it again is no guarantee of serenity, happiness, or wisdom. For that we must go beyond our intellect.

The individual who attains the peak of intellectual understanding is called a sage. Such an individual lives a profound life and is a gift to humankind. The individual who goes beyond intellect to discern the very nature of self and life is called a spiritual being. This individual achieves human flourishing for himself, and simultaneously brings goodness to the world through selfless service.

Full-Knowing Wisdom

So how do we arrive at full-knowing wisdom, the comprehensive, precise and complete wisdom of a spiritual being? Unlike informational and intellectual knowledge, full-knowing wisdom is non-cognitive. It transcends the thought process. It can only be attained through direct experience. When you go to a grocery store and ask about the taste of a mango it will be described to you by the grocer—informational knowledge. If you are a biologist you will understand the biological characteristics which give rise to this taste—intellectual analytic knowledge. However, if you taste the mango you will actually know its taste *directly*, from the actual *experience* of tasting it. Full-knowing wisdom includes informational and intellectual knowledge, but simultaneously goes beyond to offer a final, complete, and whole understanding that is achieved only through direct experience.

As we settle into our authentic self, we progressively experience five key insights or wisdoms. Although they appear to unfold sequentially, they actually arise as one. But it is easier to describe them individually. Before we begin let me add one note of caution. I am including this material here to offer you a panoramic view of the full scope of knowledge that is possible for each of us. But be very patient. Take what you can and move past what is meant for another time.

Let us start with the first, "the wisdom which knows our authentic self."

The Wisdom Which Knows our Authentic Self

Each of the five insights and wisdoms arise from the *direct experience* of our authentic self. That is why practice is so essential. The wisdom that knows our true self can distinguish our usual mental identity, our ego, from our deeper, natural ,and indestructible essence. It knows who we are at the core of our being. This critical wisdom is lacking in ordinary life, which is mired in confusion.

When you recognize your authentic self through practice, you *know* your true essence. That knowing or wisdom does not confuse your true being with your outer identity. It knows the difference. This requires a stable experience of your inner home, a glimpse will not do. That is why we practice to gain familiarity with our authentic self. Until stability is gained, glimpses of recognition will be quickly covered over by the overactive mind, and knowledge of your natural self will be covered over as well. We then forget who we are, and all of our rich qualities.

When we know the essence of our life we know the essence of all life. That knowing is the basis for living in truth—the truth of our self, the truth of others, and the truth of existence. When we live truth we have satisfied life's yearning to know itself and simultaneously achieved a natural harmony of body, mind, and spirit. We rest in that truth of being. That is the wisdom of knowing the truth of who you are.

The Wisdom of Naked Awareness

But to effortlessly rest in the truth of our being, we must better understand the mind so that we can overcome its tendency to pull us back to a mental world. As long as we have a mind and sense organs, thoughts, emotions, mental images, and sense impressions will continue to appear in awareness. Unless we know the true nature of these mental movements they will invariably pull us away from our authentic self.

Mental activity is the natural energetic play and display of awareness. The natural play and display of the mind are simple *unelaborated* mental movements. They are experienced "nakedly" without the addition of preference, grasping, attachment, or the illusion of permanence, and solidity. They are experienced just as they are, as ever-changing bare mental movements that are unconditioned by past experience stored in memory. That is why we call this "naked awareness." *The wisdom of naked awareness knows mental activity as it actually is before it is contorted and confused by mental stories.*

Let us use the metaphor of a mirror and the reflections which come and go on its surface. The reflections can be likened to the rising and falling of mental activity which appears in our mind. The reflections on a mirror's surface are transient. They come and go unchanged by the mirror. The mirror is merely a passive reflective surface on which reflections appear. Similarly, mental appearances arising in awareness are unchanged by awareness. Awareness is merely a passive expanse, an open space which allows for the continuous flow of mental activity.

An easy way to notice that is to observe your mind when you first awaken in morning. Open your eyes and quickly look around before your mind begins to label and elaborate your experience. For a brief moment you will experience things just as they are. You will experience objects without labels or any other superimposed meaning or distinctions. What you experience will be naked awareness. You will experience *what is as is*. As you continue to observe your mind, you will notice that within seconds it begins to elaborate these naturally naked mental appearances. A mental appearance which in actuality is no more than a bare mental movement then becomes a complex thought, feeling, or image with its own name and assigned characteristics.

The metaphor of the mirror and its reflections gives us a sense of the simple, naked, and continuous flow of the mind's magical play and display. When we experience what is as is without elaboration, that recognition is what we call the wisdom of naked awareness. When we fail to realize this and get caught up in its elaboration that is called confusion.

To realize the actual nature of mental activity is extremely important as it undermines our tendency to get stuck in made-up stories that run our lives, leading to confusion and suffering. This recognition brings us in alignment with experiences as they actually are, the truth of what is. We experience the moment precisely how it is without any mental add-ons. That is true reality. That is the insight of "naked awareness."

The Wisdom of One Taste

From the perspective of the mirror, what appears on its surface is an image. Whether it is an apple or an orange, for the mirror it is all the same. It is simply a reflected image. From the perspective of pure and simple awareness what appears in its expanse—thoughts feelings, images, and sensory impressions—are all mental movements, neurological blips. From the perspective of awareness, all images have the same essence. They all have one identical "taste"—they are the energetic play and display of awareness itself.

The insight or wisdom of one taste is a critical realization of the ultimate sameness and oneness of all experience. This does not deny that appearances have distinctive characteristics and functions in our conventional day-to-day life—a car is different than a tree, good is different than evil. However, from the perspective of a passive and open awareness all appearances are similar energetic displays—identical, insubstantial transient mental movements, which come and go leaving no trace. Although varying appearances will appear and function differently in daily life, their essence is the same.

To the extent that we can see that everything shares the same essential characteristics—a lack of permanence, unique identity, or substantiality—our mental afflictions will diminish in intensity. We go on with life as it is, but soften our tendency to attach to one thing or another, as in the end they are all "mere" mental movements. The understanding of the similar nature of mental activity is called the wisdom of one taste.

Discerning Wisdom

Discerning wisdom simultaneously comprehends the nature of our authentic self, the play and display of the mind, and the process of elaboration and conditioning. Discerning wisdom knows precisely how mind and life work. It knows all levels of reality. Because it can see all of reality, it does not get stuck at one level and forget the other. *Discerning wisdom frees us from the problem of losing our authentic self or losing our daily world.* We can have and live in both worlds. That is the gift of discerning wisdom.

All-Encompassing Wisdom

Awareness is the basic space of all experience. That is the realization of an all-encompassing wisdom. That is the deepest truth we can arrive at. We experience the appearance of an outer world of objects, mountains, rivers, and people. And they are all inseparable from our awareness. How could it be otherwise? We cannot put people and objects on one side of the room and our awareness of them on the other side. Try it. It simply cannot be done. Nothing is separate or distinct from our awareness.

It is important to note here that some may refer to this state of unity and wholeness as an all-encompassing awareness, as we have done here, while others may experience the unifying source as a creator. The point I am making here is the same in both instances. Life is a harmonious, seamless whole.

Let me summarize the five wisdoms which together constitute "full-knowing wisdom."

- The Wisdom Which Knows Our Authentic Self

- Naked Wisdom That Knows the Nature of Mental Activity

- The Wisdom of One Taste

- Discerning Wisdom That Knows and Can Distinguish All Levels of Reality

- All-Encompassing Wisdom That Knows the Oneness of Life

We progressively experience these five wisdoms as we stabilize an undistracted awareness. First we recognize our authentic self in the stillness of being. Then we observe and recognize the magical, insubstantial, and transient play and display of the mind. This leads to the realization that all mental movements are similar in their basic nature. We then recognize the distinction between the illusory day-to-day world that arises from these mental movements and our authentic home. Finally, we realize that it is all mind. It is all awareness. It is all one. If you have an intellectual sense of these five wisdom truths you can, in time, watch them unfold during practice.

No other living creature has access to these five wisdoms which enable us to understand the invisible nature and truth of life. It is only possible in human life, and only if we are willing to develop our inner life. Full knowing wisdom is the second quality of human flourishing.

chapter 16

Enduring Happiness

We can all agree on one fact: we each value and seek happiness. All humans share this universal aspiration. Achieving genuine and lasting happiness can be said to be a central goal of human life. There can be no argument here.

But if we so strongly desire happiness, why are our lives so often filled with dissatisfaction, distress, and suffering? Why does sustained happiness seem so elusive? Is life by its nature a cycle of pleasure and suffering with suffering winning in the end when we arrive at the unavoidable realities of aging, disease, and death? If distress and suffering is hardwired into human existence then there is little more to say, except to learn to bear it as gracefully as possible.

But let us take a radical view and suggest, as we have in this book, that happiness is innate to human life and that suffering is a reversible add-on, a contaminant which can be removed. If we assert this to be true, we must show how we can actually and finally attain our birthright of enduring happiness. Failure to do so would render this unconventional viewpoint untenable.

But we are fortunate here. For millennia very wise individuals, throughout time and across diverse cultures, have explored the issue of happiness. They have carefully examined their own experience and remarkably they have arrived upon the same universal conclusion: happiness is in our "genes" and dissatisfaction, distress and suffering can be largely eradicated. Even further, we are now confirming this assertion through the methods and tools of modern science. Neuroscience is demonstrating that inner development results in physiological and structural changes in the brain which are consistent with higher levels of happiness and well-being. It appears that happiness can be cultivated, revealed, and realized through inner development.

So where do we start the journey which takes us towards authentic happiness? We start by removing the major obstacles to happiness. We start by looking at a widely-held illusion, a powerful illusion which we have already discussed, one that keeps us from pursuing authentic and enduring happiness. It is a tenacious illusion that bears repeating many times. *It is the mistaken belief that pleasure and enduring happiness are the same.* We generally make no distinction between the two. Yet, until we decisively realize that pleasure and happiness are profoundly different we will neither be satisfied by pleasure nor achieve genuine happiness.

When we have finally seen the futility of investing in fragile and ultimately unsatisfying outer stimulus-driven pleasures, we turn toward inner development. We pursue it through inner development. Within weeks we begin to experience the early results—a decrease in reactivity, increased mental calm, and improved relationships—the foundation of a happier life. We are finally looking in the right direction—inside rather than outside.

What we find in our inner life is what we have been previously searching for in the wrong place—the gem of happiness which is our innate birthright. When we touch it, even for a moment, we immediately know how dramatically it differs from ordinary outer pleasures. Given our endless and exhausting efforts in the outer world we are amazed to discover how easy, effortless, simple, and ordinary it is.

To enable us to better understand this final stage of development let us trace the steps that lead us toward its full flowering.

Pleasure

First, we will once again take a look at what we call pleasure. Pleasure, which is mistaken for authentic happiness, is the experience of satisfaction which we attribute to an external stimulus. Simply stated, we find certain people, objects, and experiences to be satisfying and others unsatisfying. We orient our self towards what is pleasant and avoid what feels unpleasant. Pleasure is seen as residing in an outer person, object, or experience. It is seen as an unchanging quality of the outer experience.

When we seek pleasure in the external world—mistaking it for authentic happiness—we become like scavengers searching here and there to gather what we can from a seeming scarcity of such experiences. When we find islands of transitory pleasure we protect them against any threats, real or imagined. That is the Achilles heel of pleasure. It degenerates into a cycle of unrelenting desire, craving, attachment, and addiction. This is further complicated by possessiveness, protectiveness, jealousy, and anger. The seed of distress and dissatisfaction is already part of and inseparable from "pleasurable" experiences.

That does not mean that we must completely and forever turn away from the pleasures of day-to-day life. When we know with certainty that all outer things are impermanent and we have accessed our inner source of authentic happiness, we can actually enjoy outer pleasures without courting future suffering. Why? Because we already know they are impermanent, we can fully enjoy them when they are present and do not mourn their loss when they are gone.

That is how it is when we enjoy a rainbow, isn't it? We find great delight in its presence because we know it is impermanent and fragile, and we are not saddened when it disappears. We know its transient nature and that intensifies its beauty and joy. It is that way with all of life. With the knowledge of impermanence and the joy of an inner-generated happiness we can experience all of life's pleasures without suffering attachment or loss.

Once we have decisively realized the futility of relying on people, objects, or experiences as enduring sources of happiness, we are ready to turn our attention toward the attainment of the real thing. We turn toward inner development, the only guarantee that we will find what we are seeking.

Inner Peace and Delight

Wise men and women have pointed us toward the inward journey as the only true path to an enduring happiness.

We are told that the initial effort must be to tame our overactive mind. As we progress, we diminish afflictive emotions and increasingly experience the delight of a peaceful, calm mind. This is not like the intense highs and lows of pleasure. It is more like a steady contentment. It is sweet and delicious. You have to taste it to know it.

In contrast to stimulus-generated pleasure, which degenerates into dissatisfaction and suffering, inner joy and delight grows and expands with time. We feel in control. We feel in charge. We have established a "base camp" of trustworthy happiness within. Its basis is an increasingly stable inner life. No one can take it from us. That is a great relief and accomplishment.

We are now on our way toward what our wise ancestors have promised us—a profound, expansive, and enduring happiness, the great gem of life.

Enduring Happiness

As we address the full development of enduring happiness, it is essential to remember that this is a final accomplishment which may take many years. However, each step on the way, each moment of study and practice, progressively takes us in this direction. The fruits begin very early and grow over time. So be patient in regard to this final achievement. Focus on your day-to-day growth.

As a result of eliminating afflictive emotions and stabilizing an authentic inner presence we bring a final end to suffering. This parting of the clouds reveals what was already and always there, our natural easeful abiding nature, our authentic self.

Enduring happiness is wisdom-generated. It is truth-given in contrast to stimulus-driven. What is stimulus-driven is ephemeral and transitory. What is truth-given is permanent and irreversible, like a ripe fruit that cannot reverse itself and unripen. We now apprehend where we went wrong in our outer search. Pleasure rises and falls according to circumstances. Authentic happiness has no causes. It is not dependent on circumstances. It resides at the center of our being. You cannot create it. It is naturally present. It is indestructible. It is permanent, and steadfast.

Authentic and enduring happiness is unaffected by the intermittent adversities of life, including loss, disease, aging, and death.

Outer circumstances do not alter our basic state of happiness. At first, this may be quite difficult to grasp. However, consider the following. Does a cloud, however dark, alter the basic nature of the sun or does a wave, however menacing, alter the basic nature of the ocean? These are surface disturbances. They do not change the basic nature of the sun or the ocean. The same is true for us. Adversity does not change our natural state of happiness.

How do we experience this in daily life? Early in practice students will often notice that they respond differently to the usual difficulties with family or friends, problems at work, and so on. In the midst of these difficulties they maintain an inner calm that is new and unexpected. When individuals relate these experiences in class there is always a sense of awe on their face. "How could this be possible? How could something I've struggled and reacted to all of my life now be experienced with a state of calm?" I always point out that nothing changed outside. But things have begun to change within. They were peaceful and content inside, even though things were difficult and complex outside. This is a small but important taste of what I am speaking of here.

The capacity to remain serene and happy within while confronting challenges on the outside may be at first difficult to comprehend. However, with experience gained from practice you will better understand how this is possible. You will understand why authentic happiness, which arises from our natural inner state, is permanent, unchanging and steadfast, even in the face of adversity.

Inner-generated happiness is like the rays of the sun which embrace and nurture all that it touches. We become like farmers cultivating an endless crop. There is so much that we have no place to store it. It seeps out of us. We give it away. It touches everything and everyone.

A profound and enduring happiness is the third quality of human flourishing. It is a direct result of inner development. It is an experience I want you to know and feel in your lifetime. That is as important to me as it is to you.

chapter 17
Natural Self-Arising Compassion

We have now arrived at a discussion of the fourth quality of human flourishing, self-arising compassion. Compassion is innate to our authentic self. It effortlessly arises on its own when we experience and live in this essential core of our being. Natural compassion and its companion, boundless love, are precious fruits of the journey home to our deepest self.

From Serenity to Happiness to Wisdom to Compassion

Once we rest in our natural state, we will experience and progressively stabilize inner serenity, the first quality of human flourishing. Full-encompassing wisdom, the second quality of human flourishing, arises in the still and clear mind. It comprehends the true nature of human existence. It understands and cuts through the root causes of suffering. That allows for an enduring inner-generated happiness, the third quality of human flourishing.

What occurs next is both quite simple and yet quite extraordinary at the same time. Full-encompassing wisdom realizes that the root sources of distress and suffering that poisoned our own life similarly disturbs others. We realize that most individuals live their lives unaware, as were we, of the causes of their distress. Unnecessary and pointless suffering touches our heart. As a result, concern and compassion spontaneously arise. We know that we want to, and more than that, we must do something about unnecessary human suffering. We feel compelled.

Accompanying this realization is a burst of energy. I have ended my outward search. I have achieved what I longed for. I have brought suffering to an end in my own life, and as a result discovered personal authenticity, goodness, and beauty. "What else is there to do with my life?" The only thing left is to use my life as an instrument for compassionate service to others, participating through my efforts in ending the scourge of suffering which envelops humankind, great poverty, and devastation. All of the energy once tied up in cherishing and protecting our false "I" is now available for compassionate service. All of the energy involved in stress, distress, and suffering can now be turned towards others.

In this way natural self-arising compassion is a result of the sequential process of inner development. In the Christian tradition beings endowed with all-encompassing and far-reaching compassion are called angels. In ancient Greece they were called philosopher-kings. In the Hindu tradition they are called holy men. In Buddhism they are called bodhisattvas.

There are many ways of serving to eliminate suffering. In some instances it is helping to provide the basic needs of life for others who are struggling. At other times it may be providing safety for those who live in fear or care and medications for those who are suffering illness. And there may be times when serving as a teacher of life through example and guidance may be the proper action. There is not one single way to assist with diminishing and ending suffering in the world. The approach must fit the need.

Let us now review and explore the stages of evolution that takes us toward natural self-arising compassion, the fourth quality of human flourishing.

Self-Cherishing

Self-cherishing is our usual way of living. Our primary concern is to protect and care for ourselves, even when our basic needs, and more, are fully met. We may deny this, but when we look very carefully at our behavior we discover that it is primarily motivated by self-interest. The tendency for self-cherishing and its excesses is buried deep in the human condition. It begins early in life.

There comes a time in life when whatever gains we accrued from placing ourselves first are overtaken by the isolation, afflictive emotions, and loss of intimacy and love that result from an exclusive focus on self. That insight forces a reevaluation of our relationship with others, and initiates a progressive movement from self-cherishing to otherness, which we discussed in chapter nine.

Let's recall the words of Shantideva:

> Whatever joy there is in this world
> All comes from desiring others to be happy.
> And whatever suffering there is in this world
> All comes from my desiring to be happy.

Altruism

Altruism is the practice of concern and care for the welfare of others. We recognize that an excessive and exclusive focus on self is not self-serving. It is actually self-betraying. It does not bring us enduring happiness. It brings us isolation and disconnection. We begin to concern ourselves with others. We do this first in sitting practice through the giving and taking exercise described in chapter nine. We then move this intention into daily life by extending kindness, listening, patience, and understanding, and when appropriate material assistance. Slowly we develop a new habit—giving to others in the same way in which we previously gave to our self.

A wise teacher once called this smart selfishness. We get what we want by giving to others. Of course this is not the highest motivation, but it is a beginning. Over time we experience an increasing sense of happiness in seeing the happiness of others. We rejoice in their happiness. What began as somewhat of an effort becomes increasingly effortless, and our giving becomes more natural and altruistic.

However, it is never completely selfless at this level of development. There remains a cherishing "I," albeit far more subtle. There is usually something we seek in return, even if it is as subtle as a sense of self-satisfaction related to giving. So altruistic giving is never completely selfless. It is important to remember that, lest we get too puffed up. However, this is a vast improvement over unabated self-cherishing. It will prepare us for the progressive development of the transcendent quality of natural self-arising compassion, which is the pinnacle of selfless giving.

It is important to add a word here about the distinction between compassion and empathy. The discomfort and suffering of another person can evoke a sympathetic and similar feeling in our self. This is the result of recollecting our personal experience of loss and suffering. Such empathy is more about us than it is about the other person. To feel another's grief through one's personal experience is a wonderful human quality. But it is not the same as compassion. Empathy is an emotion that arises within our self. It can be painful, difficult, and at times exhausting, particularly if the circumstance persists for an extended period of time. It can be as disabling to us as it is admirable. And because it is an emotion and feeling it is basically unstable and can come and go at any time. Compassion, the basis of altruism, is not a reaction, emotion, or feeling. It results from an insightful understanding of the human condition. Its basis is wisdom, a wisdom which understands the suffering of the unexamined human condition. It is heartening rather than exhausting, permanent rather than transient.

Naturally Self-Arising Compassion

When we are resting in our natural self all speech and action occurs in direct relationship to the experience of the moment. There is no intervening thought process. When a mother's infant falls into the water the mother automatically jumps into the water to rescue the child. When our left hand is on fire our right hand automatically reaches for it to extinguish the fire. Our mind and body know what to do. Our speech and action are activated by the present moment experience itself. Can you imagine what would happen if your mind intervened. The baby might drown and your hand might burn.

Nature provides many other examples of this. A flower or tree knows to turn towards the sun. A great turtle knows to return to the same beach year after year to hatch its young. Monarch butterflies make the same yearly journey to their breeding grounds and then back again to our front yard. How does life know what to do? This is a difficult question to answer. But when the mind is clear and unconditioned and the heart is fully open we somehow know what to do. However, we have not yet learned to trust that innate knowing, but we can.

In the great traditions, selfless compassion spontaneously arises in direct relationship to what is occurring in the moment, like the mother jumping in the water to rescue her child. Natural self-arising compassion shows up in life as authentic and direct speech and action. It is neither calculated nor measured by the mind. It is a precise and perfect match to the needs of the moment.

That is what distinguishes natural and spontaneously self-arising compassion from a mental-based altruism. It needs nothing back. It is effortless, natural, courageous, and fearless.

The progression from self-cherishing, to altruism, to selfless compassion, is non-linear. There is great overlap of these stages of development. The point is to be aware of the entire process and to regularly inquire about our motivations so that we may measure our progress and identify those moments when it would be best to upgrade our motivation. Through ongoing development we slowly mature our natural desire to be of help to others, and in time we will, in all of our actions, be as selfless and spontaneous as the mother jumping into the water to save her drowning infant.

A Final Word About Love

Love and compassion are inseparable. Compassion is the desire that all beings be free of suffering and the causes of suffering. Love is the desire that all beings live in happiness. As you can see, they are seamlessly interwoven. When we wish one we wish the other as well.

Of course, the usual love we are accustomed to is highly personal in nature, and often quite full of dependency and attachment. Here we are speaking of a far greater love. We are speaking of a selfless love that transcends mind, transcends "I," and fully and equally embraces all. It is a simple, pure, and clean love that seeks happiness for all others. Nothing more and nothing less. Without asking, this selfless gift is fully returned, and more so.

A selfless compassion and love joined together is the fourth transcendent quality of human flourishing.

chapter 18

Boundless Freedom

There are three types of freedom—outer, inner, and innermost or boundless freedom. The latter is a profound, yet extraordinarily simple, freedom *to be*. It is the fifth quality of human flourishing.

Outer freedom is political and economic. It is the absence of perceived political, social, and economic restrictions. Inner freedom is freedom from afflictive emotions, Innermost or boundless freedom is freedom from the known—freedom from the influence of old mental habits and fixed and outdated perspectives. The latter is the freedom *to be* in the freshness, nakedness, and fullness of each moment—a complete presence which is unaltered and unshaped by past experience. We call the first type "conventional" freedom, the second type "psychological" freedom and the third type "spiritual or boundless freedom."

In the West we have come a long way in assuring outer freedoms. However, we have failed to understand, value, or address inner and innermost freedom. Without these subtler aspects of freedom we are anything but free. Regardless of our customary notions about freedom, we are as enslaved to our misunderstandings and mental afflictions as the prisoners in Plato's cave. Like them, we neither comprehend nor miss the possibility of boundless freedom, as we are completely unaware of our predicament, our lack of freedom. Yet, boundless freedom is the pinnacle of human achievement without which our lives are closer to the animal kingdom than to the human one.

If I were to make a general inquiry into the question of freedom, as it applied to my own life, my initial response would be one of certainty. I am free—free to choose to be here or there, write these words, organize my life as I wish, make choices free from compulsion, assert views arrived at without undue influence, choose friends, career, home, and dinner. A simple review of my life would assure me of this.

So why not leave it at that? Why go further? Why inquire more deeply? The answer is clear, yet somewhat difficult to grasp. Because I appear to be free does not necessarily mean that I am actually free, any more than the appearance of water on the distant desert road means there is actually water there. The same can be said for the railroad tracks which seem to meet in the distance, the echo and the night dream with all their vividness and apparent truthfulness. Mental and sensory illusions can be quite convincing. Nevertheless, they are illusions. They are untrue. They do not exist the way they appear. What these examples teach us is that many life experiences appear one way but actually exist in quite another.

Consider this possibility. What if our sense of freedom were similarly an illusion? What if we are actually living in an invisible prison, built by time, thought, mental habit, and fixed perceptions, but cannot see it? If our sense of personal freedom is really an illusion, wouldn't it be worth knowing that? Wouldn't it be important to know if we are unknowingly enmeshed in a self-betraying myth, a myth which limits our life and possibilities?

As humans this should be of particular concern as we have the unique capacity to attain a profound, authentic, and boundless freedom. So you might agree that it is worthwhile to undertake a personal inquiry which can establish whether we live in total freedom or whether we are in a prison of our own making which is hidden from ordinary sight. If the latter is the case, we will have surrendered one of our deepest possibilities to a comforting myth.

That brings us to the exploration of the progressive evolution of the fifth quality of human flourishing—boundless freedom.

Outer Freedom

I will not discuss outer freedom—political and economic freedom—in great detail, as our focus here is to explore the subtler and more expansive aspects of freedom. But even when it comes to political and economic freedom—the freedom to express our beliefs and be free from focusing on essential material needs—there are a few important questions to consider.

Is the ability to express our beliefs the only measure of political freedom? Are we truly free if our beliefs themselves—our ideologies, thoughts, and strongly held feelings—arise from complex and unseen religious, cultural, and personal influences, influences which were unconsciously acquired and then fixed in place rather than freely chosen? Are we truly free when these powerful influences automatically *predetermine* and *compel* our viewpoint? Consider whether any ideology based on thought, based on the known, based on the past can ever be free.

If our viewpoint is already established, it is related to the past. Where is its flexibility, openness, and relevance to the actual unique experience of the moment? When you have a fixed viewpoint are you able to respond to the facts of the moment as they are with an open mind and heart? Or, are you limited to seeing and responding with your set political perspective? If so, are you coming from habit and the past rather than a spontaneous responsiveness to the truth of the moment? It may seem like political freedom, but is it?

The same can be said for economic freedom. Are we economically free if we are influenced and compelled by a cascading series of wants that are confused with needs? Are we economically free when we are chronically dissatisfied with how we live, fearful that we may fall back, or constantly reaching for more and more? Are we economically free when we lack contentment and gratitude for what is given? When the mind is involved in ever-increasing desires and wants can we be economically free, regardless of what we have?

We are like wind-up toys, wound up in youth with ideas, attitudes, and perceptions which robotically and predictably unwind over the course of our lifetime. That's what we call political freedom. Our desires are continuously shaped and influenced by endless advertising and marketing. That's what we call economic freedom.

I would like to leave these questions here and ask you to consider them further. Inquire, reflect, and examine whether you can be free when the mind is constructing and pledging allegiance to ideologies or enslaved to ceaseless desires. When you analyze this to its end you will discover that, even in the most politically open and economically secure culture, outer freedom is not possible without inner freedom. It is a convincing and comforting illusion, but that is not the way it is.

Inner Freedom

Inner freedom is the freedom from mental disturbances. It is freedom from afflictive emotions and the overactive mind. Do I have control over my mental activity or does my mental activity have control over me? Can I be free when I ceaselessly and involuntarily attach to random mental activity and automatically act it out in the world through my speech and action? Is my reactivity and automatic behavior freedom? Few of us would allow another to control our lives to the extent that we are already controlled by mental activity. Yet, we allow this to happen each moment, never recognizing our enslavement to this inner tyranny of mental chatter.

The initial step in gaining inner freedom is to recognize this dilemma. The second step is to resolve it. For this we apply our self to inner development. That effort progressively slows ceaseless mental activity and creates a clearing in our mind. We now have a mental clearing in which we can begin to see the mechanics and horror of inner enslavement.

We get our first taste of inner freedom at the very earliest stages of practice. It shows up as diminished reactivity, increased clarity and stillness, and greater understanding of our mind. That can be seen in the first few weeks of practice.

As we progressively take charge of our inner life, we discover a previously unknown inner freedom. Our life is no longer a response to random mental activity, but rather, a vital presence based in the actual moment. Our speech and actions are reflective of current circumstances and far less influenced by past experience.

We discover that inner freedom is staying fully in the moment. We experience and let go, experience and let go. Everything is new. Everything is fresh. We are liberated from the enslavement of mental chatter. That is the nature of inner freedom—freedom from afflictive emotions and the out-of-control mind. We have each had experiences of this. They are sometimes referred to as "being in the flow." At such moments we are unchained from our overactive mind and feel the simple freedom to be. Such moments are often brief and transient. But with practice they expand and stabilize. Inner freedom is the basis for the emergence of boundless freedom.

Boundless Freedom

When we have achieved a carefree and easeful mind, isn't that all there is? Aren't we there, finally? Not quite; there is one further obstacle. That obstacle is our subtlest conditioning—largely unseen propensities and tendencies which continue to subtly shape our lives.

When a child sees a tree for the first time it has no previous knowledge with which to categorize it. The child experiences it "nakedly" and "unadorned," with a sense of awe and wonder, free of labels and mental elaborations. The child lives the moment as it is, totally free to experience the tree as it actually is *in that moment.* The present remains unshaped by past experience—both overt patterning and subtle propensities. Because the child lacks accumulated past experiences, its moment-to-moment experience is completely free from the "known." We can see this in the awe and wonder of a young child meeting life for the first time, each moment and each day.

In *your* adult life have you ever seen a tree for the first time? Have you seen its texture, movement, rhythm, colors, or relationship to its environment *as it is* in the moment, free from images and information stored in memory? Have you ever seen a tree with your entire being? Have you ever seen a tree by being one with the experience itself? Have you seen the actuality of this experience as it is and has never been before? Have you ever seen a tree exactly as your sensory system sees it without the label "tree" and the subsequent superimposition of preconceived ideas?

Consider your closest relationships. Is it possible to experience family, friends, or lovers as if you were meeting them each moment for the first time? Can you see, hear and experience these precious individuals with a freshness and firstness that is unaltered by past perceptions? Are you able to let go of your prejudices and judgments and likes and dislikes? Are you able to meet this individual in total freedom without constricting beliefs—just as he or she is in that moment? If not, you are meeting the past rather than the present. You are meeting an unchanging mental image of the person rather than the person. The moment and meeting is conditioned and determined by what was.

When old perspectives, stories and propensities influence us, however subtle they may be, we are not totally free. As long as what we know, conscious or unconscious, shapes our present moment experience, we cannot experience life freely. This is the subtlest form of conditioning and the subtlest yet most powerful limitation to freedom.

When we rest in our natural state cognition is stilled. We live in open awareness rather than in thought. When we need our thought and reasoning capacities they are available to sort out this or that problem, drive a car, or attend to daily activities. In our natural state of being cognition is a mental instrument that we *use* when we need it. It is not our default state-of-being. It does not dominate our lives. It does not take us away from the direct and full experience of life. So we learn to use the cognitive mind as an instrument of life when needed, but we do not allow it to obscure our direct and unfiltered experience of life.

Boundless freedom is a noble gift and possibility for each of us. It transcends and includes all lesser aspects of freedom. It cannot be seen, as it is not visible. It cannot be touched, as it is not material. It cannot be created, as it is already there in the ground of our authentic self. It cannot be destroyed, as it is independent of all causes. It is pure and uncontaminated, as it is no longer influenced by afflictive emotions, the pervasive influence of the past, or the powerful constraining forces of culture. It is simple and remarkably ordinary. It is profound and extraordinary. It is a human treasure.

Boundless freedom is the fifth quality of human flourishing.

chapter 19

The Perfection of Health

Aurobindo, the noted Indian scholar and sage, spoke about the perfectability of human life. He viewed our condition as a work-in-progress, evolving from ignorance and confusion to the pinnacle of development—a flourishing and prospering of body, mind, and spirit. He called this final accomplishment the perfection of health.

Aurobindo was born thirty years after Charles Darwin published his seminal work, *Origin of the Species*. He applied Darwin's new theory of evolution to human development. Like nature itself, our lives, he said, were not static but rather in the process of evolving. However, unlike other aspects of nature we have the unique opportunity to take a direct role in our development. He believed that through inner development we could flourish into our fullest humanity. He had no illusions as to the effort involved in accomplishing this evolutionary feat. But he, like all great masters, understood the potential and destiny of human life, and the importance that each of us plays in the unfolding of our greatest possibilities.

However, in modern times health has been viewed from a different and far more limited perspective. We view health in exclusively biological terms, measuring it solely by physiologic parameters and overall life expectancy. That is why it is so difficult for us to imagine a sustained state of optimal well-being.

But that is not how the wise ones saw it. They viewed health through a very different lens. They saw it as an ongoing dynamic process through which we perfect our humanity, to the fullest extent possible, from cradle to grave. Growth, development, and flourishing were the signposts of health. *Health, they declared, is the realization of our fullest humanity*. It is not defined by the presence or absence of disease. It is defined by the quality of our life.

We have already spoken about the progressive realization of

the qualities of human flourishing—serenity, full-knowing wisdom, enduring happiness, natural self-arising compassion, and boundless freedom. We have discussed the evolution of each of these qualities as they develop through study, reflection, and practice. The perfection of health is the culmination of this process. It is the final fruit of human flourishing. It encompasses all of the qualities we have spoken of. It spontaneously and naturally arises through the force of inner development.

For us this is a new way of envisioning health. However, in actuality it is quite traditional. It is not what I learned in my modern day medical education. But it is there, as it has always been, at the core of the Western and Eastern understanding of health. The durability of this ancient view results from its alignment with the truth of the human condition and its unique possibilities.

We are not animals destined to live and die in ignorance of our basic nature. We are not animals that are incapable of bringing suffering to an end. We can intentionally influence the unfolding of our lives. We have the capacity to transcend the limitations of our biology and live in the fullness of life. We can flourish. To accomplish this is to perfect both health and life.

Our understanding of health matures in a sequential manner. We will look at these steps one-at-a-time. However, it is important to remember that health can appear in its perfected form at any time, even at the moment of death. Why? Because it is innate to and always present in our authentic self. When we touch the core of our being, it is spontaneously there.

Biological Health

There is not much that we need to say about biological health, as we know it well. It is a major accomplishment of modern times and modern science, an accomplishment that deserves praise and ongoing support. The origin of biological and medical science dates back to two seminal events. The first occurred in ancient Greece. It was the intentional turn towards rationalism, which was most embodied in the medical writings of the physician Hippocrates. The second source was the application of rationalism to the great scourge of the Middle Ages, the infectious epidemics that devastated civilization and led to immeasurable suffering.

The meeting of rational inquiry and the epidemics of infectious disease led to the emergence of the fields of bacteriology and medical diagnostics and therapeutics. We are very fortunate to be recipients of these advances.

Over the past decades we have seen a further evolution of biological medicine with the attention given to wellness initiatives, mind/body strategies, integrative medicine, and health promotion activities. Although still a distant cousin to the medical establishment, these initiatives are a response to the realization that biological medicine is limited in its ability to promote and sustain a larger vision of health. These complementary approaches point towards something that is still missing from our modern view of health and healing—a concern with the role of mind and spirit in health and disease.

Integral Health

The word "integral" means unitary or one. It refers to a far-reaching health and well-being that addresses all of the important aspects of our lives. There are four components of an integral health. They correspond to the four central aspects of our life. The first two are highly personal—our physical and mental well-being. The second two relate to our interaction with others—our interpersonal relationships and our relationship to the larger culture and planetary community. These four aspects of life are interconnected. They are always impacting upon one another. Each contributes to the quality of life—health and illness, happiness and suffering. A concern for each of these aspects of life is essential if we are to resist and recover from disease, optimize well-being and reach towards our full human potential.

Medical science has noticed this as well. There are no shortages of studies that demonstrate the effect of stress, distress, and mood disorders on physical health, and the other way around. Similarly, there are no shortages of studies that demonstrate the effect of relationships, good and bad, on our physiology. And there are as well many studies which demonstrate the effect of job stress, job strain, and unemployment on physical health and well-being. The problem is not a lack of information to support the well-established view that multiple factors impact on our health. The problem is that our singular focus on biology keeps us from implementing this knowledge. An integral perspective insists on this integration. It is holistic in nature.

Just as a car needs a driver so does our life. Without the driver, the car could not properly arrive at its destination. *Inner development is the driving force that takes us toward integral health.* It touches each of the three other aspects of our life. Loving-kindness and a universal embrace become possible with inner development. The subtlest form of mind/body healing becomes possible with inner development. Compassionate service becomes possible with inner development. That is why inner development, as we have been discussing it throughout this book, is the next essential step in our quest for a larger health and life. *Inner development is the basis for the attainment of integral health.*

The embrace of the far-reaching vision of integral health is a significant departure from an exclusive focus on biological health. It is a major change in focus and allocation of resources. But we must be careful here. It is easy to mistake alternative therapies and treatments, however valuable, for an authentic shift in vision. Remember that the central characteristic of the shift towards an integral approach is the turn inward and the reliance on our inner capacities, rather than on remedies and therapies. The reliance is on ourselves rather than on practitioners. So you must know the difference between a variation on biological medicine, which merely increases our medical tool kit, and an authentic vision of integral health that results from inner development. They are not the same.

There are many ways to approach integral health. The most critical approach will be your focus on inner development, as described in this book. I have discussed integral well-being more completely in my previous book *Integral Health* (Basic Health, 2006.)

The Perfection of Health

The comprehensive integral approach, driven by inner development, can take us far along the path toward a far-reaching well-being. However, when we speak about the perfection of health we are speaking about something quite different than the mechanics of optimizing all of the individual factors that impact on body, mind, and spirit. The perfection of health embraces all aspects of biological medicine and integral health. However, it goes beyond these approaches. The perfection of health, as we are speaking of it here, is rooted in the vastness and essence of our being. It is inseparable from our authentic self. It is our authentic self.

A perfected health is, in Aurobindo's language, divine life on earth. When we are settled in our authentic self an optimal sense of well-being permeates and harmonizes body, mind, and spirit, irrespective of our physical condition. We can and should apply ourselves to developing our physical life, mental life, and relationship to others, but this is developmental. It is gradual in its approach. When we are settled in our natural state-of-being all aspects of our life are in perfect harmony and balance, right there in that moment. We have all had glimpses of such moments. I am sure you will notice that at such times, irrespective of outer conditions or adversities, all is well, all is complete and all is at peace. There is nothing more that is needed. Life seems full and perfected. You are fully alive and well. And that is it.

Yes, that is it. When we have stabilized a full presence in the moment all the qualities of human flourishing are present, and we have attained the perfection of health.

All that is necessary is to move beyond your overactive mind, recover your authentic self, and stabilize your capacity to live life in the immediacy of the moment. If you do so, you will naturally experience a state of well-being which goes far beyond any previous notions of health. That is the singular purpose of inner development—to live in the present moment, experience the richness and vastness of life, and know a perfected state of health.

You may ask, "What if I am ill or experiencing stress or distress? Is it still possible to experience a through and through well-being."

Again, my answer to you is a definite yes. At the core of your distress and suffering is a profound well-being. I have uncovered this essential well-being in many individuals precisely at the moment of great suffering. However, to create the stability of that experience requires the inner development which we have spoken of in this book. With this preparation, aging, disease, and death will not be experienced as they now are. That is a certainty.

There is a profound health that is available to each of us, right now and forever. This all-encompassing health embraces and transcends all lesser understandings of health. It is immune to outer adversity including disease, aging, and death. It spontaneously arises when we abide in the center of our being. It is reliable, steadfast, and permanent. It has never left us. We have left it.

Aurobindo called it divine health because it is *permanent, indestructible,* and goes beyond anything we know through conventional understanding. He called it *noble and sacred* because it is the highest achievement of humankind.

This call to human flourishing is not a new call. It is an old one found in the West the East and in every culture and age where visionaries sought to explore the unique nature and potential of human life. The wise ones know that human life is still an unfinished project, a work in progress. They sought to elevate the quality of our existence by urging us toward the perfection of our unique possibilities. They tell us that sustained health, happiness, and serenity are natural to the human condition. But natural, they caution us, does not mean immediately available. They urge us to go beyond human instincts, stubborn holdovers from the animal kingdom, and our cultural training to look within at our humanity. They remind us that we are not animals disguised as humans. Unfold your nature they tell us. Become what a human is capable of becoming. Look within to the authentic source of enduring health, happiness, and serenity. Flourish!

PART IV

The Integration

I am a physician. That is where this work began. During my twenty years of full time internal medicine practice I saw far too many individuals confront the catastrophe of mental and physical illness in a system that limits itself to biological diagnosis and therapies. The opportunity that such a pivotal moment in life affords goes unseen, and is lost. Perhaps more than any other time in life that moment is ripe for growth and transformation. The individual is open to change, time becomes fully available, and the ego lies low. In the midst of tragedy lies the precious seed of human flourishing. In the midst of suffering lies the potential to prosper. However, that requires that healers seize this precious moment and guide individuals towards the richer life that suffering is pointing towards. Then, suffering becomes meaningful rather than meaningless. Life becomes larger rather than smaller.

In the chapters that follow, consider how a broad-based integral approach, one that guides us toward human flourishing, can complement and enhance conventional approaches to the major epidemics of our time. Holding the view that health is always a possibility even in the midst of life's greatest adversities, let us explore together how we can apply the approach of inner development discussed in this book to the difficult disorders of our time. Let us explore how we can find our essential self and the qualities of human flourishing in the very wounds that break our life open. Let us see if there is a blessing and grace that cannot be broken by disease, aging, and death.

chapter 20

Addiction Disorders

W e begin our exploration with a discussion of addictive disorders. Here is the question we will attempt to answer. Can we, by applying what we have learned about mind and heart, help to bring this epidemic to an end? Let us examine this possibility.

We could begin this discussion in the customary manner by presenting statistics which define the prevalence and cost of addictive disorders—the percentage of population addicted to alcohol and drugs and the related economic burden to society. However one draws the line in defining addiction, the numbers are staggering. Let us leave it there.

Rather than focus on the disturbed psychology or the physiology of addictive disorders, it is my intent to explore addiction from a broad-based integral perspective, which can offer us new insights and approaches to this difficult and tenacious problem. I shall define addiction here as a mind/body disturbance resulting from an undeveloped inner life. *What I am suggesting is that the psychological and physiological disturbances of addiction are secondary to an undeveloped inner life. The latter is seen as the root cause of addiction.*

That is not the modern day perspective. The contemporary perspective asserts that addiction is primarily a psychological and physiological disorder. There are psychological triggers, circumstances, and patterns of behavior that initiate and reinforce addictive behavior as well as physiological consequences of addiction which further compel it. Alcoholism is viewed as being triggered by a variety of identifiable psychological circumstances and sustained by physiological dependence.

The customary approach to treatment is multimodal, addressing both the psychological and physiological aspects of addiction. Twelve Step programs such as Alcoholics Anonymous, currently the mainstay of treatment for addictive disorders, have expanded this perspective by emphasizing the role of spirituality. Because of its success in treating addiction it is important to carefully examine the original vision and intent of AA. This understanding will point us in the direction of a very different understanding of this disorder.

Roland H., Carl Jung, and AA

Earlier we spoke of a fascinating exchange of letters in 1961 between Bill Wilson, the founder of AA, and the famed Swiss psychologist Carl Jung. As you may recall, Bill Wilson wrote to Jung of his desire to share with him the fate of one of Jung's patients, Roland H., who Jung had treated for alcoholism years before. He reminded the doctor about his final advice to his patient and related how this counsel ultimately led to the founding of AA. Bill Wilson writes in his note that during Roland's last visit to Jung he was advised that neither medicine nor psychiatry had a cure for alcoholism and that his case was therefore "hopeless." When Roland further inquired of Jung whether there was any hope to be found Jung answered yes, "… if he could become the subject of a spiritual or religious experience."

　　　Unknown to Jung, who never saw Roland H. again, he left Jung's office and subsequently joined the Oxford Group, an evangelical movement in Europe which emphasized meditation and prayer. Through his spiritual efforts he overcame his addiction. He returned to New York and through a series of interconnections Bill Wilson became aware of the experience of Roland H. with Jung and the Oxford Group, and following his example, similarly achieved remission from alcoholism. Wilson then went on to start what we now know as AA.

　　　What were Jung's recollections about his final meeting with Roland H.? What did he write in response to Bill Wilson's thank-you note to him? Here are Jung's words:

> His craving for alcohol was the equivalent, at a low level, of the spiritual thirst of our being for wholeness; expressed in medieval language: the union with God.

- - - - - - -

> You see, "alcohol" in Latin is *spiritus,* and you use the same word for the highest religious experience as well as for the most depraving poison.

Jung understood that the driving force and root cause of addictive behavior was the addict's *unrecognized and unmet spiritual need.* In order to heal addiction at its source this natural and unmet spiritual need must be responded to and satisfied in an appropriate and authentic manner through inner development.

In Exile

Jung was correct, very correct. He knew and could articulate what we each know and feel—that we are in exile from our true home, our spiritual home, our authentic self. We know this place of exile. We know it through a persistent and vague discontent, dissatisfaction, meaninglessness and longing for something more to live by. We know it from those rare glimpses when we touch a deeper presence that removes us from our day-to-day world and briefly opens a doorway to the transcendent and divine. But we can neither hold nor abide in this essence for more than a few moments. Yet neither can we let it go.

Each of us carries within our self the remembrance of this inner presence, timeless serenity, wholeness, and well-being long after we have wandered from our soul essence early in life. It is this vague but extraordinary remembrance of our true nature which drives us to reunite with it once again. The authentic search and reunion with our inner home is the genuine spiritual path of inner development.

It can be said that all addictions—emotional and physical, positive and negative—arise from the natural impulse for spiritual experience, even if we are unconscious of this inner longing. But addictions are mistaken perversions of this natural impulse. They obscure the true path while intoxicating us with temporary pleasures, pleasures which are inadvertently substituted for the "real thing" which can only be found within.

The authentic path home to the center of our being, to our authentic self, has been well described for millennia and across diverse cultures. It is present in the Judeo-Christian tradition, in the Eastern philosophies and if we choose to look closely at the roots of Western rationality we will find it there as well. But in modern times most authentic spiritual paths have been obscured, diluted or distorted—their core essence has been lost from view. As a result we can no longer access a genuine spiritual life, and that inability is the source of all addictions. That is the core of the problem.

Unless we can diagnose the problem correctly we cannot apply the correct therapy. It is easy and customary to respond to addiction with pharmacological and psychological measures. And they are certainly of value in managing addictions. But they work on the surface, rather than at the source. They pull out weeds rather than destroy the root system. That is why in modern times we consider addictions lifelong problems. Like weeds, which return once again in the spring, recurrences of addiction are commonplace until we address the problem at its root source.

But what if we could understand addictions correctly—not so much as physical, emotional, and psychological disorders—but recognize them at their source as spiritual problems—as an absence of inner development and spiritual realization? Then we could apply the correct antidote, the only authentic and enduring healing elixir. To do so we must approach what is essentially a problem of the mind *through the mind*—through an expansion of consciousness which arises through inner development.

The Spiritual Perspective on Addiction

The problem of addiction is really quite simple to understand when approached from the direction of inner development. Here is how it goes. Our natural state is one of simple open awareness, a natural and easeful presence and being. However, our day-to-day mind is so overactive that there is little contact with this natural state. Yet, in those rare moments when mental chatter ceases we are fully present in the moment.

For a moment we are in the center of our being. All is complete. There is no further longing, and certainly no addiction. We all know this place. It is the authentic object of our longing. It is the essence of life itself. But we are unable to sustain that experience because our mind has been trained to default to its tenacious mental activity—from the authentic experience of life as it is in the moment to a world lived in an abstract mental imagination with all its mental chatter and emotional afflictions. We lose our center and once again seek to mistakenly replace it with outer pleasures, which over time become our addictions.

Yet we continue to long for this heaven on earth. We tire of being refugees in the inhospitable land of ceaseless mental chatter. We long for home. We long for our self. We seek it everywhere, except where it is—within. Therein lies the entire problem and solution of modern addiction. In our mistaken search for our native home—in our effort to re-experience the serenity, happiness and wholeness of the spiritual life—we reach outwards toward counterfeit experiences and turn them into counterfeit gods, believing all the time that we have found our lost world, our lost self. Addiction results from this grand, pervasive and convincing delusion.

"Pleasure" is the name we give to these counterfeit experiences. Seen superficially they are just that - pleasurable. Seen more deeply they are distractions and diversions, which, by taking us further and further from our authentic self, assure distress and suffering. How could this be? How could we be so mistaken? How could a temporary outer pleasure be mistaken for the real thing? The answer is simple and clear. A lifetime habit of turning our gaze outwards, a habit learned in childhood and supported by our culture, has made us vulnerable to the seduction of temporary outer pleasures. We are taught to seek these pleasures as if they were the real things. In fact, the entire marketing and advertising industry exists to create, control, and sustain this delusion, and they have done a very good job.

What must be apparent by now is that we are all, to one degree or another, addicted to outer pleasures. Some of our addictions are socially unacceptable and overtly destructive while others are socially encouraged even though they similarly rob us of life and health. From a conventional perspective the first is termed "addiction" and the second "normal."

The Spiritual Approach

For greater than two millennia Eastern philosophies and methodologies have directly addressed the core issue of addiction by addressing inner development.

Why begin with inner development? Because the dysfunctional mind is the root source of all addictions. Learning to calm the mind allows us to observe, investigate, and understand its dynamics. In this way, we progressively gain control over habitual behavior and progressively reacquaint ourselves with our natural and settled state of presence and being. Inner development offers us the opportunity to progressively discover our authentic self, the source of a satisfying and rich spiritual life which, as Jung noted, is the only cure for addiction.

As we progress in inner development, the issue is no longer whether addictions can be permanently overcome, but rather, one of extending and stabilizing the addiction-free mental space discovered within. We have discussed this approach throughout this book. I am not suggesting that the individual suffering addiction should stop any of the varied methods used to combat this problem. What I am suggesting is that you study the readings in this book, begin the practices, and if possible find a competent guide to assist you. That will *add* another dimension to your efforts, and over time you can judge the results for yourself.

The Larger Issue

As I have said here, addictions are reflections of an untrained and undeveloped mind that is incapable of living in its natural essence. The individual with an overt and dysfunctional addiction is the proverbial tip of the iceberg. We, you and I, are the remainder of that iceberg. Our addictions do not show up in the usual ways. They show up in dysfunctional relationships, uncontrolled ambition, striving, and the excesses of consumerism, to name a few.

The disabilities experienced by the addict can be seen as visible examples of the less obvious attachments and addictions challenging all of us. Our aim should not be limited to healing overt symptoms.

We should aim at eradicating all aspects of addiction—gross and subtle—in order that we may become whole once again and gain access to the greatest possibilities of our life—human flourishing. *Addictions, a most tragic human problem, are a potential gateway to a larger life and health.*

chapter 21

Heart Disease and Chronic Disorders

In this chapter we will address heart disease and other common chronic disorders. Once again we will inquire whether applying the approaches of inner development can assist in overcoming these disorders and promoting well-being.

I will use heart disease as our prime example because it is the leading cause of death in both men and women. In 2006 heart disease accounted for 25 percent of all deaths in the United States. The annual cost of caring for heart disease—health care services, medications and lost productivity—is estimated to be $316 billion dollars and rapidly rising. The personal cost is inestimable.

As with most chronic illness, heart disease is caused by the conjunction of multiple risk factors. These include: hypertension, genetic tendencies, elevated cholesterol, diabetes, obesity, smoking, inactivity, and emotional stress and distress. Measuring the relative importance of any one factor is extremely difficult. The aim of prevention, risk reduction and treatment is to address and reverse as many of these contributing factors as is possible. That approach has been shown to be effective in slowing the progression of heart disease, reducing heart attacks and extending life. There is even reason to believe that it may be possible to reverse the progression of heart disease with lifestyle change.

If we separate these factors into two main categories we can identify physical or biological factors as well as psychological or mental factors. Scientific medicine emphasizes diagnosis and treatment of the physical and biological risk factors for heart disease. Much work has been done in this arena, so it is not necessary to address this further here. However, that is not the case for mental factors. Although there is considerable research which demonstrates the importance of mind in heart disease and other chronic ailments, there is considerably less attention given to them.

There are two ways in which mental stress and distress contribute to the development and progression of heart disease. First, they are significant factors in the development and perpetuation of physical and biological risk factors such as hypertension, cardiac arrhythmias, obesity, smoking, and inactivity. Second, mental stress and distress appear to be independent risk factors which cause adverse effects on the health and stability of the endothelial lining of coronary blood vessels, activate and sustain the inflammatory response which impacts on plaque build-up, increase vasoconstriction in abnormal coronary blood vessels, disturb the delicate balance of life-sustaining hormones, alter blood clot formation and platelet aggregation, as well as negatively effecting other biological systems. The main point here is that both indirectly, by its adverse impact on other risk factors, and directly, through its own effects, the mind plays a significant role in the development and progression of heart disease. There can be no argument about these facts.

Not surprisingly, the incidence of heart-related problems has been shown to increase significantly following the acute stress of natural disasters like hurricanes, earthquakes, and tsunamis. Much the same can be said regarding more personal "life disasters." Studies have conclusively documented that individuals who have undergone a recent major life changes—for example, loss of a spouse or other close relative, loss of a job or moving to a new location—have a higher incidence of disease and death.

More recently, researchers at Harvard Medical School analyzed 10 years of medical data on more than 17,000 women in the health profession. The women, who were enrolled in a long-running study on heart disease, were in their 50s or early 60s when the study began. Those who said their job requires them to work "very hard" or "very fast" but who have little say over their day-to-day tasks—"job strain"—were 88 percent more likely than those in less-stressful jobs to have a heart attack. They were also 43 percent more likely to need heart surgery, according to the study. In addition, women who were stressed out by work or worried about losing their jobs were more likely than those with steady employment to be physically inactive and to have high cholesterol.

Multiple studies have consistently linked stress—personal, interpersonal, and occupational—to heart disease and other chronic ailments. That conclusion seems equally apparent to common sense. Here is the question that all this is pointing toward. "Given the challenges of modern day life, can we resolve the issue of unrelenting mental stress?"

Hardiness, Resilience and Inner Development

Why is it that certain individuals react to specific life events with unrelenting stress, some with middling stress and others with no stress at all? If stress were *inherent* in each of these trigger factors then everyone would react the same way. Of course, that is not the case. Individual variations show us that each individual responds to life's challenges in a highly personal way.

Two sociologists, Suzanna Kobasa and Aaron Antonovsky, examined the stress response from another direction. They looked at individuals who exhibited hardiness and resilience when confronted with adversity. They wanted to know the difference between these individuals, and others, who succumbed to difficult circumstances. Kobasa articulated three common traits shared by these individuals. First, they perceived *challenge* as an opportunity to grow and change. Second, a clear sense of and strong *commitment* to their values and goals conveyed a steadiness and resilience. Perhaps one could say they have an unwavering view of their life direction. And finally, their sense of confidence, called an *internal locus of control*, was a source of ongoing mental stability irrespective of outer circumstances.

Antonovsky identified three further but related factors. He found that individuals that were resilient when confronting stressful circumstances were able to "make" sense" of their situation. They believed that everything happened to them in a way that could be understood. They also believed that they had the personal resources to cope with life as it unfolded. And finally, these hardy individuals believed that life in its entirety had meaning and purpose, a meaning and purpose which flowed through all of life's experience, challenging or not. Kobasa and Antonovsky identified specific psychological factors which assisted individuals in minimizing the stressful response to outer stimuli.

We can now go a further step and consider the impact of mind training and contemplative practice. Can inner development result in a mental state that is even more resistant to life's challenges? Can we find through mind training the "ultimate" source of hardiness and resilience? *Can we find through inner development a valuable new approach to heart disease and other chronic ailments? The answer appears to be a definite yes.*

With mind training, our mind can become increasingly stable and progressively immune to the adversities and challenges of day-to-day life. This can serve to prevent the development of illness, to slow its growth, or potentially reverse its direction. Because the source of stress, a major contributing factor to heart and chronic disease, is in the mind, the solution is similarly in the mind. It is now time to make use of this knowledge.

The Medical Office Visit

The meeting between a healer and an individual confronting heart disease or other chronic ailments can be limited or profound, depending on the intention, skill, understanding, and capacities of the practitioner and his patient. Inner development, combined with biological knowledge and psychological skills, offers the possibility of greatly assisting recovery, reducing risk factors, preventing recurrence, transforming illness into optimal well-being, and catalyzing the progressive movement toward human flourishing. *From this viewpoint, heart disease and other chronic ailments can be seen as hidden opportunities of immense importance.*

chapter 22

Depression

D epression, by any measure, is a devastating epidemic of modern times. It destroys happiness and personal relationships. It destroys our spirit and too often destroys life as well. By the year 2020 it is estimated that depression will become the second most common health problem in the world. Currently, 7 percent of individuals over the age of eighteen suffer from clinical depression, and this includes one in eight adolescents. Suicide is the leading cause of death for ages 18-24.

Clinical depression, depression that is characterized by overt and disabling symptoms, is the coarsest form of this disorder. It is certainly the proverbial "tip of the iceberg." We lack statistics that quantify the subtler forms of depression which are characterized by far less apparent mood disorders. We all know the feeling of being "down," disinterested in life, unmotivated, and dispirited. For some this may occur for brief moments here and there, but for many others these symptoms of subtle depression are a life-depleting and long-term emotional burden which has cumulative and devastating effects over time. Too often the duration of these symptoms allows them to pass for "normal." We think that life is just that way. So we make adjustments and move on, failing to recognize the slow and insidious way that subtle depression robs life of vitality and richness.

Depression is not merely an emotional disorder. It is a physical disorder as well. Individuals with depression are four times as likely to develop heart disease than those without depression. Depression following a heart attack substantially increases the risk of death or another heart attack. Depression is also known to suppress the immune system. It is our immune system which protects against infectious disease and cancerous growths. Twenty-five percent of cancer patients experience clinical depression, which compounds and perhaps even undermines efforts to reverse the disease process. Half of the patients with Parkinson's disease suffer from depression. Fifty percent of individuals with eating disorders suffer from depression and it is estimated that up to one third of individuals suffering from addictive disorders similarly suffer from depression.

In addition to being an emotional and physical disorder, depression is a spiritual disorder as well. It depletes our life energy, enthusiasm for living, the joy of life's offerings, and the beauty of intimacy and connection. It fractures our sense of wholeness. We become isolated in a mental world of distress and despair from which there appears to be no exit.

Whether in its course or subtle forms, depression is a pervasive disorder of body, mind, and spirit calling out for greater understanding and far-reaching approaches that can cut to the root of this problem and bring it to a decisive end. Is this possible? Is it really possible to end the epidemic of depression? The answer is an emphatic *yes*!

The Causes of Depression

Depression has multiple causes. In modern times these are classified as biological, psychological and situational. They include: genetic risk factors, serious illness, side-effects of prescribed medications, death or loss of a loved one, social isolation, interpersonal conflict, and work stress, among others. Individually or together these factors are cited as the major causes of depression—subtle or severe.

Once again the problem here is the nagging observation that two individuals may have the same risk factors, encounter similar adverse circumstances, and share family genetics but are not, for an unknown reason, equally susceptible to depression. Medical science, whose interest is disease and dysfunction, rarely studies such individuals. But for some researchers, individuals who are considered "anomalies" to modern science may offer the key to understanding the factors which push one individual into depression while a similar individual remains unaffected.

I previously discussed the research of Aaron Antonovsky and Suzanne Kobassa. They carefully studied individuals who, when compared to their counterparts, were resistant to adversity and described personality traits which appeared to account for individual hardiness. Dr. Martin Seligman at the University of Pennsylvania, has developed a further list of personality characteristics that appear to convey resistance to emotional stress, distress and depression. He calls this *positive psychology*. This list includes qualities such as *courage, persistence, wisdom and knowledge, hope, humor, kindness, creativity, open-mindedness*, and so on.

If we go further and examine the spiritual literature we will find additional answers. Wise women and men, throughout time and across varying cultures, explored their own spiritual life, achieving a profound understanding of the true nature of self, life, and living. They transcended the usual reactions and responses to adversity, which are found in those lacking a spiritual life. Their hardiness was based on a wisdom which understood and mastered the human condition.

There is an essential thread which weaves itself through the findings of Antonovsky, Kobassa, Seligman, and the great spiritual masters. It is a simple and important one. Neither difficult and stressful circumstances nor biologic propensities can alone account for the occurrence of stress, distress, and depression. *An undeveloped inner life is a key factor enabling the progression of the sequence of events which lead from adversity to depression.*

These observations expand our limited biological and psychological understandings of depression. They enable us to more fully comprehend its causes. Therefore we are able to more precisely and effectively apply the correct and permanent remedies—biological, psychological and *spiritual*. We discover that we are not helpless victims when confronting life's challenges. There is a way out of depression.

Conventional Approaches to Depression

There are a limited number of treatments for depression. Those with mild or subtle symptoms usually do not receive treatment. They just grin and bear it until it passes. However, if mild depression persists it may, unknown to the individual, become a way of life. In time it may even seem normal. Although unseen and taken for normal, it insidiously and silently destroys the rich possibilities of living and loving. That is often the course of subtle depression, and the reason why estimates of the overall prevalence of depression are likely quite understated.

When the symptoms of depression are sufficiently noticeable or disabling, the next stop is usually a psychologist. There are many psychological approaches to depression. In any one instance some may work better than others. The aim is to assist the individual in gaining insight into the factors that led to the depressive episode, expand personal resources, enhance supportive relationships, develop new coping strategies, and modify dysfunctional behaviors. To some extent these efforts may assist individuals in minimizing symptoms or recovering from the mood disturbance. And, the therapeutic relationship itself may serve as a source of support and healing.

However, psychological approaches are often unable to control or significantly modify symptoms. When this occurs the referral is usually to a psychiatrist for a brief and focused "medication" visit. The physician may prescribe one or more medications, describe potential side effects and then refer the individual back to the psychologist for ongoing care. There is a place for medications in the treatment of severe depression. Medications can often lift the depression and allow the individual to take an active role in working with the psychologist and integrating new insights into day-to-day life. They can serve as a bridge across the severest and most disabling symptoms.

But that is not what usually happens. Too often, medications become a way of life. Minimal to no effort is made to "grow" the positive psychological traits and spiritual qualities that undermine the deeper sources of depression and simultaneously convey an enduring hardiness. As a result, medications cannot be stopped and the transition to personal resources is not achieved. When I practiced internal medicine I always insisted that such medications be accompanied by specific efforts in these directions so that medications, serving only as a bridge, could be discontinued as the individual grew in understanding and capacity. However, in our culture, it is too often easier to pop a pill and live with the side effects then work on one's life.

There is now an increased interest in the use of herbal remedies, which may have a positive impact on mild depression. However, there is insufficient evidence to give much guidance here. My suggestion is simple—if they help, use them. Their side effects will certainly be less than the usual medications. However, the same issues persist. Unless we use these remedies as a bridge while we simultaneously work to grow our lives, we will miss, as we do with regular pharmaceuticals, the true gift of depression which is the call to a larger life.

In recent years electroconvulsive therapy (ECT) has once again become an accepted approach when the usual forms of therapy fail to arrest disabling symptoms. There is also experimental research investigating the effects of electrical stimulation of specific brain areas. The hope of modern science is that this intervention will alter the neurophysiology of depression in a positive direction. Currently, such approaches are only a last resort.

These are the standard psychological and medical approaches to depression. They may improve or reverse symptoms but most often they do not lead to the psychological and spiritual insights and practices which are necessary to address the problem of depression at its source.

Clinical Research

There is a small but growing body of clinical research, which focuses on the relationship between inner development and depression. Let us take a look at two examples of this research.

John Teasdale and colleagues in the United Kingdom reported on the use of "mindfulness-based cognitive therapy" in a group of individuals suffering from recurrent depression. Mindfulness is a basic inner practice which trains the mind in attention, seeking to break the rumination process which is characteristic of depression. The mindfulness breathing practice described in chapter four is an example of such a practice. Patients (145) were placed in two groups. One received the mindfulness training and the other served as a control group. Relapse or recurrence of depression was assessed over a 60-week study period. For patients with three or more previous

episodes of depression the addition of mindfulness meditation significantly reduced the risk of further relapse when compared to the
control group.

Dr. Paul Grossman and his colleagues at the Department of
Psychosomatic Medicine at the University of Basel Hospital conducted another well-quoted study. That research was published in
the journal *Neurology*, the medical journal of the American Academy
of Neurology. Dr. Grossman addressed the problem of depression in
patients with multiple sclerosis. They assigned 150 patients to either
an eight-week mindfulness meditation program or regular medical
care without the added program. Participants in the mindfulness
meditation program reported lower levels of fatigue and depression for up to six months following the intervention, as compared
to those receiving standard care alone. Individuals in the meditation
program improved in almost all measures studied—fatigue, depression, anxiety—and overall quality of life. Patients who participated
in mindfulness training saw their depressive symptoms drop by
more than 30 percent as compared to study participants who did not
participate in the mindfulness training. Individuals assigned to usual
medical care alone declined slightly on most of the measures.

These are two examples of newly-emerging research which
examines the role of contemplative practice in the care of depression. It should be noted that these programs focus only on the use of
mindfulness meditation, which is a basic entry-level contemplative
practice. That approach is generally taught without the level of content or sophistication of practice found in the preceding chapters.
One could only imagine the impact on depression if the full scope
of inner development, its techniques and understandings, is applied
to this pervasive problem. I suspect that further, more sophisticated
research will confirm what to most scholars of the mind is already
quite evident: tame and develop the mind and heart and you will go a
long way towards resolving the modern day epidemic of depression.

The Contemplative Approach to Depression

Sages and mystics throughout time and across diverse cultures have intensively studied mind and spirit. Their findings are the basis of a comprehensive and precise understanding of our inner life. The process of inner development draws upon this extensive and comprehensive knowledge. Its goal is an understanding of mind and its processes, the relief of distress and suffering and the development of the qualities of human flourishing. That allows for health-enhancing insights and understandings, a stable experience of inner peace, and a psychological and spiritual *stamina* which can withstand the influence of negative thoughts, afflictive emotions and adverse circumstances.

Inner development provides the basis for the sense of coherence postulated by Antonovsky, the hardiness described by Kobassa and the positive psychology of Seligman. It provides the skills, resources, know-how, and capacity to meet life and its adversities with a steadiness and confidence which withstands their corrosive effects and lays the proper foundation for a peaceful and joyful life. Both are possible. We can experience adversity, work with it, and at the same time maintain a stable and joyful inner presence. That may seem impossible at first. However, with mind training and regular practice it is quite possible.

An "Exit" Strategy

Imagine for a moment that you lived in a culture which taught you something very different. Imagine that from a very young age you were taught by example to value your inner life and to seek the peace and stillness of your natural self as an antidote to life's adversities. Imagine how different it would be if, when life became difficult, you were not merely thrown a toy or "comfort" food. How would you be if you hard learned by example that there was a way through difficulty and distress, and that way was to turn inward to your natural self while opening your heart to others?

Perhaps your parents would teach you about daily sitting practice, loving-kindness, generosity, patience, and the value of silence and innerness. When your intellect began to mature your parents would read you bedtime stories about the great teachers who had mastered mind and heart and were of service to others. You would slowly become aware that there was a path of study, reflection and practice, a path which could provide you with the inner resources and capacities to move through adversity with peace, ease, and even joy. Imagine that your extended family, teachers, and community supported this emphasis on inner development. How would you be different?

If early in life we developed a stable inner life, understood the nature of transient emotions and thoughts, and stabilized a calm and serene inner self, we would have cultivated a lifelong antidote to depression. *To know there is an indestructible place of inner harmony, peace and happiness is to have a way out, a powerful exit strategy accompanied by renewed hope and possibility.* In modern times we are unaware of this option, of this exit strategy. The result is frustration and despair. However, if as adults we pursue inner development we will have found the doorway out of depression.

Of course such development takes time, as we follow the path described in the preceding chapters. However, the moment we start down the path of inner development we begin to shift our life. We turn inward rather than outward. We come to understand the nature of our mind and life. We develop the qualities described by Antonovsky, Kobassa, and Seligman and the insights of spiritual beings. This will not happen all at once, but it will definitely begin the moment we turn our gaze in the correct direction. I have seen this with my clients time and again.

There is another aspect of contemplative practice which is of great importance and must be part of our exit strategy. Isolation and dysfunctional relationships are major contributing factors to depression. There are a variety of contemplative practices which help to open the heart and cultivate the quality of loving-kindness. We have reviewed some of these in chapter nine. They can be very important in enhancing the quality of our relationships and diminishing isolation. They empower the individual to reconnect with family, friends and society. Interpersonal connection, as we well know, is a very powerful healer.

A Summary

The process of inner development is not a source of instantaneous relief. It is a long-term solution to depression. That is why the time to start is now, when we are healthy and well. However, if we are in the midst of a mental disturbance we can begin with simpler techniques and more personalized guidance.

The approach of inner development does not negate the value of conventional approaches to depression. It merely views these as ways to buy time and afford immediate relief as we develop the one sure and lasting antidote—the development of mind and spirit.

Beyond Depression

Our aim here goes beyond reversing the causes of depression. Our aim is to bring forth human flourishing. It is to enable each of us to reclaim the full possibilities and richness of human life. There is no human who is exempt from this possibility.

Much as we have harnessed an outer technology to defeat infectious disease, developed the technology for safe surgery, traveled to the moon, and increased the comfort and ease of human life, we can as well harness the age-old wisdom which reveals the secrets of our mental and spiritual life. As we gain the resources and capacity to understand and overcome the disorders of our mental life, we will find that depression, once thought to be difficult to reverse, can potentially be brought to a final and complete end. We may even discover that in our darkest hour lies the seed of our brightest days.

chapter 23

Attention Deficit Disorders

It is estimated that between 3 and 5 percent of children are currently diagnosed with attention deficit hyperactivity disorder (ADHD,) approximately 2 million children in the United States. This disorder is characterized by a combination of symptoms including inattention, hyperactivity, and impulsive behavior which is age inappropriate, and significantly interferes with appropriate age-related activities.

As there are no objective diagnostic markers for ADHD, diagnosis involves standardized subjective evaluations and judgments performed by qualified professionals. Although there may be multiple factors which contribute to the development of ADHD—ranging from genetics, to early brain trauma, nutrition and environmental influences—the source or cause of this disorder is unknown. ADHD can be accompanied by alterations in normal brain development and morphology which are most likely correlative rather than causal.

The inability to identify a singular causative agent has led to multimodal treatment efforts. These include singly or in combination: medication, behavioral therapy targeted at skill building, environmental adjustment, and coordinated and supportive efforts of family, practitioners, counselors, and teachers. Combined treatment appears to offer some relief, although medications are often accompanied by significant side effects. Symptoms may diminish or dissipate as adulthood is approached, although a significant number of individuals may carry these symptoms, with varying intensity, into later life.

An Integral Perspective

Given the absence of specific identifiable causal agents or circumstances, the limited effectiveness of current approaches and the significant and often unacceptable side effects of medications, it may be of value to consider alternative understandings and approaches to this disorder.

From an integral perspective, the individual experiences life through consciousness, biology, social interactions, and cultural institutions. When addressing health and disease we must understand and consider each of these factors in order to embrace the wholeness of human life. Failure to do so results in partial understandings and limited and fragmented approaches to therapy. The value of a comprehensive broad-based perspective is that it considers the multi-dimensional nature of the human experience. However, it is essential to remember that although these four aspects of human experience may appear distinct and can be addressed separately they are inseparable from each other. Human life is a unified and integrated whole.

In contrast to the integral approach, current understanding and treatment of ADHD is limited to conventional perspectives and understandings—biological and psychological. For example, given our cultural bias, we usually attribute health and disease to biological factors. As a result, changes in brain function and morphology are implicated and emphasized as potential causal agents. That emphasis, and the corresponding de-emphasis of non-biological factors, is largely a result of a bias towards the physical, a bias which is specifically found in modern medical science.

Psychological interventions such as behavioral therapy have entered the mainstream of Western culture following the work of William James in the late nineteenth century. As a result, this contribution toward treatment of ADHD is a natural extension of psychological theory and methodologies developed in the West since that time. Finally, a more recent understanding of social and cultural influences on health and disease has further broadened our understanding. We now consider the role of educational approaches and environmental factors as well. To comprehensively address the complex and poorly understood phenomenon of ADHD it is best to consider all potential contributing factors.

Inner Development and Health

We are lacking a very significant perspective on this disorder and its treatment. Western culture, as a result of its concern with the biological and psychological sciences, has failed to fully explore the uniquely human domain of consciousness. Yet, the mind is central to ADHD, and the full development of its capacities offers a potentially powerful and untapped approach to ADHD.

There can be no argument that ADHD is a particular human phenomenon which is related to mental function, much as is stress, anxiety, depression and suffering. I propose that further advances in the understanding, treatment, and potential alleviation of ADHD may depend on our willingness to consider the important role of mental and spiritual development. That requires incorporating the understandings and practices of contemplative methods into current multimodal treatment approaches.

Contemplative Theory and ADHD

Contemplative theory poses two levels of distraction or inattention. The first level, the most fundamental one, is a loss of our natural state of open awareness—our mind's still and pervasive essence. A simple way of grasping this is to experience the brief gap between two thoughts. That gap offers a glimpse of this natural state. However, we cannot sustain this gap of open awareness beyond such brief glimpses. As a result of conditioned mental habits, we unknowingly wander away from our natural inner home towards mental chatter.

Distracted from our authentic self we are then drawn into a tight relationship with mental activity—the abstract world of thoughts, feelings, and mental images. The habit of straying from our natural resting state of presence into mental activity soon becomes our default mental state. By adulthood it becomes a deeply ingrained mental habit. We live in unfocused random mental chatter rather than in a stable open and undistracted awareness. Loss of the natural undistracted resting place of our mind, according to contemplative theory, is the primary cause of mental distraction. *When we rest in our natural state of being neither inattention nor hyperactivity is possible.*

The second level of mental distraction follows from this loss of open awareness and the subsequent enmeshment in mental activity. In modern times the mind is trained to be overactive. We experience the overactive mind as filled with random and ceaseless thoughts, feelings, mental images and sensory impressions. We may fix or ruminate on a single mental movement—thought, feeling, or visual image. This results in anxiety and worry. Or, as is most common to ADHD, the overactive mind may show up as a floating distraction. The mind floats from one mental movement to another—the hallmark of inattention. The enmeshment with the overactive mind is simultaneously embodied in our physiology and expressed in the outer world through speech and action. What follows in the instance of floating distraction is an outward projection of impulsive and hyperactive behavior which corresponds to and is caused by hyperactive mental activity.

In summary, the cycle of mental events is as follows: the initial distraction from our naturally settled state of undistracted open awareness—the primary distraction—is followed by the automatic emergence and dominance of the out-of-control cognitive process—thoughts, feelings and images, leading to the second distraction. We are then subject to floating inattention which mirrors this mental overactivity. That result is hyperactive speech and action. *From the perspective of contemplative theory ADHD is viewed as a habitual and learned dysfunctional disturbance of the mind.*

Contemplative Practice as "Therapy"

Contemplative practice follows contemplative theory. Its aim is to alleviate inattention, hyperactivity and other forms of distress and suffering, and in its place promote a profound well-being of body, mind and spirit. This is accomplished by the alleviation of dysfunctional mental processes and the simultaneous expansion of the mind's capacities. There are various steps in the pursuit of this goal. I will address only the more basic and essential steps, reviewing briefly what we have covered in previous chapters.

Central to inner development is the role of the teacher/healer.

In modern times this is frequently ignored or considered of secondary importance. However difficult it may seem in modern times, the relationship between the patient with ADHD and the teacher/healer must be reinvigorated with loving compassion, patience, availability, presence, and trust. That is at the core of all healing and in particular the healing which arises from contemplative practice. Group activities, brief visits, or team approaches cannot substitute for this one-to-one engagement. Each individual is unique in capacity, temperament, and needs. Diagnosis and care cannot be generic. The one-to-one healing relationship at the core of contemplative practice must be close, personal, and present.

The teacher/healer must be well-trained in the practices of inner development much as the biological scientist is well-trained in his area of expertise. "Learn one, do one" does not work here. There are many shortcuts to learning specific contemplative techniques. They are all partial and flawed. The process of inner development ultimately relies on a sophisticated series of methodologies whose aim is to understand the nature of mind, release its habitual and dysfunctional patterns and enable the unfolding of the qualities of human flourishing. It is not a mere technical treatment targeted at a specific dysfunction.

Contemplative Methodologies

For greater than two millennia contemplative theory and practice has directly addressed the issue of inattention, distraction, and dysfunctional behavior with countless methodologies—contemplative and behavioral. Contemplative methodologies begin with one of various techniques whose aim is to train attention through the use of the mental faculties of mindfulness and vigilance. These approaches are best tailored to the individual, their age, capacities, and temperament.

Assisting an individual in training attention requires great flexibility on the part of the healer/teacher. When proper motivation is present and the appropriate practice is skillfully taught and applied, every individual can experience a capacity to work with his/her mind. Although the experience of attention or inner stillness may at first be quite brief, the fact that it is possible at all is a relief and revelation to the individual enmeshed in a wandering mind. It is essential to clearly point out and reinforce this possibility the moment it is realized by the individual. The issue is now extending and stabilizing these initial islands of attention. Helplessness and confusion is replaced by hope and empowerment.

What is important to reemphasize here is that the human mind is maleable and trainable. If this were not so there would be little use for any form of education. This is supported by neuroscientific research which demonstrates that functional and morphologic change in the brain *is* possible through mental training well into adult life.

The Larger Issue

The individual with ADHD is the proverbial tip of the iceberg. Inattention and mental distraction are the result of an over-stimulated, untrained and undeveloped consciousness. For most of us we call this lesser level of ADHD "normal." It *is* the social norm in Western culture. However, when seen from the perspective of a fully-developed inner life, it is more accurately viewed as a culturally-acceptable level of dysfunction.

The greater teaching of ADHD may be its role in highlighting the universal and pervasive dilemma of an undeveloped inner life. The disabilities experienced by the individual with ADHD may one day be seen as an instructive microcosm of the accepted and less-seen disabilities challenging all individuals in modern times, robbing each of us of the serenity and happiness of a healthy and well-developed mind.

Our aim should not be limited to returning those with overt symptoms to "normal," but rather, assisting all individuals in attaining the full possibilities of human existence that result from the intentional development of our inner capacities. *ADHD, when properly approached, can be the gateway to a far-reaching health and well-being. That is the opportunity at the core of this disturbance.*

In Summary

By adding contemplative practice to the multimodal approach now used to control the symptoms of ADHD we can bring to bear a powerful set of methodologies specifically directed at training attention, facilitating inner calm, and enhancing the overall quality of life. These methodologies, whose theoretical base and practical application have been well-developed and time-tested, are diverse and highly nuanced. They are grounded in the practitioner/client relationship and can be tailored to a wide range of individual capacities, temperaments, and dispositions.

Beyond their capacity to train attention, these very same techniques can assist the individual in moving beyond the relief of symptoms toward a greater well-being. Exposure to age appropriate approaches in childhood or young adulthood will allow individuals many years in which to learn and fully develop an important group of life-enhancing skills and practices. Although our initial effort is to ameliorate disturbing and dysfunctional symptoms, our larger goal should be to assist the individual in "using" the gift of ADHD as a step to a higher level of living.

chapter 24

Post-Traumatic Stress Disorder

Post-Traumatic Stress Disorder is not a new problem. One of the first purported descriptions of PTSD was recorded by the Greek historian Herodotus. In 490 BC he described, during the battle of Marathon, an Athenian soldier who suffered no injury from war but became permanently blind after witnessing the death of a fellow soldier.

Outer conditions may change, cultures may change as well as approaches to health and healing, but the human condition—body, mind, and spirit—is unchanging. In modern times, the development of the field of psychology in the late nineteenth century, sophisticated assessment and research capabilities, diagnostic labeling, rapid global communication, and the diminishing prevalence of life-threatening physical events have together focused a more intense spotlight on this very difficult but ancient challenge to well-being.

Scientific interest and understanding of stress-related disorders can be traced back to the work of the famed Canadian physiologist Hans Selye. In his seminal book, *The Stress of Life,* Selye detailed the physiological responses to psychological stress. He spoke of two aspects of stress: the *acute* stress response which is a normal protective response to an imminent life-threatening situation. The second, the *chronic* stress response, is an ongoing dysfunctional and destructive response to imagined mental threats. The first saves us. The second, over time, threatens our lives.

The chronic stress syndrome referred to by Selye is characterized by low-level mental distress accompanied by subtle physiological changes, which are persistent and responsible for long-term damage to body, mind and spirit. The symptoms of chronic stress include anxiety, fear, varying levels of depression, fatigue, irritability, disenchantment, interpersonal conflict, and a subtle but persistent malaise.

The Signs and Symptoms of PTSD

PTSD can be considered a third and more intense aspect of the stress response. Unlike the acute stress syndrome, PTSD persists beyond the culmination of the initial triggering event. Unlike chronic stress, this syndrome begins with a specific, sudden, terrifying and dramatic insult to life—an intense psychological and physical trauma. This may be violent personal assaults such as rape or severe emotional abuse, natural or human-caused disasters, accidents, or military combat. This list has been extended to include the effects on medical personnel of ongoing exposure to severe trauma, teenage bullying, and major childhood trauma. In vulnerable individuals such traumas are etched into consciousness and result in specific, severe, persistent, and disabling mental and physiologic symptoms.

The symptoms of PTSD equal the severity of the trauma. These fall into three categories: re-experiencing symptoms, avoidance behaviors and hyperarousal symptoms. The initial trauma is recurrently re-experienced by both an involuntary reliving of its psychological elements—painful thoughts and emotions—and the occurrence of frightening night dreams. Disturbing and potentially disabling physical symptoms accompany these experiences. Objects or situations that are reminders of the initial event may trigger this replay of the original experience. Avoidance behaviors include the avoidance of places, events, or objects that are reminders of the trauma. The affected individual may also suffer from other emotional disturbances such as persistent guilt, depression, anxiety, and loss of interest in previously pleasurable circumstances. Hyperarousal is the susceptibility to being easily startled as if one was continually on edge. It is characterized by the presence of a persistent tenseness as well as unexpected angry outbursts.

Any of these symptoms may make it difficult to accomplish daily tasks such as sleeping, eating, or concentrating. Individuals can suffer such symptoms temporarily. In this case they last several weeks after the trauma and then dissipate. However, if they continue for weeks, months, or longer they are often termed PTSD. What was an expected short term response to trauma now becomes fixed in place as a dysfunctional, persistent, and highly painful series of disabling symptoms.

Yet there is more. There are the heart wrenching personal stories which highlight this human tragedy. Dr. Katalin Roth, from the Department of Medicine of The George Washington University School of Medicine and Health Sciences, relates in the following passage her evaluation interview with Annie, a young Cameroonian woman who was seeking asylum in the United States. We are told that Annie was not easy to interview. She spoke in a whisper, made little eye contact, and sat in an attitude of fear, her shoulders hunched and knees drawn in. When she was 20 years old she was arrested and abused in prison. For two weeks, she suffered daily beatings, food deprivation, and multiple sexual assaults. Here is an excerpt from a report by Dr. Roth.

> She suffered hourly reminders of her ordeal. Every meal in Maryland reminded her of the great hunger she had felt in prison; every morning wash reminded her of the lack of water and filth in jail; and every night's nightmares reminded her of the screams of fellow prisoners and of her own weeping. She suffered the persistent pelvic pains and fears of genital infection that plague most victims of rape, and despite a normal examination, she did not seem to accept my reassurances. She carried with her the physical scars of bleeding wounds that had healed without stitches.

And there are more stories, many more each with their unique and painful details, each with a life devastated with no apparent clear exit from this ceaseless nightmare of existence.

Conventional Approaches to Treatment

All three forms of stress are fundamentally disorders of mind and spirit which simultaneously express themselves in a disordered biology and neurobiology that is likely more correlative than causal. These difficult and tragic dilemmas can be approached from a biological, psychological, or spiritual perspective. Psychological and biological approaches, the customary tools of conventional medicine, are commonly used in a treatment plan that tailors "what works" to the specific symptoms of the affected individual.

As it is my intent to discuss PTSD from a consciousness perspective, I will only briefly review current medical and psychological approaches to this disorder.

Psychological interventions include: psychotherapy with a particular focus on the specific symptoms of PTSD, various forms of behavioral therapy, EMDR (eye movement desensitization and reprocessing), exposure therapy, and family counseling. These approaches as well as others can be used alone or in combination.

Biological approaches focus on the use of pharmacologic agents. Pharmacologic interventions are considered of potential use in preventing PTSD after the exposure to major trauma and in the ongoing treatment of persistent symptoms. Multiple classes of psychoactive pharmacologic agents are used alone or in combination to lessen the symptoms of PTSD. Regardless of the availability and use of physiological and psychological approaches, PTSD remains a difficult and potentially intractable problem.

The Integral Approach

According to the integral perspective, it is essential to consider the role played by *all* the factors which give rise to an experience such as PTSD. Unless we do so we can neither fully understand nor comprehensively address it. When we are unaware of or only work with one or more of the causative factors, we arrive at a partial healing. To *fully* succeed in alleviating the problem, healing must be whole healing, particularly in a disturbance as complex as PTSD.

Because of the long-held bias of Western medicine, biological diagnosis and treatments are generally the first concern. Biology and psychology are the two main elements in the conventional approach to PTSD. My purpose here is to show how the addition of contemplative understandings and practices, as discussed in this book, can serve as an essential addition to current efforts to prevent and heal PTSD.

The Response to Major Trauma

Medicine has a highly unfortunate habit of studying what makes people ill. It has shown far less interest in understanding why some individuals are highly resistant and resilient to illness. It is far less interested in what keeps people well. Look at any study in a major medical journal and you will note how the "outliers," those that seem to remain well when experiencing the same conditions to which others succumb, are treated as anomalies and rarely studied. Wouldn't we want to know why these individuals remained well while others fell ill? It seems logical, doesn't it? The problem is that modern medicine is primarily concerned with disease, not health.

Let us look at PTSD as an example of this. It is estimated that 50-90 percent of individuals encounter significant trauma in their lifetime. Only about 8 percent of these individuals develop the full blown symptoms of PTSD. Why is this? We are learning more and more about those who are vulnerable and develop PTSD. Can a study of those who are resilient to traumatic events teach us something that will help both prevent and treat this illness? The answer is a firm yes. That is just common sense.

I have discussed in earlier chapters the work of Suzanne Kobassa, Aaron Antonovsky, and Martin Seligman in identifying personality traits that convey resistance to the damaging effects of adverse circumstances. Of particular importance here is the work of Antonovsky whose subjects included individuals that survived the horrors of life in a concentration camp. This work is supported by Viktor Frankl's observations in his book, *Man's Search for Meaning*, in which he describes his personal experience in a concentration camp. The research by these and other individuals partially explain why certain individuals seem resistant to the corrosive effect of major trauma while others succumb.

What we are discovering is that an individual's preexisting mental state plays a significant role in who becomes ill and who remains well. This opens an entirely new possibility for us. If the development of certain personality traits can protect an individual against the long-term consequences of trauma, what would be the result of a greater level of inner development which addressed not only the personality, but consciousness itself? Could it possibly convey full immunity to post-trauma symptoms? If so, we may have a way to prevent this problem in high-risk individuals such as soldiers entering combat who will predictably confront high levels of psychological trauma.

Inner Development as Prevention

I would like to relate to you a real life story that I heard shared on several occasions by the Dali Lama. However, before I share this with you I must say a few words in preparation. There are many examples of very special individuals that exhibit personal capacities which result from the lifelong cultivation of their inner life. I take these stories as inspirational accounts that show me what is possible for human life. I realize I have neither reached nor may ever reach their level of attainment, but, nonetheless, the knowledge of what is possible for any one human being can be reassuring and encouraging for all of us. When hearing these stories I neither see myself as less nor hold myself to a standard that I may never attain. However, I am motivated to study and practice with greater intensity so that I may reach as far as possible towards the human possibility demonstrated by the lives of such individuals.

I first heard this story in Dharamsala, India, which is the home of the exiled Tibetan people. Each day individuals cross over the high Himalayas from Tibet to reach safety and freedom in India. Each has a story to tell. The Dali Lama spoke to us one day about a very old monk who had been imprisoned and tortured for many years in a Chinese jail. When asked what was the worst moment in his almost two decades of imprisonment, the answer was simple and quick. The old monk responded, "It was the moment when I feared I might lose compassion for my captors."

The Dali Lama went on to make the point that this monk, who lived under the most awful and fearful conditions, left this experience in complete mental health. He was happy, compassionate and at peace. He had no post-trauma symptoms. In fact he had sustained a high level of well-being regardless of imprisonment, humiliation, deprivation, and torture which occurred over a period of two decades.

Of course, as a monk this individual had gone through decades of inner development prior to his incarceration. He had learned to fully develop mind and heart and through his efforts had attained a high level of inner stability. He was *fully prepared* for the unfortunate and unexpected trauma that was imposed on his life. As a result, he was able to maintain, and perhaps even strengthen, his mental clarity and loving-kindness throughout this experience. That is a remarkable observation. But it is not exceptional.

Throughout history there have been examples of many others who have developed this level of mental fortitude. In our time we immediately think of Nelson Mandela and Mahatma Gandhi. But there are ordinary individuals who have achieved much the same, some through an intentional process of inner development and others through the grace of a natural spiritual inclination. The point is that it can happen. It is a human possibility. Psychological and spiritual development can most assuredly prepare individuals to better resist the tragic consequences of profound trauma. It is that process of inner development that we have been discussing in this book.

Each of us will meet adversity in life. For those less fortunate, it will be the tragic traumas of imposed violence. For the remainder of us it will be life's more minor adversities culminating in the great transitions of disease, aging, and death. We do not ask for adversity or trauma. But when it meets us the question is how will we respond? Will we collapse and contract, or rise up and expand? Surely we all wish the latter, and we *do* have an ability to prepare for this preferred outcome. We can all gain from the wisdom, heart, and fortitude provided by inner development. Inner development will enable us to meet life's adversities with greater equanimity, potentially prevent the serious and disabling effects of post-traumatic symptoms, and perhaps even enable us to grow and flourish as a result of these life traumas. That is the role of inner or spiritual development in the *prevention* of PTSD.

Inner Development as Treatment

In modern times we live very busy lives. We are unaware of or devalue the importance of mind and heart. We have little time for those aspects of life which are not considered "productive." As a result of this deficiency in our education and personal life, we are unprepared to traverse the great adversities of life and even less so, tragic and violent traumas. Soldiers prepare their bodies for combat but not their mind and spirit. We emphasize care and protection of our body but do not afford the same to mind and spirit. So all of us, to one extent or another, are at high risk of succumbing to the adverse effects of life's difficulties. We have neither the knowledge nor mind and heart skills to overcome the powerful negative forces of life's challenges.

Regardless of this lack of preparation for life, we can, even in the midst of trauma, call upon inner development as an important process to be added to current approaches to PTSD. Of course it is one thing to plan ahead and quite another to begin an education of mind and heart in the midst of great fear and trauma. Nevertheless, with skilled teachers and committed individuals, progress is definitely possible.

There are four goals in the treatment of PTSD through inner development. The first is to introduce the individual to an inner experience of peace and serenity that exists independently of, and is never compromised by, life's adversities. This inner home, our naturally settled self, is ours from the very beginning. It is the essence of our being. It exists before, during, and after trauma. The fact that we do not experience it is not a result of its absence but rather the result of thick covering layers of mental chatter that obscure this natural refuge and home that is innate to our being. To know that this place exists within us, a place of peace that is free of symptoms and suffering, is an unimaginable relief to individuals struggling with PTSD. It foreshadows a potential exit strategy!

I have worked with many individuals who are in the midst of great suffering. It is definitely possible, even under these most troubling conditions, to bring forth this experience. However, if you are lacking previous inner development or inner stability this recognition and experience may be quite brief. The work ahead lies not in creating a refuge of inner peace free of suffering and trauma, as it is already there, but rather, undergoing the personal development that can sustain it over time. The introduction of the individual to this ever-present inner source of peace and serenity, and its subsequent stabilization, is the first goal of inner development applied to the treatment of PTSD.

A second goal is to provide the individual with an accurate and comprehensive understanding of how the mind works with thoughts, feelings, visual images, and sensory impressions. Central to PTSD is the recurrence and dominance of mental experiences that replay the underlying trauma. In a sense these recurring mental experiences "take over" the mind and imbue it with unrelenting fear and anxiety. How does the mind create a vivid and intense experience that mimics real life when all that is happening at the moment is a function of the imaginative mind? How do these thoughts, visual images, feelings and sensory experiences, which are nothing other than neuro-electrical blips, take over and run our mind, body, and life?

The answer to these questions is no more mysterious than learning the mechanics of a car. To accomplish the latter we hire a master mechanic. Similarly, we need a master inner guide who can teach us about the nature of our mind, help us understand how it works, and point out how it mistakenly fools us by drawing our attention to the imaginary as if it was real. With a progressive understanding of the mechanics of the mind the individual can progressively be released from the faulty mind mechanism which keeps one caught in a post-traumatic dream world.

Like any other education this takes time, effort, study, reflection and practice. But once the light is turned on the darkness dissipates. Once we begin to learn about how the mind has created and sustained the symptoms of PTSD the individual is progressively freed from the intensity and tenaciousness of this false daydream. Learning about the mind is the second goal of inner development when applied to treating and overcoming the symptoms of PTSD.

The third goal is to gain skill in using the techniques of mind training, particularly the development of the mental capacity for mindfulness. Mindfulness is the process by which we become aware of mental movements—thoughts, feelings, visual images, and sensory impressions—as they are occurring in the mind. There is a critical distinction between being enmeshed and identified with the imaginary content of the mind and standing separate from this content as an observer. In the first instance there is no "I" separate from mental activity. Therefore, there is no one "home" to work with what is happening. We are carried away by our mind like a flag following wind currents. Through a variety of techniques we can develop mindfulness to a level sufficient to enable the individual to "separate" from their painful daydream.

What do I mean by this? To be an observer of one's experience provides a very important insight and capacity. The insight is simple yet profound: *I am not my thoughts, feelings, imagery, or sensory experiences.* When I can observe and name these inner experiences they lose their intensity and persistence. I may even discover that they are not constant or fixed. They are impermanent. They change moment-to-moment in intensity and character. And even more, when left alone—that is not dwelled on or elaborated—they rapidly dissipate on their own. They are empty of any real substance. They are ghosts of time past, electrical discharges, *not real events.* When we can determine this directly and decisively for ourselves, these mental events progressively lose their power and influence. Training in mindfulness is the third goal of inner development as applied to the treatment of PTSD.

The fourth goal involves a series of practices that open the heart, simultaneously diminishing self-absorption and isolation and extending and enhancing interpersonal relationships. By developing the attitude of loving kindness and gratitude towards others, we reach out to others. We discover that kindness, connection and compassion are powerful antidotes to the symptoms of PTSD. At first glance this may seem difficult if not impossible for the individual suffering such disabling symptoms. But we know of many instances in which individuals have used their suffering as a means to further understand the suffering of others. They transform their personal suffering into heartfelt compassion, and in some instances, into meaningful service. The cultivation of loving-kindness and compassion through specific techniques and methods can be a highly effective antidote to the symptoms of PTSD. This is the fourth goal of inner development applied to the treatment of PTSD.

We have now covered the role of inner development in preventing PTSD by creating an inner hardiness and resilience to trauma as well as the role of inner development in treating PTSD.

The Larger Picture

PTSD is an extreme dysfunction of the innate stress response that is a natural coordinated mind/body response to acute stress. It is meant to bring our entire system to a state of immediate alertness to cope with impending danger. It is designed to shut off as soon as the danger has past. In both chronic stress and PTSD this system remains inappropriately activated and results in a progressive set of disabling emotional and physiological symptoms.

In modern times most individuals live under a cloud of persistent stress. In this sense we are each somewhere on the continuum that stretches from the acute stress response to PTSD. We are so accustomed to stress and its less-apparent symptoms that we consider them "normal." However, we should each consider the possibility that modern women and men suffer an ongoing stress disorder that is a microcosm of PTSD. This is not to minimize the level of disability associated with PTSD, but rather, to point out that we each may have a piece of that problem and thus be a part of the solution for ourselves and for others.

To bring this truth to awareness may be difficult but it may also motivate each of us to engage inner development, as described in this book, as a way of moving beyond the distress and suffering of daily life towards a life of human flourishing.

In Summary

PTSD is a complex disorder of body, mind, and spirit. To adequately address this tragic human dilemma it is essential that we bring to bear all three approaches—biological, psychological, and spiritual. As inner development is the least understood and least applied approach to PTSD, I have used this chapter and book to illustrate how we can facilitate inner development over the short and long term.

If we are willing to do so, we will most certainly enhance our ability to resist the corrosive effects of adversity and simultaneously develop the skills and capacities to grow through life's challenges. And, if we are truly committed and devoted to this approach, we may also find that in the midst of this great challenge is found the seed of human flourishing which can turn tragedy into fortune.

We may yet realize that at the core of all of life's adversities can be a breaking open that reveals what is most rich in humankind. That is what the wise ones across time and culture have told us.

Fore-Thought

There was a time in my life when I thought that inner exploration would come to an end. However, that has not been the case. What I discovered was that inner development and the pursuit of a full awakening is an ongoing journey. So here we are at a perpetual beginning. The basic process and the essential understandings have been reviewed in this book. There are other resources and suggestions I have listed in the appendix. And for me, it is my intention to continue with *you* on this journey in any way that I can. We are in this together. We cannot flourish alone. We can only flourish together.

What I have shared with you in these pages is not mine. It is important for me to acknowledge its true authors. The knowledge and practices I have passed on to you belong to others who, throughout time and across diverse cultures, have pioneered the path to a larger and healthier life. We renew and reinvigorate their efforts with our own. Much as they did, we study, reflect, practice, and integrate what we have learned into worldly life. We have patience with the obstacles we confront and the back and forth of the process. We know we are creating a new and deeply satisfying life. We know we have finally found the right direction. We know we are making good use of our life, and that is a great relief. We are finally coming into our own and arriving at the center of our being. And it is there that we will find the truth of life, the extraordinary goodness of our nature, and the beauty of every moment and particle of existence.

So set your course and follow it. Chart the next step and the next, and the life you discover will be the one that you have longed for. You will never again question whether there is more to life. You will be living it. You are blessed and graced with a precious life. Do not waste it. Please use it well for yourself, others, and our planet.

Appendix #1: The Center for Human Flourishing

We began our journey towards human flourishing by exploring the Aesclepian healing centers of ancient Greece. It is now time for us to use what we have learned in the preceding pages to upgrade and extend our ancestor's vision. It is time to create *Centers for Human Flourishing*. These centers will enable us to support our personal efforts in shared community and bring to others the realizable goal of ending the distress and suffering of modern life and cultivating the unique qualities of human flourishing. This is more than an opportunity. It is an imperative. It is a good use of our precious lives.

Now, as in ancient times, we cannot do this alone. To heal ourselves, our culture, and our planet, we need to join together in sharing this noble vision. We need a place for healing, skilled guides, and a supportive community to accompany us on the journey. We need time away from the rapid pace of day-to-day life. We need an opportunity to regularly remove ourselves from daily life so that we can once again touch the essence of our being—the ordinary, simple and ever-present authentic self. We need places where we can gather in stillness, silence, beauty, and truth for the sole aim of healing our lives so that we may become instruments of healing for others and our planet. This is not a luxury. It is food for the heart and spirit.

We need havens of sanity which will allow us to discover the folly of our endless and mistaken striving, ambition, doing and busyness. We need to meet individuals who live differently, individuals who live a whole and healthy life permeated by happiness, peace, and an open heart. We need examples of the power of being over doing, truth over illusion, happiness over pleasure and sanity over insanity. We need the opportunity to sit still, clear our minds, and discover who and what we are. We need the opportunity to travel to, and rest in, the center of our being, our only true and permanent home. For these purposes we need places of refuge so that we may together come home to the precious possibilities of life. We need *Centers for Human Flourishing.*

The Vision

The Center for Human Flourishing (CHF) would serve as a home-away-from-home for the purpose of assisting individuals, irrespective of their state of physical health, in alleviating distress and suffering, and promoting the qualities of optimal well-being. It is the intention that these achievements would be the basis for serving others, our culture, and planet.

The CHF is meant to serve the same purpose as the Aesclepian healing temples. For 800 years, spanning the birth of Western civilization, these centers were places of refuge and learning for individuals such as you and I who sought the fullness and richness of life. They were the result of a wisdom culture which remembered and retained a knowledge and fluency with both inner and outer aspects of healing. They knew the nature of whole healing. They knew that every individual arrives at a moment in life when there is no choice but to step out of day-to-day experience and join others in a healing community. Their aim was as simple and as radical as is ours—to create a physical space and living community which could assist the individual in restoring basic well-being and cultivate the qualities of human flourishing. That was their purpose. And now, it must be ours as well.

The CHF is not a place one comes to for the sole purpose of taking a course or two. It is not a place for intellectual speculation or stimulation. It is not a place to try out all kinds of new ideas and techniques. It is where we follow a modern update of an ancient formula. It is a place for ongoing study, reflection and practice in the embrace of a like-minded community. It is where we incubate a larger life. It is where we recover our basic humanity. It is where we prepare ourselves to become instruments of services to others and our planet. That is the vision of the CHF.

Retreat: Outer, Inner, and Innermost

The CHF is a place of retreat. There are three types of retreat—outer retreat, inner retreat, and innermost retreat. The outer retreat is the physical place we go to in order to remove ourselves from the pushes and pulls of day-to-day life. Jesus did this in the desert, Buddha under the Bodhi Tree, and seminarians and monks in silent and devotional retreat. You and I follow the same tradition when we choose to enter the environs of the CHF. However, our modern lives do not allow for long-term retreat. Therefore our retreat center will be easily accessible to urban centers and offer programs of varying duration, as well as distant outreach.

Outer Retreat

There are certain qualities of an outer retreat that we should mention here. The first is the naturalness of its setting. We are seeking to rediscover our authentic self. By experiencing the unadorned beauty of nature we are reminded of the unelaborated simplicity and beauty of our own being. The openness and spaciousness of nature reminds us of our inner spaciousness. Its stillness and tranquility evoke the innate serenity at the heart of our being. Stillness outside catalyzes stillness within. Beauty outside touches our experience of inner beauty. Simplicity outside evokes simplicity within. In this way the physical environment of the CHF will serve as a healing refuge which is the container for our work together.

The CHF will be permeated by loving-kindness. That will be the sweet heart essence of the community. Its relationships and activities will exude this heartfeltness. There will always be a helping hand and a patient ear. Teachers, staff, and guests will be interconnected in shared community which models peaceful and healthy dialogue.

Inner Retreat

The second type of retreat is the inner retreat. The outer retreat is a retreat from the overactive outer world. The inner retreat is subtler. It is a retreat from the overactive mind and its afflictive emotions. The qualities of the outer retreat greatly assist in calming the mind, but this will neither be sufficient nor stable in itself. We cannot forever be dependent on outer circumstances. We must develop the "portable" skill and capacity to stabilize inner calm.

In order to accomplish that, we pursue study, reflection and practice to gain insight into mental misunderstandings and afflictions. In that way we learn to maintain inner calm regardless of outer circumstances. The inner retreat, the calm mind, is mobile, unlike the physical environment of the CHF; it can be with us wherever we go. We have already discussed in detail the progressive steps in taming and stabilizing the mind. This is the second aspect of retreat, inner retreat. It is the ongoing individual learning process which is the core of study and practice at the center.

Innermost Retreat

The third form of retreat is the innermost retreat. That is no more or less than living in the present moment in our authentic self. Time away from day-to-day life enables us to once again gain familiarity with and stabilize the essence of our being. That is our ultimate goal. Once we achieve this final innermost refuge we no longer require the first two types of refuge. Settled in our natural home of presence and being, we have cut through the root sources of dissatisfaction, distress, and suffering to reveal the precious gift of human flourishing. We will no longer be dependent on specific supporting circumstance nor study, reflection, or practice. Our practice will be our life and our life will be our practice. We will become teachers by example for others.

However, this is a high level of development which will naturally evolve as we cultivate the outer and inner aspects of retreat. The outer retreat gets us started. It provides us with a "jump start." The real focus at the CHF is inner development, which alone insures mental stability. As our inner life becomes increasingly stable, the innermost retreat, your authentic self, will spontaneously arise on its own.

These are the three types of retreat. They support each other and together allow the time and proper environment to focus on inner development and optimal well-being.

Activities

The activities at the Aesclepian center were diverse. They touched all essential aspects of health and healing. Theirs was an integral approach, rooted in a profound and holistic understanding of the inner and outer aspects of health and healing. The same approach would fit the CHF. There is one difference. Modern times have completely denied and devalued the inner life. That was not so in ancient times. As a result, the major emphasis of a modern day Aesclepian center must be a focus on inner development and the recovery of the truth, goodness, and beauty of our authentic self.

There will be study programs, seminars, intensive retreats, and time for reflection. There will be opportunities to engage in activities related to physical well-being as well—fitness, movement practices, nutritional counseling, and related programs. The center will nurture personal relationships which model the qualities of openheartedness, full listening, and otherness. Service-oriented outreach programs will extend beyond the environs of the CHF. And we will use what our Aesclepian ancestors did not have available. We will use Internet programming to support the ongoing programs at the center for those who have returned home. The activities at the center will be dynamic, tailored to the individual, and available on- and off-site, as long as needed by each individual.

Mentoring

It is important that each of us have access to skillful, reliable, and trustworthy guides who can help us travel the path to human flourishing. Although we may share the same goal, we have different temperaments, capacities, and life experiences. There is not a single formula which fits all. We must be able to tailor our process to suit our nature, life experience, and current capacities. No more than we would attempt to build a boat without the assistance of a master boat builder should we attempt to develop our life without the assistance of master teachers, teachers who have walked this path themselves, gaining the knowledge and experience necessary to guide others.

That is not as easy as it may appear at first glance. We must choose carefully, as once we invest in a teacher we rely on them for proper guidance and instruction. In my view, any prudent and discerning individual can assess the necessary skills and qualities of a teacher/guide. Here are some of the questions we would ask. Does this teacher carry forth a tradition of teaching and learning which is time-tested? Has he or she adequately prepared their own lives as instruments of service to others? Does this individual's demeanor fit their words? Stated another way, does this individual walk his or her talk? Do we sense an inner stillness and loving-kindness in this individual? How have his others student's fared? Does this teacher remain part of a growing community of peers with teachers of his own? Is his attitude selfless, kind, humble, caring, and supportive? Does he or she listen well and respond appropriately? These would be the guidelines for choosing teachers.

Now, let us take an imaginary journey to the CHF.

The Journey to the Center for Human Flourishing

Close your eyes for a moment and imagine embarking on the same journey which the ancient Greeks undertook on their way to the Aesclepian healing temple. You know—perhaps through suffering, illness, or the calling of your soul—that you are ready to turn a corner in your life. Fortunately, there is a place for individuals seeking a larger health and life. You place a phone call to the center and are warmly received and encouraged to visit. You plan and prepare for your visit. You make final preparations on the day of departure. As you travel to the center your thoughts about daily life and its routines drop away, and your focus slowly turns toward your own life. You feel a mixture of hope and excitement.

You arrive at the center and feel at home in the natural beauty, stillness, and warmth which welcome you. You meet the staff, find your room, get settled in, and sit back and read a bit about the center, its mission, and its activities. Then, you join other new guests to learn more about what lies ahead. At this initial meeting several practitioners serve as guides. They introduce themselves one at a time, speaking about their life, work, and interests. With whom do you feel a sense of connection or initial chemistry? Perhaps this is the first practitioner you will interview. Is he or she a match for your needs? Chemistry and intimacy are essential aspects of the healing relationship.

Imagine meeting with this healer/helper. Imagine your story is fully heard from beginning to end, acknowledged, understood, and embraced. Experience the sense of stillness that enters your mind and heart. How does it feel to experience this inner stillness, peace, and ease? How does it feel to be home again? Your practitioner will point out that this is your inner healer, your ultimate place of refuge, and reliance. Sitting in communion, imagine how you and your mentor will slowly arrive at a decision regarding the resources and activities to explore in your personalized healing process.

Each day you engage in activities which nourish body, mind, and spirit. Gradually, you begin to gain new understandings which blossom into important realizations. You can now sense how it is possible to change from the inside out. Your faith is transformed into confidence. You feel movement. Your life is no longer standing still. You trust there is a way to find what you have been seeking. You now know that optimal well-being is available to you, regardless of your circumstances. Health, happiness, and wholeness can be self-cultivated, grown and achieved, even by you. You feel a release accompanied by great relief.

There will come a time when your visit to the center will be complete and you will be ready to integrate what you have learned into day-to-day life. Although returning home, you will continue to remain connected to the retreat and healing community. The center will always be a home away from home.

Things may be a bit different. You will have new priorities and perhaps some readjustments will occur. You and others will notice that you are changing. You are less reactive, more patient, and increasingly clear about your direction and the work ahead. You will need solitude and time for study and reflection. You will need time to just be. You will certainly sense the early awakening of a new-found health, happiness, and wholeness. Would you like this to be more than an imaginary journey? Let's make it happen.

This appendix has offered a brief overview of a new and very different type of healing center, one which can serve as a resource for individuals—adults and children—a teaching center for practitioners-in-training and a research center for those who wish to more deeply study this expansive healing process. Everything we need in order to create such a center is waiting and ready. All that is needed is to implement the vision we have described here. Now is the time to bring it to life. To do so will be an act of healing not only for ourselves and others, but for our culture and planet as well.

Appendix #2: Resource Guide

There are many possible resources available to assist you in expanding what you have learned in this book. There are books, DVDs, seminars, and retreats. There are also many good teachers. As mentioned previously it is very important, if you seek a teacher, to choose one who follows a time-tested path of study, practice, and reflection. It is also important that your teacher be part of an ongoing learning community. In the resource guide that follows I have offered a few suggestions to help you on your way. I have tried to be focused rather than extensive.

Finally, I want to emphasize that the material in this book is sophisticated and subtle and can be read and re-read many times, and experienced each time at a different level.

Suggested Reading

Rather than provide an extensive list I am offering this short reading list for further study. I would rather target a few key books that I feel will follow-up on the work in this book. I will give you a sense of each book and you can choose as you wish.

Ricard, Mathieu, *Happiness: A Guide to Developing Life's Most Important Skill,* Little, Brown and Company, New York, 2006.

This is a wonderfully written and insightful book that is an excellent complement to the course manual. It touches on many of the topics we've discussed: happiness, suffering, compassion, cultivating and abandoning, human flourishing, and meditation.

Salzberg, Sharon, *Loving-Kindness: The Revolutionary Art of Happiness,* Shambhala Press, 2002.

The development of loving-kindness, that is, the focus on others, is one of the key elements of moving towards a larger life and health. This skillful book furthers the relevant sections in the course manual. It covers the understandings and practices that are essential to the development of an open heart. Opening the heart is an essential part of our journey towards a larger life of health, happiness, and wholeness.

Dacher, Elliott, *Integral Health: The Path to Human Flourishing*, Basic Health, 2006.

Further Reading

Dalai Lama, and Howard Cutler, *The Art of Happiness: A Handbook for Living*, Riverhead, 1998.

    This book is written for the general public. It addresses many of the basic issues we have discussed during this program. It adds a Buddhist flavor.

Begley, Sharon, *Train your Mind and Change Your Brain*, Ballantine Books, 2007.

    This book is a well-written and fascinating account of a *Mind and Life* meeting (regular meetings of Western scientists and Buddhist scholars) that focuses on the mind/body relationship, happiness, and well-being. It is a comprehensive look at the current research on contemplative adepts and human flourishing.

Resources

I would strongly urge you to consider programs and retreats which can extend from a long weekend to 10 days. The following are three centers I recommend.

Shambhala Centers, all major cities, www.shambhala.org.

Insight Meditation Society, Barre, Massachusetts, www.dharma.org.

Spirit Rock Meditation Center, Woodacre, California, www.spiritrock.org.

About the Author

Photo courtesy of Tami Kauakea Winston

Elliott S. Dacher, M.D., practiced full-time internal medicine from 1975 to 1996. In 1996 he left his medical practice to begin an in-depth study of the principles and practices of consciousness and health—an ongoing study of the subtlest mind/body medicine which he pursued for many years amongst the wisdom traditions of Asia. He is also the author of *Integral Health: The Path to Human Flourishing (Basic Books, 2006,) Whole Healing* (Dutton/Plume, 1996) and *Intentional Healing* (Marlowe, 1996).

Dr. Dacher currently studies, practices, and teaches the principles and practices of health and healing with a special focus on inner development and human flourishing. His work emphasizes the traditional goals of medicine: the end of distress and suffering, and the promotion of each individual's fullest potential, the innate capacity for human flourishing.

The author has two wondrous daughters, Alison and Jessie, and two equally wondrous grandchildren, Zoe and Pela.

For Further Information

Inner development is an ongoing way of life. The information and practices in this book are a strong beginning. The text can be reviewed again and again, and in time the practices will become a daily habit.

Please visit my website and keep in touch.

www.elliottdacher.org